Velázquez Spanish and English Glossary for the Mathematics Classroom

Spanish - English/English – Spanish

D1114708

Velázquez Spanish and English Glossary for the Mathematics Classroom

Spanish - English/English – Spanish

List of Contributors,	**v**
Preface,	**vi**
User's Guide,	**x**
Section I,	**1**
Español - Inglés,	
Section II,	**117**
English - Spanish	

Velázquez Press: 9682 Telstar Ave. Ste 110
El Monte, CA 91731 USA

Visit www.VelazquezPress.com or www.AskVelazquez.com

ISBN 10: 1-59495-017-2
ISBN 13: 978-1-59495-017-9

Printed in the United States of America

First Edition

14 13 12 11 10   2 3 4 5

The Library of Congress has cataloged this edition as follows:
Library of Congress Control Number: 2010927034

List of Contributors

Lexicon researched and compiled by
Arthur C, Rachel L and the editors at
Velázquez Press

Thanks to Sandra Strikovsky for her review of
Spanish-English terms

Thanks to Diego A Medina for the cover design

Preface

Limited English speakers in United States schools are faced with a double hurdle. They not only must learn a second language in an ESL setting, but also must keep up with their peers in terms of content. In the case of abstract thought, such as mathematics, a student may enter an ESL program already with well-formed concepts in his or her native language. The student and the teacher must bridge this gap, especially if this student is to succeed in the current American educational system.

The *Velázquez Spanish and English Glossary for the Mathematics Classroom* is a newly compiled work that presents a breadth of vocabulary that all bilingual students and teachers will find to be an indispensable supplementary resource. This new bilingual glossary is convenient and relevant to classroom study and examinations because it offers a comprehensive array of lexical terms and translations. Here, the ESL student and math teacher will find not only technical terminology presented in English and Spanish, but also entries for the type of discourse most commonly used to discuss mathematics.

This glossary fills a specific niche in elementary, middle and high school ESL and bilingual education by aspiring to the following objectives. First, it is a resource used by limited English speaking students in the classroom to aid them in the comprehension of abstract mathematical terms and in their own expression of the language of math. Second, it is designed to be used by these same students during standardized math exams. Finally, the *Velázquez Spanish and English Glossary for the Mathematics Classroom* can be used as a handy reference tool for bilingual math teachers who must overcome questions of translation equivalents of specific terminology. Look no further than the *Velázquez Spanish and English Glossary for the Mathematics Classroom* for all student, teacher and administrative math needs!

Velázquez Press

Prefacio

Los estudiantes que asisten a escuelas norteamericanas y que hablan un inglés limitado tienen que confrontar principalmente dos obstáculos: no sólo deben aprender el inglés como una segunda lengua sino que también deben permanecer a la par de sus compañeros de clase en las demás materias. En los casos de asignaturas de pensamiento abstracto, como lo son las matemáticas, un estudiante puede ingresar a cualquier programa bilingüe con ciertos conceptos bien formados en su primera lengua. De cualquier forma, el estudiante y el maestro deben trabajar para hacer más pequeña esta diferencia lingüística, sobre todo si el estudiante pretende tener logros importantes dentro del sistema educativo estadounidense.

El glosario bilingüe de términos matemáticos para uso en salones de clase, *Velázquez Spanish and English Glossary for the Mathematics Classroom*, es una moderna compilación que presenta un vocabulario amplio, indispensable como recurso suplementario para todo estudiante y maestro bilingüe. Este nuevo diccionario bilingüe resulta muy conveniente y relevante para su uso tanto en salones de clase como en exámenes estandarizados, debido a su gran abanico comprensible de términos y traducciones. En este libro, el estudiante de inglés como segunda lengua y su maestro de matemáticas

Guía del usuario

Este glosario es único ya que su formato de presentar las traducciones palabra por palabra cumple los requisitos para exámenes escolares estandarizados. No están permitidas la pronunciación fonética, las categorías gramaticales ni las palabras para guiar la traducción.

Este glosario incluye vocablos en orden alfabético que están en negrita. Los homónimos que tienen diferentes categorías gramaticales están indicados con un superíndice. Las comas se usan para sentar los equivalentes sinónimos en una lista. Las palabras asociadas están dentellados de bajo de la entrada principal y están en negrita para facilitar la búsqueda.

Vocablo en negrita

Homónimo con diferente categoría gramatical

poder[1], can, to be able to,
poder pagar, to afford

Traducción del vocablo

Section I
Español – Inglés

a razón de,
in the amount of
ábaco, abacus
ábaco de Napier,
Napier's bones
abajo, down
abajo de,
below
abalorio, bead
abanico, fan, range
abastecer, to supply,
to provide
abasto, supply
abecedario, alphabet
aberración, aberration
abierto, open
abreviación, abbreviation
abreviar, to abbreviate
abreviatura, abbreviation
abrir, to open
abrir hacia abajo,
open downward
abrir hacia arriba,
open upward
abscisa, abscissa
absoluto, absolute
abstracción, abstraction
absurdo, absurd, irrational,
senseless
abundancia, abundance
abundante,
abundant, ample
academia, academy
académico, academic
acarreo negativo,
negative carry
acceder, to access
accesar, to access

acceso, access, approach
aceleración, acceleration
acelerar, to accelerate,
to speed up
aceptar, to accept
acerca de,
about, concerning
acercamiento, approach,
approaching
acercarse, to approach,
to go near
acertar, to guess correctly
acertijo, riddle
aclarar, to clarify
acompañar, to accompany,
to go along with
acordarse, to agree,
to remember
acorde, chord
acortar, to shorten
acostumbrado, customary
acotado, bounded
acre, acre
activación, activation
activar, to activate
actividad, activity
activo, active, asset
actual, current
actuar, to perform
acuerdo, accordance
de acuerdo con,
in accordance with
acumulación,
accumulation
acumulado, cumulative
acumulador, accumulator
acumular, to accumulate,
to accrue
acuñar, to coin
adaptar, adapt
adecuado, suitable,
appropriate, adequate
adelantar, to go ahead

adelanto, advance
adentro, inside
adherente, adherent
adherirse, to adhere,
to follow
adhesión, adhesion
adhesivo, adhesive,
cinta adhesiva, tape
adición, addition
adicional, additional, extra
aditivo(a), additive
adivinanza, guess
adivinar, to guess
adjuntar, to attach
adjunto, adjoint, attached
adyacencia, adjacency
adyacente, adjacent
aerodinámico,
aerodynamic
aeronave, airplane
afectar, to affect
afilado, pointed, pointy,
sharp
afirmación, affirmation
afirmación deducida,
deduced statement
falsa afirmación,
false positive
afirmar, to affirm, to state,
to assert
aflojar, to loosen
afortunado,
fortunate, lucky
agotamiento,
exhaustion, depletion
agotar, to exhaust,
to deplete
agrandamiento,
enlargement
agrandar, to enlarge
agregado, aggregate
agregar, to add
agrupación,

grouping, cluster
agrupado, grouped
agrupar,
cluster, arrange, group
agudo, acute, sharp
ángulo agudo,
acute angle
triángulo agudo,
acute triangle
ahorrar, save
ahorros, savings
aislar, isolate
aislar el radical,
isolate the radical
ajustable, adjustable
ajustar, to adjust
ajuste, adjustment
alambre, wire
alámbrico, wired
alargar, to elongate,
to stretch
alcance, reach, scope,
overtaking
alcance medio,
mid-range
alcanzable, achievable
alcanzar, to reach
aleatorio, random
alfabeto, alphabet
álgebra, algebra
álgebra de Boole,
Boolean algebra
álgebra de lógica,
algebra of logic
álgebra lineal,
linear algebra
álgebra matricial,
matrix algebra
algebraicamente,
algebraically
**algebraicamente
equivalente,** algebra-
ically equivalent

algebraicamente independiente, algebraically independent

algebraico, algebraic

algoritmo, algorithm

algoritmo de Euclides, Euclid's algorithm

algoritmo de la división, division algorithm

algoritmo de la raíz cuadrada, square-root algorithm

algoritmo estándar, standard algorithm

algunas veces, sometimes

alineado, aligned

no alineado, unaligned

alinear, to align

almacenaje, storage

almacenar, to store

almanaque, calendar

alrededor, around, surrounding

alteración, alteration, change

sin alteración, unchanged, unaltered

alternancia, alternation

alternante, alternating

alternar, to alternate

alternativo, alternative

altímetro, altimeter

altitud, altitude

alto, high

el más alto, highest

más alto, higher

más alto que, higher than

altura, height, altitude

altura (de un triángulo), perpendicular height (of a triangle)

altura de los ojos, eye level

altura del cilindro, height of a cylinder

altura del cono, height of a cone

altura del pendiente, slant height

altura inclinada, slant height

alturas coexistentes de un triángulo, concurrent altitudes of a triangle

ambición, ambition

ambicioso, ambitious

ambiguo, ambiguous, unclear

ámbito, boundary line

amortización, depreciation

ampere, amp, ampere

amplificación, amplification

amplificar, to amplify

amplio, wide, ample

amplitud, amplitude

añadir, to add

análogo, analogous

análisis, analysis

análisis algebraico, algebraic analysis

análisis de varianza, ANOVA, analysis of variance

análisis matemático, mathematical analysis

análisis no estándar, nonstandard analysis

análisis de Fourier, Fourier analysis
analítico, analytic
analizar, to analyze
analogía, analogy
análogo, analog, analogous
ancho, breadth, width, wide
anchura, breadth, width
anchura de un intervalo, width of an interval
angular, angular
ángulo, angle
ángulo agudo, acute angle
ángulo alterno, alternate angle
ángulo alterno externo, alternate exterior angle
ángulo alterno interno, alternate interior angle
ángulo bisector, angle bisector
ángulo central, central angle
ángulo central de un polígono regular, central angle of a regular polygon
ángulo coexistente de un triángulo, concurrent angle of a triangle
ángulo cóncavo, concave angle
ángulo congruente, congruent angle
ángulo contenido, included angle
ángulo convexo, convex angle
ángulo correspondiente, corresponding angle
ángulo cuadrantal, quadrantal angle
ángulo de contingencia, angle of contingence
ángulo de depresión, angle of depression
ángulo de elevación, angle of elevation
ángulo de fase, phase angle
ángulo de incidencia, angle of incidence
ángulo de la base, base angle
ángulo de la circunferencia, angle of circumference
ángulo de orientación, orientation angle, bearing
ángulo de posición, position angle, bearing
ángulo de referencia, reference angle
ángulo de reflexión, reflex angle
ángulo de refracción, angle of reflection
ángulo de un segmento circular, angle of a circular segment
ángulo del cuarto cuadrante, fourth-quadrant angle
ángulo del primer cuadrante, first-quadrant angle

**ángulo del
segundo cuadrante,**
second-quadrant angle
**ángulo del
tercer cuadrante,**
third-quadrant angle
ángulo del vértice,
vertex angle
ángulo diedro,
dihedral angle
ángulo dirigido,
directed angle
**ángulo en posición
normal,** angle in a
standard position
ángulo esférico,
spherical angle
ángulo exterior,
exterior angle
**ángulo exterior
de un triángulo,**
exterior angle of a
triangle
ángulo inscrito,
inscribed angle
**ángulo inscrito
en un círculo,**
angle inscribed
in a circle
**ángulo inscrito
en un semicírculo,**
angle inscribed in
a semicircle
ángulo interior,
interior angle
**ángulo interior de
un triángulo,**
interior angle of a
triangle
ángulo llano,
straight angle
ángulo obtuso,
obtuse angle

ángulo plano,
flat angle
ángulo principal,
principal angle
ángulo recto,
right angle
ángulo reflejo,
reflex angle
ángulo reflexivo,
reflex angle
ángulo sólido,
solid angle
ángulo subpuesto,
subtended angle
ángulo superior,
superior angle
ángulo triedro,
trihedral angle
ángulo z,
z-angle
ángulos adyacentes,
adjacent angles
**ángulos complemen-
tarios,** complementary
angles
ángulos conjugados,
conjugate angles
**ángulos consecu-
tivos,** consecutive
angles
**ángulos correspon-
dientes,** correspond-
ing angles
**ángulos cotermina-
les,** coterminal angles
**ángulos interiores
remotos,** remote
interior angles
**ángulos no
adyacentes,**
nonadjacent
angles
ángulos opuestos,

opposite angles
**ángulos suplementa-
rios,** supplementary
angles
ángulos verticales,
vertical angles
anillo, annulus
año, year
año luz,
light year
anormal, abnormal
anotación, notation
anotar, to jot down, to take
notes, record
ante merídiem,
ante meridian (a.m.)
antecedente, antecedent
antemeridiano (a.m.),
ante meridian (a.m.)
anterior, previous
antes, before
antiderivada,
antiderivative
antidiferenciación,
antidifferentiation
antilogaritmo, antilog,
antilogarithm
antinomia, antinomy
antiprisma, antiprism
antisimétrico,
antisymmetric
anual, annual
anualmente, annually
anular, delete
ánulo, annulus
anverso, front side,
front page
aparece, appear
apéndice, appendix
ápice, apex
aplicable, applicable
aplicación, application
aplicación algebraica,

algebraic application
aplicación biyectiva,
bijection
aplicar, to apply
**aplicar diversas
estrategias,** apply a
variety of strategies
apotema, apothem
apoyar, to support
apoyo, support
apreciación, appraisal
aprender de memoria,
memorize
apropiado, appropriate
aproximabilidad,
approximability
aproximación,
approximation
**aproximación al
promedio,** approxima-
tion of the average
**aproximación
alternativa,**
alternate approach
**aproximación de
primer grado,**
approximation
of 1st degree
aproximación de raíz,
approximation of root
**aproximación
óptima,** optimal
approximation
**aproximación
sistemática,**
systematic approach
**aproximación
sucesiva,** successive
approximation
**aproximación
trigonométrica,**
trigonometric
approximation

aproximaciones sucesivas, trial and error method, trial and error procedure

aproximadamente, approximately, around, about

aproximado, rough

aproximarse, to approach, to approximate

apuntar, to point

arbitrario, arbitrary

archivar, to file, to record, to save

archivo, record, file

arco, arc, loop, arch

  arco abierto, open arc

  arco cerrado, closed arc

  arco circular, circular arc

  arco interceptado, intercepted arc

  arco mayor, major arc

  arco menor, minor arc

  arco segmental, segmental arc

  arco sujeto por una cuerda, arc subtended by a chord

  arco superior, superior arc

  arcocoseno, arccos

  arco congruente, congruent arc

  arcoseno, arcsin

  arcotangente, arctan

área, area, field

  área bajo una curva, area under a curve

  área de superficie, surface area

  área de superficie lateral, lateral surface area

  área de un círculo, area of a circle

  área de un rectágulo, area of a rectangle

  área lateral del cono, lateral area of a cone

argumento, argument

  argumento lógico, logical argument

  argumento válido, valid argument

arista, edge, border

  arista lateral del prisma, lateral edge of a prism

aritmético(a), arithmetical, arithmetic

  aritmética binaria, binary arithmetic

armazón, frame

armónico, harmonic

arqueado, arched

arquear, to arch

arreglar, to arrange, to fix, to mend

arreglo, array, arrangement, ordering

arriba, up

  arriba de, above

ascendente, ascending

ascender, to rise, to ascend, to climb

asentar, plot

  asentar puntos, plot points

aseverar, to state
así que, therefore
asignación, assignment
asignar, to assign
    asignar valores,
    assign values
asignatura,
    subject, course, class
asimetría, asymmetry
asimétrico(a), asymmetrical, asymmetric
asíntota, asymptote
    asíntota rectilíneo,
    rectilinear asymptote
    asíntota vertical,
    vertical asymptote
asociabilidad, associativity
asociación, association
asociar, to associate,
    to match, to pair up
asociativa, associative
áspero, rough
asterisco, asterisk
asumir, to assume
atajo, shortcut
atar, to tie
atípico, atypical
atmósfera, atmosphere
atrasado, behind, late
atrasarse, to get behind
atravesar, to span,
    to pass through
atribuir, to attribute
atributo, attribute, feature,
    property
aumentar, to increase,
    to raise, to augment
    aumentar infinitamente, infinitely
    increasing
aumento, increase
ausente, absent
auténtico, authentic

autoevidente, self-evident
autonomía, autonomy
autónomo, autonomous
auxiliar[1], to aid, to help
auxiliar[2], auxiliary
auxilio, aid, help
    primeros auxilios,
    first aid
avance, advance
    avance de fase,
    phase lead
avanzado, advanced
avanzar, to advance
averiguar, to figure out,
    to check
avión, airplane
axioma, axiom
    **axioma de clausura
    de adición,** Closure
    Axiom of Addition
    **axioma de clausura
    de la suma,** Closure
    Axiom of Addition
    **axioma de clausura
    de multiplicación,**
    Closure Axiom of
    Multiplication
ayuda, aid, help
ayudar, to aid, to help
azar, randomness
    al azar,
    random, randomly
    elegir al azar,
    draw at random
    escoger al azar,
    to randomly draw,
    to randomly choose
    evento al azar,
    random event
    muestra al azar,
    random sample
    selección al azar,
    random selection

B

bajada, drop
bajar, to drop, to go down
bajo, short, under
> **bajo cero,**
> below zero
> **el más bajo,**
> shortest
> **más bajo,**
> shorter
> **más bajo que,**
> shorter than

balanceado, balanced
> **no balanceado,**
> unbalanced, uneven

balancear, to balance
balanza, balance, scale
> **balanza de platillos,**
> pan balance

banda, band
barata, sale
barato, inexpensive, cheap
baricentro, barycenter
barométrico, barometric
barómetro, barometer
barra, bar, beam
> **barra de fracción,**
> solidus

barrido, mapping
> **barrido biunívoco,**
> one-to-one mapping
> **barrido inducido,**
> induced mapping
> **barrido inverso,**
> inverse mapping
> **barrido isogonal,**
> isogonal mapping

barril, barrel
basado, founded

basado en hechos,
factual
basar, to base
báscula, scale, balance
base, base
> **base algebraicamente**
> **independiente,**
> algebraically indepen-
> dent basis
> **base común,**
> common base
> **base de datos,**
> database
> **base de un logaritmo,**
> base of a logarithm
> **base de una figura,**
> base of a figure
> **base de una función**
> **exponencial,**
> base of an exponential
> function
> **base de una potencia,**
> base of a power
> **base del cilindro,**
> base of a cylinder
> **base diez,**
> base ten
> **base inferior,**
> lower base
> **base inferior del**
> **cilindro,** lower base
> of a cylinder
> **base ortonormal,**
> orthonormal base
> **base superior,**
> upper base
> **base superior del**
> **cilindro,** upper base
> of a cylinder
> **en base 10,**
> power of 10

básico, basic
beneficio, benefit, profit

bicondicional, biconditional
bicuadrada, biquadratic
bidimensional, two-dimensional
bien, well
   bien formado, well-formed
bienes, property
bilateral, bilateral
billón, trillion
bimodal, bimodal
binario, binary
binomial, binomial
binormal, binormal
bisecar, to bisect
bisecarse entre sí, bisecting each other
bisector, bisector
   ángulo bisector, angle bisector
   bisector de un segmento, bisector of a segment
   bisector externo, external bisector
   bisector interno, internal bisector
   bisector perpendicular, perpendicular bisector
bisectriz, bisector, bisecting line
bit, bit
bloque, block
bola, ball
boleta de calificaciones, report card, transcript
boleto, ticket
bondad de ajuste, goodness of fit
borde, border, edge
   borde lateral, lateral edge
borrador, eraser, rough draft
borrar, to erase
bosquejar, sketch
bosquejo, outline, trace
breve, brief, short
brújula, compass
bruto, gross
buscar, look for
   buscar la correspondencia, match
byte, byte

cada, each, every
   cada vez, every time
cadena, chain
caer, to fall
   dejar caer, to drop
caída, fall
calculabilidad, calculability
calculable, calculable
calculadora, calculator
   calculadora científica, scientific calculator
   calculadora de gráficos, graphic calculator
   calculadora gráfica, graphing calculator
   calculadora programable, programmable calculator

calcular, to calculate,
to compute, to tally
    **calcular aproximada-
mente,** estimate
    **calcular el presu-
puesto,** to budget
    **calcular el volumen
de,** calculate the
volume of, cubicar
    calcular los factores,
to factor, factor
a number
cálculo, calculation,
tally, calculus
    cálculo aproximado,
rough estimate, ap-
proximate calculation
    **cálculo aproxima-
do a partir de los
primeros dígitos,**
front-end estimation
    cálculo aritmético,
arithmetic calculation
    cálculo diferencial,
differential calculus
    cálculo integral,
integral calculus
    cálculo mental,
mental math
    cálculo numérico,
numerical calculation
calendario, calendar
calibrador, caliper
calidad, quality
calificación,
grade, report card
calificar, to grade, to score,
to assess
cambiar, to change, to alter
cambio, change
    cambio de volumen,
volume change
    cambio porcentual,
percentage change
    sin cambio,
unchanged
camino, path
campana de Gauss,
bell curve
campo, field
    **campo de flujo
conservativo,**
solenoidal field,
zero-divergence field
    campo eléctrico,
electric field
    **campo electromagné-
tico,** electromagnetic
field
    campo escalar,
scalar field
    campo finito,
finite field
    campo irrotacional,
irrotational field
    campo magnético,
magnetic field
    campo ordenado,
ordered field
    campo solenoidal,
solenoidal field,
zero-divergence field
    campo tensorial,
tensor field
    campo vectorial,
vector field
    campo visual,
line of sight
cancelación, cancellation
    **cancelación del
lado izquierdo,**
left-hand cancellation
cancelar, to cancel
cancha, field
canicas, marbles
canjear, to exchange

canónico(a), canonical
cantidad, quantity, amount
  cantidad conocida,
  known quantity
  cantidad del vector,
  vector quantity
  cantidad escalar,
  scalar quantity
  cantidades idénticas,
  identical quantities
  **cantidades inversa-
  mente proporciona-
  les,** inversely proportional quantities
  **cantidades propor-
  cionales,** proportional
  quantities
caos, chaos
caótico, chaotic
capacidad, capacity
  **capacidad de memo-
  ria,** memory capacity
capital acumulado,
  accumulated capital
capital inicial,
  initial capital
capturar, to input
cara, face
  **cara (de una mone-
  da),** head (of a coin)
  cara de un poliedro,
  face of a polyhedron
  cara lateral,
  lateral face
característica,
  characteristic, attri-
  bute, feature, property
  **característica de
  identidad de la
  multiplicación,**
  identity property
  of multiplication
  característica de

  identidad de la suma,
  identity property of
  addition
cardinal, cardinal
carga, charge
cargar, to carry, to charge
caro, expensive
carta, card
cartesiano, Cartesian
cartilla de calificaciones,
  report card
casi, almost, close
  casi igual a,
  approximately equal to
casilla, cell
caso, case
  caso cierto,
  certain case
  caso especial,
  special case
  caso general,
  general case
  caso imposible,
  impossible case
  caso particular,
  particular case
catenaria, catenary
cateto, leg
  **cateto de un triángu-
  lo isósceles,** leg of an
  isosceles triangle
  **cateto de un triángu-
  lo recto,** leg of a right
  triangle
  cateto opuesto,
  opposite leg
  catetos congruentes,
  leg triangle congru-
  ence
causa, cause
causalidad, causation
causar, to cause
cavidad, cavity

circunferencia, circumference
circunferencia de un círculo, circumference of a circle
circunscribir, circumscribe
circunscrito, circumscribed
　circunscrito a, circumscribed about
cisoide, cisoid
clarificar, to clarify
claro, clear
　no claro, unclear
clase, class, course, type
clasificación, classification
　clasificación de ángulos de acuerdo al cuadrante, classifying angles by quadrant
　clasificación de triángulos, classification of triangles
clasificado, classified
　no clasificado, unclassified
clasificar, to classify, to sort, categorize
clausura, closure
clave, key
cobrar, to charge, to collect
cociente parte-parte, part-to-part ratio
cociente parte-todo, part-to-whole ratio
codificar, to codify, to encode
código, code
codominio, codomain
coeficiente, coefficient

coeficiente binomial, binomial coefficient
coeficiente conductor, leading coefficient
coeficiente constante, constant coefficient
coeficiente de correlación, correlation coefficient
coeficiente de regresión, regression coefficient
coeficiente de un producto, coefficient of a product
coeficiente entero, integer coefficient
coeficiente indeterminado, indeterminate coefficient, undetermined coefficient
coeficiente integral, integral coefficient
coeficiente literal, literal coefficient
coeficiente multinómico, multinomial coefficient
coeficiente numérico, numerical coefficient
coeficiente principal, lead coefficient
coeficiente racional, rational coefficient
cofunción, cofunction
　cofunción trigonométrica, trigonometric cofunctions
coherencia, consistence
coherente, coherent
　coherente total, coherent whole

coincidente, coincident
coincidir, coincide
co-interno, co-interior
cola, tail
colaboración, collaboration
colaborar, collaborate
colección, collection,
    colección de datos,
    collection of data
colectar, collect
colina, hill
colindante, adjacent
colinealidad, collinearity
    **colinealidad pre-
    servada,** collinearity
    preserved
colineal, collinear
    no colineal,
    noncollinear
colocar, put
cologaritmo, cologarithm
color, color
columna, column
    columna inicial,
    initial column
    columna terminal,
    terminal column
    matriz columna,
    column matrix
combar, to warp
combinación, combination
    **combinación con
    repetición,** combina-
    tion with repetition
    **combinación sin
    repetición,** combina-
    tion without repetition
combinar, combine
    **combinar
    los radicales,**
    combine the radicals
    **combinar los radi-
    cales semejantes,**

combine like radicals
    **combinar los tér-
    minos semejantes,**
    combine like terms
comercial, mainstream
cometa, kite, comet
comisión, commission
compactación,
    compactness
compacto, compactness,
    compact
comparable, analogous
comparación, comparison
comparar, to compare
compartir, to share
compás, compass
compeler, to compel
compensación,
    compensation
competencia, competency,
    competition
competente, competent
competidor, competitor
competir, to compete
competitivo, competitive
complejo, complex,
    unsimplified
complementar,
    to complement
complementario,
    complementary
complemento, complement
completar, to complete,
    to fill in
    **completar el cua-
    drado,** complete
    the square
completo, full, complete
complicación,complication
complicado,
    complicated, complex
    no complicado,
    uncomplicated

complicar, to complicate
componente, component
   componente imaginario, imaginary component
componer, to compose
comportamiento,
   behavior, conduct
composición, composition,
   conjugacy
   composición de las funciones, composition of functions
   composición de las transformaciones, composition of transformations
comprar, buy, purchase
comprender,
   to understand,
   comprehend
comprensible,
   comprehensible,
   understandable
comprensión,
   comprehension
comprobable, verifiable
comprobación, verification
   comprobación de una hipótesis, hypothesis testing
comprobar, to prove,
   to check, to verify
   comprobar por factoración, check by factoring
compuesto, compound,
   composite
computable, computable
computación,
   computer science
computacional,
   computational

computadora, computer
   computadora análoga o analógica, analog computer
computar,
   to compute, to tally
cómputo, tally, count,
   computation
común, common
   poco común,
   uncommon
comunicar, to interconnect, to communicate
con, with
   con reemplazo,
   with replacement
   con repetición,
   with repetition
   con respecto a,
   concerning,
   with respect to
concavidad, concavity
cóncavo, concave
concéntrico, concentric
concepto, concept
conceptualizar,
   to conceptualize
concluir, to conclude
conclusión, conclusion
   conclusión lógica,
   logical conclusion
   sacar conclusiones,
   draw conclusions
concluyente, conclusive
concordar, to match
concreto, concrete
concurrencia, concurrence
   concurrencia de bisectrices perpendiculares, perpendicular bisector concurrence
concurrente, concurrent
concurrir, to concur

concurso, contest
condición, condition
    condición inicial, initial condition
    condición necesaria, necessary condition
    condición necesaria pero no suficiente, necessary but not sufficient condition
    condición necesaria y suficiente, necessary and sufficient condition
    condición suficiente, sufficient condition
condicional, conditional
    condicional oculta, hidden conditional
conducir, to conduct, to drive
    conducir a, to lead to
conducta, behavior, conduct
conductor, conductor, driver
conectar, to connect
    conectar con, link up
conexión, connection
confiable, reliable
confianza, confidence
confirmado, confirmed
confirmar, to confirm
conflicto, conflict
conforme, congruent
    conforme a, according to, consistent with
conformidad, accordance
confundido, confused
confundir, to confuse

confuso, confusing, unclear
congruencia, congruency, congruence
congruente, congruent
cónico, conic
conjetura, conjecture, guess
    conjetura de Goldbach, Goldbach's conjecture
    conjetura matemática, mathematical conjecture
    formular una conjetura, formulate a conjecture, form a conjecture
    última conjetura de Fermat, Fermat's last theorem
conjeturar, conjecture
conjugado(a), conjugate
    conjugado complejo, complex conjugate
    conjugado de un número complejo, conjugate of a complex number
conjunción, conjunction
conjunto, set, group
    conjunto abierto, open set
    conjunto de datos, set of data
    conjunto de diferencia, difference set
    conjunto de diferencia simple, simple difference set
    conjunto de números, set of numbers

conjunto de números reales, set of real numbers
conjunto de números irracionales, set of irrational numbers
conjunto de números racionales, set of rational numbers
conjunto de objetos, set of objects
conjunto de puntos no colineales, noncollinear set of points
conjunto de reemplazo, replacement set
conjunto de verdad, truth set
conjunto no numerable, non-denumerable set
conjunto finito, finite set
conjunto imagen, image set
conjunto infinito, infinite set
conjunto no enumerado, non-enumerable set
conjunto no vacio, non-empty set
conjunto nulo, empty set, null set
conjunto propio, proper set
conjunto resultado, outcome set
conjunto solución, solution set
conjunto solución de un sistema de ecuaciones, solution set of system of equations
conjunto universal, universal set
conjunto vacío, empty set
conjuntos disyuntivos, disjoint sets
conjuntos equivalentes, equivalent sets
conjuntos mutuamente excluyentes, mutually exclusive sets
conmutar, to commute
conmutatividad, commutativity
conmutativo, commutative
cono, cone
cono autoconjugado, self-conjugate conic
cono circular, circular cone
cono circular recto, right circular cone
cono circunscrito, circumscribed cone
cono de revolución, cone of revolution
cono recto, right cone
cono truncado, frustum
conocer, to meet, to know
conocido, known
consecuencia, outcome
consecutivo, consecutive
conseguir, to get, to obtain
conservación, conservation
conservar, to conserve
considerablemente denso, nowhere dense
considerar, to consider
consiguiente, consequent

consistencia de axiomas,
consistency of axioms
**consistencia de ecuacio-
nes,** consistence of
equations
consistente, consistent
consolidar, consolidate
constante, constant
constante arbitraria,
arbitrary constant
**constante
de dilatación,**
constant of dilation
**constante de
proporcionalidad,**
constant of propor-
tionality
constante física,
physical constant
constante literal,
literal constant
constante numérica,
numerical constant
constatar,
to confirm, to verify,
to check, to show
constituir, to constitute
construcción, construction
**construcción aproxi-
mada,** approximate
construction
**construcción geomé-
trica,** geometric
construction
construido, built,
constructed
construir, to build,
to construct
contable, countable,
denumerable
contactar, to touch
contacto, contact
en contacto,

touching
contador, counter
contar, to count, to tally
contar por,
count by
**contar en
forma regresiva,**
count back,
count backwards
**contar por múltiplos
de un número,**
skip count
contenedor, container
contener, to contain
conteo, tally, count
conteo con palitos,
tally mark
contestar, to answer
contexto, context
contiguo,
adjacent, bordering
continuación, continuation
a continuación,
as follows
continuar, to continue
continuidad, continuity
**continuidad por
piezas,** piecewise
continuous
continuo, continuous,
unsegmented
contorno cerrado,
closed path
contra, against, counter
contra la intuición,
counterintuitive
contra los hechos,
counterfactual
contradecir,
to contradict, to con-
flict, to go against
contradicción,
contradiction

contradictorio, contradictory, conflicting

contraintuitivo, counterintuitive

contrapositivo, contrapositive

contrariar, to disagree

contrario, opposite

contrastante, contrasting

contrastar, to contrast

contraste, contrast

contribución, contribution

contribuir, to contribute

contundente, compelling, convincing, conclusive

convencer, to convince

convención, convention

convencional, conventional, mainstream

    no convencional, non-conventional

conveniente, convenient

convergencia, convergence

convergente, convergent, converging

convergir, to converge

conversión, conversion

converso, converse

    converso de una frase, converse of a statement

convertir, to convert

    convertir las medidas, convert measures

    convertirse en, to become

convexidad, convexity

convexo, convex

    ángulo convexo, convex angle

convincente, convincing, compelling

coordenada, coordinate

    coordenada polar, polar coordinate

    coordenada x, x-coordinate

    coordenada y, y-coordinate

    coordenadas baricéntricas, barycentric coordinates

    coordenadas cartesianas, Cartesian coordinates, coordinate grid

    coordenades lineales, linear coordinates

    coordenada rectangular, rectangular coordinate

coordinar, to coordinate

copiar, to copy

coplanar, coplanar

    no coplanar, non-coplanar

corchete, bracket, square bracket

    corchete circular, round bracket

    corchete cuadrado, square bracket

corolario, corollary

corona circular, annulus

correctivo, corrective, remedial

correcto, correct, right

corregir, correct

correlación, correlation

correlación inversa,
inverse correlation
correlación negativa,
negative correlation
correlación positiva,
positive correlation
correlacionar, to correlate
correspondencia,
correspondence
**correspondencia
biunívoca,**
one-to-one
correspondence
**correspondencia
de muchos a uno,**
many-to-one
correspondence
**correspondencia
de uno a muchos,**
one-to-many
correspondence
**correspondencia
de uno a uno,**
one-to-one
correspondence
**correspondencia
isométrica,** isometric
correspondence
corresponder,
to correspond
correspondiente,
corresponding
corriente, current
corriente dominante,
mainstream
corriente eléctrica,
electric current
corriente principal,
mainstream
cortar, to cut
corto, short, shortcircuit
más corto,
shorter

más corto que,
shorter than
el más corto,
shortest
cortocircuito,
shortcircuit
cosecante, cosecant
coseno, cosine
costado, side
al costado de,
alongside
costar, to cost
costear, to afford
costo, cost
cotangente, cotangent
cotejar, to match,
to compare
cotidiano, everyday
covarianza, covariance
crear, to create
crecer, to grow
**crecer exponencial-
mente,** increase
exponentially
**crecer logarítmi-
camente,** increase
logarithmically
creciente,
ascending, growing,
increasing
crecimiento, growth
**crecimiento
exponencial,**
exponential growth
crecimiento lineal,
linear growth
crédito, credit
creencia, belief
creer, to believe
creíble, plausible,
believable
criba de Eratóstenes,
Eratosthenes' sieve

criterios

criterios, criteria (sing. criterion)
  prueba de igualdad de fracciones, equality test of fractions
crítica, criticism, critique
criticar, to criticize, to critique
crítico(a), critical
cronológico, chronological
cronometrar, time
cruce, intersection, crossing
crucial, crucial
cruzar, to cross, to intersect, to span
cuaderno, notebook
  cuaderno de ejercicios, workbook
cuadrado, square (sq.)
  completar el cuadrado, complete the square
  cuadrado de un número, square of a number
  cuadrado inverso, inverse square
  cuadrado perfecto, perfect square
  diferencia de cuadrados, difference of two squares
  diferencia de dos cuadrados perfectos, difference of two perfect squares
  trinomio cuadrado perfecto, perfect square trinomial
cuadrángulo, quadrangle

cuadrar, to square
cuadrático, quadratic
cuadratriz, quadratrix
cuadratura de una sección cuadrático-lineal, quadrature of a conic
cuadrícula, grid
cuadrilátero, quadrilateral
cuadrilla de coordenadas, coordinate grid
cuadro, square (sq.), chart
cuadruplicar, to quadruple
cualidad, quality
cualquier, any
cuantificador, quantifier
  cuantificador existencial, existential qualifier
  cuantificador universal, universal quantifier
cuantificar, to quantify
cuantitativo, quantitative
cuartil, quartile
  cuartil superior, upper quartile
cuarto[1], fourth
  cuarto grado, fourth degree
cuarto[2], quarter
  cuarto de círculo, quarter-circle
cuarto de galón, quart (qt.)
cuaternión, quaternion
cuatro, four
cubicar, calculate the volume of
cúbico, cubic (cu.)
cubo, cube
cuboide, cuboid
cubrir, to cover
cucharada,

tablespoon (tbsp.)
cucharadita,
teaspoon (tsp.)
cuenta, count, tally
cuerda, chord
cuerda común,
common chord
cuerda de contacto,
chord at contract
cuerda de curvatura,
chord of curvature
cuerpo, body
cuesta, hill, slope
cuesta abajo,
downhill
cuesta arriba,
uphill
cuestión, question, issue
cuestionable, questionable
cuestionar, to question
cuidadoso, careful
cumplir con,
to meet, to fulfill
cuociente, quotient
cuota, quota
curioso,
curious, inquisitive,
strange, unusual
curva[1], curve
curva[2], curved
curva abierta,
open curve
curva algebraica,
algebraic curve
curva analítica,
coordinate curve
curva áspera,
unsmoothed curve
**curva básica del
coseno,** base cosine
curve
curva binómica,
binomial curve

curva cerrada,
closed curve, sharp
curve, sharp bend
curva cerrada simple,
simple closed curve
curva circular,
circular curve
curva compleja,
complex conjugate
**curva compleja
cerrada,** complex
closed curve
curva cóncava,
concave curve
curva continua,
smooth curve
curva cuadrática,
quadratic curve
**curva de coordena-
das,** coordinate curve
**curva de distribu-
ción normal,**
bell curve
**curva de la frecuen-
cia,** frequency curve
**curva de seguimien-
to,** curve of pursuit
curva degenerativa,
degenerative curve
**curva en forma de
campana,** bell curve
curva escalonada,
step curve
curva espacial,
space curve
curva inversa,
inverse curve
**curva logarítmica
recíproca,**
reciprocal logarithmic
curve
curva normal,
normal curve

curva orientada, oriented curve

curva paramétrica, parametric curve

curva periódica, periodic curve

curva reglada, ruled curve

curva secante, secant curve

curva simétrica, symmetrical curve

curva simple cerrada, simple closed curve

curva tangente, tangent curve

curva trascendental, transcendental curve

curvado, curved

curvatura, curvature

curvilíneo, curvilinear

D

dado, die (pl. dice)

dado(a), given

dados, dice (sing. die)

dar, to give

dar a, give to

dar de sí, to stretch

dar forma, to shape

dar la vuelta, to revolve, to rotate

darse cuenta, to realize, to notice, to observe

dato, datum

datos, data (sing. datum)

datos agrupados, grouped data

datos base, raw data

datos bivariados, bivariate data

datos crudos, raw data

datos de fundamento, raw data

datos de salida, output

datos originales, raw data

datos univariados, univariate data

de acuerdo con, in accordance with

de dirección preservada, sense-preserving

de dos en dos, two-by-two

de giro, pivoting

de lado opuesto, opposite side

de nuevo, again

de poca importancia, minor

de uno a uno, one at a time

de uno en uno, one-by-one

de varias variables, multiple variables

de vez en cuando, occasionally, sometimes, from time to time

debajo de, under

débil, weak

debilidad, weakness

débito, debit

década, decade

decaedro, decahedron

decaer exponencialmente,

decay exponentially
decágono, decagon
deceleración, deceleration
decenas, tens, tens place
decenas de mil,
    ten thousands
    decenas de millar,
    ten thousands place
decidible, decidable
decidir, to decide
decilitro, deciliter
décima más cercana,
    nearest tenth
decimal, decimal
    decimal finito,
    finite decimal,
    terminating decimal
    decimal ilimitado,
    unlimited decimal
    decimal infinito,
    infinite decimal, non-
    terminating decimal
    decimal mixto,
    mixed decimal
    decimal no periódico,
    non-repeating decimal
    decimal periódico,
    repeating decimal
    decimal recurrente,
    recurring decimal
    decimal terminal,
    terminating decimal
    **decimales equivalen-
    tes,** equivalent deci-
    mals
    decimales periódicos,
    periodic decimals
    decimales similares,
    similar decimals
    fracción decimal,
    decimal fraction
    lugar decimal,
    decimal place

notación decimal,
    decimal notation
    punto decimal,
    decimal point
décimas, tenths
decímetro, decimeter
décimo, tenth
decisión, decision
decisivo, crucial, decisive
declaración, declaration,
    statement
    **declaración geomé-
    trica,** geometric state-
    ment
    declaración inversa,
    inverse statement
    **declaración relacio-
    nada,** related state-
    ment
declarar, to declare,
    to state, to assert
declinar, to decline
declive, declination
decodificar, decode
decodificación, decoding
decreciente, decreasing
**decrecimiento exponen-
    cial,** exponential decay
deducción, deduction
deducible, deductible
deducir, to deduce
deductivo, deductive
defecto, flaw, defect
defectuoso, flawed,
    defective
defender, defend
deficiencia,
    incompleteness
definición, definition
    definición explícita,
    explicit definition
    definición recursiva,
    recursive definition

definir, to define
definitivo,
    definite, definitive
deformar,
    to deform, to warp
degradación, derangement
dejar[1], to leave
dejar[2], let
    dejar caer,
    to drop
    dejar de,
    to cease,
    to stop
del modo, modal
delantero, front
delimitante, bordering
delinear, sketch
delta de Kronecker,
    Kronecker delta
deltaedro, deltahedron
deltoide, deltoid
demanda, demand
    oferta y demanda,
    supply and demand
demostración indirecta,
    indicated demonstration
demostrar, to demonstrate,
    to show, to model
denominador, denominator
    denominador común,
    common denominator
    denominadores
    comunes, like
    denominators
    denominadores
    semejantes,
    like denominators
    máximo común de-
    nominador, greatest
    common divisor (GCD)
    menor denominador
    común, lowest com-
mon denominator
(LCD), least common
denominator
    mínimo común
    denominador,
    least common denomi-
nator (LCD), lowest
common denominator
(LCD)
denominar, to name
denotado por, denoted by
denotar, denote
densidad,
    density, compactness
    densidad real,
    real density
denso, dense
dentro, inside
    dentro de un sistema
    dado, within a given
    system
dependencia lineal,
    linear dependence
depender de, to depend on
dependiente, dependent
deplazamientos sucesi-
    vos, successive
    displacements
depreciación, depreciation
depreciar, to depreciate
depresión, depression
deprimir, to depress
derecho, right
derivación, derivation
    diferenciación
    implícita, implicit
    differentiation
derivada, derivative
    antiderivada,
    antiderivative
    derivada de
    orden superior,
    higher-order derivative

derivada parcial, partial derivative

segunda derivada, second derivative

derivar, to derive

derivar de, to follow

desaceleración, deceleration

desacelerar, to decelerate

desafiar, to challenge

desafío, challenge

desajuste, mismatch

desalinear, to unalign

desaparición idéntica, identically vanishing

desapercibido, unobserved

desaprobar, to fail

desarrollar, to develop, to expand

desarrollo, development

descartar, to discard, to rule out

descendente, descending

descender, to descend, to go down

descifrar, to decode, to decipher

descodificar, to decode

descomponer, to decompose, to break into, to break down

descomposición, decomposition, breakdown

descomposición en factores, factoring

desconectado, unrelated, unconnected, disconnected

desconectar, to disconnect

desconexión, disconnection

desconocido, unknown

descontar, to discount

descubierto, discovered, uncovered

no descubierto, undiscovered

descubrimiento, discovery

descubrir, to discover, to uncover

descuento, discount

descuidado, careless

desempeñar, to perform a duty

desempeño, performance

desequilibrado, unbalanced

deshacerse de, to get rid of

designación, designation

designar, to designate

desigual, unequal

desigualdad, inequality

desigualdad absoluta, absolute inequality

desigualdad con una variable, inequality containing one variable

desigualdad condicional, conditional inequality

desigualdad cuadrática, quadratic inequality

desigualdad de primer grado, first-degree inequality

desigualdad de triángulos, triangle inequality

desigualdad de valor absoluto, absolute value inequality

desigualdad equivalente, equivalent inequality

desigualdad inconsistente, inconsistent inequality

desigualdad lineal, linear inequality

desigualdad lineal con dos variables, linear inequality in two variables

desigualdad racional, rational inequality

desigualdades que envuelven fracciones, inequality involving fractions

desigualdades simultáneas, simultaneous inequalities

deslizar, to slide

desordenado, disordered, chaotic, unsystematic

despejar, to isolate the variable, to clear

despejar (la variable), to isolate a variable

desperfecto, flaw

desplazamiento, displacement

desplazamiento de fase, phase displacement, phase shift

desplazamiento simultáneo, simultaneous displacement

desplazar, to displace, to spread

desproporcionado, disproportionate

desprovisto de, void

después, after, afterwards

después de, after

desunir, disjoint

desviación, deviation

desviación absoluta, absolute deviation

desviación absoluta media, mean absolute deviation

desviación estándar, standard deviation

desviación normal, standard deviation

desviación típica, standard deviation

desviar, to deviate

detallar, to detail

detalle, detail

determinante, determinant

determinar, to determine

detrás de, behind

devolver, to return

día, day

diagonal, diagonal

diagonal principal, leading diagonal, main diagonal, principal diagonal

diagonalización de zuna matriz, diagonalization of a matrix

diagrama, diagram

diagrama acompañante, accompanying diagram

diagrama de árbol, tree diagram

diagrama de caja y bigotes, box-and-whisker plot

diagrama de

dispersión, scattergram

diagrama de flujo, flow diagram

diagrama de frecuencia, frequency diagram

diagrama de tallo y hoja, stem and leaf plot

diagrama de Venn, Venn diagram

diagrama lineal, line plot

diagrama ramificado, tree diagram

diamante, diamond

diámetro, diameter

diámetro de un círculo, diameter of a circle

diámetro de una esfera, diameter of a sphere

diario, daily

dibujar, to draw

dibujar al trazo, to sketch

dibujar el gráfico de, draw the graph of

dibujar en un plano, to plot

dibujar la figura, draw the figure

dibujar una imagen, draw a picture

dibujo, drawing, illustration, picture

dibujo a escala, scale drawing

diccionario, dictionary

dicotomía, dichotomy

diestro, right-handed

diez, ten

diezmilésimas, ten-thousandths

diferencia, difference

diferencia común, common difference

diferencia de dos cuadrados, difference of two squares

diferencia de dos cuadrados perfectos, difference of two perfect squares

diferencia entre dos cubos, difference of two cubes

diferenciable, differentiable

diferenciación, differentiation

diferencial, differential

diferenciar, to differentiate

diferente, different, unalike, unlike

difícil, difficult, hard

digital, digital

dígito, digit

dígito binario, binary digit

dígito significativo, significant digit

dilatar, dilate

dimensión, dimension

de una dimensión, one-dimensional

de dos dimensiones, two-dimensional

de tres dimensiones, three-dimensional

dimensiones de un rectángulo, dimensions of a rectangle

dimensional, dimensional
    bidimensional,
    two-dimensional
    multidimensional,
    multidimensional
    tridimensional,
    three-dimensional
    unidimensional,
    one-dimensional
dimensionalidad,
    dimensionality
diminuto, minute, tiny
dinámico, dynamic
diofántico, Diophantine
dirección, direction
    de dirección
    preservada,
    sense-preserving
    dirección escolar,
    principal's office
    en dirrección
    contraria al reloj,
    counterclockwise
    direction
directo, direct
director de la escuela,
    principal
directriz, directrix
    directriz de una
    parábola, directory
    of a parabola
dirigido, directed
    dirigido a,
    pointed to
    dirigidos opuesta-
    mente, oppositely
    directed
dirigirse, to direct
    dirigirse hacia,
    to point to
disco, disc, disk
discontinuo,
    discontinuous

discordar en fase,
    be out of phase
discrepar, to disagree
discreto, discrete
discriminante,
    discriminant
discriminar,
    to discriminate
diseñar, to design
diseño, design
    diseño experimental,
    experimental design
disminución porcentual,
    percent decrease
disminuir, to decrease,
    to shrink
disparejo, uneven
dispersar, to spread,
    disperse
dispersión, dispersion
disponibilidad, availability
distancia, distance,
    gap, span
    distancia desde un
    punto fijo, distance
    from a fixed point
    distancia entre
    dos puntos, distance
    between two points
    distancia entre
    dos rectas paralelas,
    distance between
    two parallel lines
    distancia entre un
    punto y una recta,
    distance between a
    point and a line
    distancia euclidiana,
    Euclidean distance
    distancia fija,
    fixed distance
    distancia horizontal,
    horizontal distance

distancia preservada, distance preserved
distancia vertical, vertical distance
distante, distant
distinción, distinction
distinguible, distinguishable
distinguir, to differentiate, to distinguish
distinto, dissimilar, distinct
distinto de, not equal to
distorsión, distortion
distorsionar, to distort
distribución, distribution
curva de distribución normal, bell curve
distribución de chi-cuadrada, chi-squared distribution
distribución de Dirac, Dirac function
distribución de la frecuencia, frequency distribution
distribución normal, normal distribution
distribución normal estándar, standard normal distribution
distribución de Poisson, Poisson distribution
distribuciones de frecuencias grupales, grouped frequency distributions
distribución de t, t-distribution
distribuir, to distribute
distributividad,

distributivity
distributivo, distributive
disyunción, disjunction
disyunción inclusiva, inclusive disjunction
disyuntivo, disjoint, disjunctive
divergencia, divergence
divergente, divergent
dividendo, dividend
dividir, to divide, to split
dividir en mitades, halving, halve
dividir en n partes iguales, divide into n evenly
dividir exactamente, come out even
dividir por la mitad, divide in half, halving, halve
dividir residuo, come out even
dividir sin resto, come out even
divisibilidad, divisibility
divisible, divisible
divisible por, divisible by
división, division, partition
división de casilla, long division
división de Horner, long division, synthetic division
división de un segmento de recta, division of a line segment
división interna, internal division
división sintética, synthetic division

división sucesiva, successive division
divisor, divisor
divisor cero, zero divisor
divisor complementario, complementary divisor
divisor común, common divisor
divisor de prueba, trial divisor
divisor nulo, null divisor
máximo común divisor, greatest common factor (GCF), highest common divisor
doblado, bent
doblaje múltiple, multi-fold
doblar, to bend, doubling
doble, double, twice
doblete unidad, unit doublet
doce docenas, gross
docena, dozen (doz.)
dodecaedro, dodecahedron
dodecaedro regular, regular dodecahedron
dodecágono, dodecagon
dólar, dollar
dominio, domain
dominio de una función, domain of a function
dominio denso, dense domain
dominio real, real domain
dominio restringido, restricted domain

dominio tridimensional, three-dimensional domain
dominó, domino
dona, annulus
dos, two
de dos en dos, two-by-two
dos veces, twice
dudoso, doubtful, questionable, uncertain
duplicado, duplicate
duplicar, to duplicate, to double, doubling
duro, hard

echar, throw away
ecuación, equation
ecuación algebraica, algebraic equation
ecuación algebraica irreducible, irreducible algebraic equation
ecuación condicional, conditional equation
ecuación cuadrática, quadratic equation
ecuación cuadrática incompleta, incomplete quadratic equation
ecuación cuadrática pura, pure quadratic equation
ecuación cúbica,

cubic equation
ecuación de la recta, equation of a line
ecuación de primer grado con una variable, first-degree equation with one variable
ecuación de regresión, regression equation
ecuación de segundo grado, second-degree equation
ecuación de suma, addition sentence
ecuación de valor absoluto, absolute-value equation
ecuación derivada, derived equation
ecuación diferencial, differential equation
ecuación diofántica, Diophantine equation
ecuación diofantina, Diophantine equation
ecuación en derivadas parciales, partial differential equation
ecuación exponencial, exponential equation
ecuación fraccionaria, fractional equation
ecuación incondicional, unconditional equation
ecuación indefinida, indefinite equation
ecuación indeterminada, indeterminate equation

ecuación inversa, inverse equation
ecuación lineal, linear equation
ecuación lineal de una variable, linear equation in one variable
ecuación literal, literal equation
ecuación polinomial, polynomial equation
ecuación polinómica, polynomial equation
ecuación punto-pendiente de una recta, point-slope equation of a line
ecuación que contiene paréntesis, equation containing parentheses
ecuación radical, radical equation
ecuación reducible, reducible equation
ecuación reducida, reduced equation
ecuación resultante, resulting equation
ecuación simple, simple equation
ecuación tangencial, tangential equation
ecuación trigonométrica, trigonometric equation
ecuaciones consistentes, consistent equations
ecuaciones dependientes, dependent equations

ecuaciones inconsis-tentes, inconsistent equations

ecuaciones lineales dependientes, dependent linear equations

ecuaciones simé-tricas, symmetrical equations

ecuaciones simultá-neas, simultaneous equations

ecuaciones equiva-lentes, equivalent equations

educación, education

educación bilingüe, bilingual education

educación especial, special education

efectivo, cash, actual

efecto, effect

efectos, property

efectuar, carry out

eficacia relativa, relative efficiency

eje, axis (pl. axes)

eje cuádrico, axis of quadric

eje de las abscisas, axis of abscissas

eje de los núme-ros reales, real number axis

eje de ordenadas, axis of ordinates

eje de rotación, axis of rotation, rotation axis

eje de simetría, axis of symmetry

eje de un cilindro, axis of a cylinder

eje de una sección cónica, axis of a conic section

eje horizontal, horizontal axis

eje imaginario, axis of imaginaries, imaginary axis

eje longitudinal, longitudinal axis

eje mayor, major axis

eje menor, minor axis

eje numérico, number axis

eje real, real axis

eje transverso, transverse axis

eje vertical, vertical axis

eje x, x-axis

eje y, y-axis

ejes de coordenadas, coordinate axes

ejecutar la operación, perform the operation

ejemplo, example, model

ejemplo contrario, counterexample

ejercicio, exercise

elaborar, to develop, to elaborate

elección, election, choice

electricidad, electricity, power

eléctrico, electric

electromagnético, electro-magnetic

elegir, to pick, to choose
    elegir al azar,
    draw at random
elemental, elementary
elemento, element
    elemento autocorres-
    pondiente,
    self-corresponding
    element
    elemento convexo,
    convex body
    elemento de
    identidad,
    identity element
    elemento de
    identidad aditiva,
    identity element for
    addition
    elemento de identi-
    dad multiplicativa,
    identity element for
    multiplication
    elemento de
    rotación,
    body of rotation
    elemento de
    un conjunto,
    element in a set
    elemento de unidad,
    unit element
    elemento de
    volumen,
    volume element
    elemento
    escalar de arco,
    scalar arc segment
    elemento
    escalar de línea,
    scalar line element
    elemento escalar
    de superficie,
    scalar surface element
    elemento finito,

    finite element
    elemento guía,
    leading element
    elemento inverso,
    inverse element
    elemento neutro,
    neutral element
    elemento nulo,
    null element
    elemento vectorial
    de arco, vector path
    element
    elemento vectorial
    de línea, vector line
    element
    elemento vectorial
    de superficie,
    vector surface element
    elementos disyunti-
    vos, disjoint elements
elevación, elevation
elevado al cubo, cubed
elevar, to elevate, to raise
    elevar a una poten-
    cia, to raise to a power
    elevar al cuadrado
    ambos lados,
    square both sides
    elevar al cubo,
    to cube
    elevar ambos
    lados al cubo,
    cube both sides
elegible, eligible
eliminación, elimination
    eliminación de fac-
    tores irrelevantes,
    elimination of irrel-
    evant factors
    eliminación de
    variables desconoci-
    das, elimination
    of unknowns

eliminación por sustitución, elimination of substitution
eliminación sucesiva, successive elimination
eliminar, to eliminate, to rule out, take out
elipse, ellipse
elipsoide, ellipsoid
elíptico, elliptical, elliptic
emparejar, to level, to equalize, to pair off, to match
emparejar mal, to mismatch
empatar, to tie
empírico, empirical
emplear, to use
en, in, on, at, onto
en todas partes, everywhere
encabezado, heading
encajar, to fit
encentrar, incenter
encerrar, to enclose
enchuecar, to skew
encima, above, over, on top
encima de cero, above zero
encoger, to shrink
encontrar, to find, to locate
encontrar la solución del conjunto, find the solution set
encontrar el valor de, find the value of
encontrar la circunferencia de un círculo, find the circumference of
encontrarse, to meet
encorvar, to curve

encuadrar, to square
encuentro, encounter, binding
encuesta, poll, survey
energía, energy
enésimo[1], nth
enésimo[2], umpteenth
énfasis, emphasis
enfatizar, to emphasize
enfocar, to focus
enfoque, focus
enfoque alternativo, alternate approach
enfoque inválido, invalid approach
engañar, to trick, to cheat
engaño, trick
engañoso, misleading
enlace, link
enlazar, to link, to bind
enmarcar, to frame
ensayar, to test, to try, to practice
ensayo, trial, test, rehersal, essay
ensayo y error, trial and error
tubo de ensayo, test tube
entender, to understand
entendible, understandable
entero[1], entire, whole
entero[2], integer
entero impar, odd integer
entero negativo, negative integer
entero par, even integer
entero positivo, positive integer
enteros consecu-

tivos, consecutive integers

enteros impares consecutivos, consecutive odd integers

enteros pares consecutivos, consecutive even integers

enteros sin signos, signless integers

entidad, entity

entonces, then

entrada, input

entrada de datos, input

entrar, to enter

entrar (una tabla o gráfica), enter (a table or graph)

entre, between

enumeración, enumeration

enumerar, to enumerate, to list

enunciado, statement

enunciado compuesto, compound statement

enunciado condicional, conditional statement

enunciado de resta, subtraction sentence

enunciado matemático, mathematical statement

envergadura, width

epiciclo, epicycle

epicicloide, epicycloid

equiangular, equiangular

triángulo equian-

gular, equiangular triangle

equidistante, equidistant

equilátero, equilateral

triángulo equilátero, equilateral triangle

equilibrar, to balance

equilibrio, balance

equipotencial, equipotential

equitativamente, evenly

equivalencia, equivalence

equivalente, equivalent

equivalente lógico, logical equivalent

no equivalente a, not equal to

equivocado, wrong

equivocarse, to make a mistake

errar, to err, to make a mistake

errático, erratic

erróneo, wrong, erroneous

error, error

error de medida, measurement error

error de muestreo, sampling error

error de porcentaje, percentage error

error de redondeamiento, rounding error

error de redondeo, rounding error

error de truncamiento, truncation error

error porcentual, percentage error

error promedio, average error

error relativo,
relative error
error tipo I,
type I error
error tipo II,
type II error
escala, scale
escala absoluta,
absolute scale
escala de la razón,
ratio scale
escala de mapa,
map scale
**escala de probabili-
dad,** probability scale
escala de un gráfico,
scale of a graph
escala interior,
inner scale
escalar[1], to scale, to climb
escalar[2], scalar
escaleno, scalene
triángulo escaleno,
scalene triangle
escalón, step
escoger, to pick, to choose
escoger al azar,
to randomly draw,
to randomly choose
escribir, to write, to record
escrito(a), written
escrutinio, scrutiny
escuchar, listen
escudo (de moneda),
tail (of a coin)
escudriñar, to scrutinize
escuela, school
escuela preparatoria,
high school
escuela primaria,
elementary school
escuela secundaria,
middle school, junior

high school
esencial, essential, key
no esencial,
extraneous
esfera, sphere
esfera circunscrita,
circumscribed sphere,
circumsphere
esfera inscrita,
insphere, inscribed
sphere
esfera sólida,
solid sphere
esférico, spherical
espacial, spatial
espacio,
space, gap, spacing
espacio de puntos,
point space
espacio en blanco,
gap, whitespace
espacio euclidiano,
Euclidean space
espacio hermítico,
Hermitian space
espacio modelo,
sample space
**espacio muestral
finito,** finite
sample space
**espacio unidemensio-
nal,** one-dimensional
space
espacio vectorial,
vector space
**espacio vectorial
de n dimensiones,**
n-dimensional vector
space
esparcir, to scatter,
to spread
especial, special
especificación,

specification
especificado, specified
no especificado, unspecified
especificar, to specify
específico, specific
espectro, spectrum
especular, to speculate
especulativo, speculative
espejo, mirror
esperar, to expect
espesor, thickness
espiral, spiral
espiral hiperbólica, hyperbolic spiral
esporádico, occasional
esquina, corner, corner point
estabilización, stabilization
establecer, to establish
estaca, peg
estación, season
estadística, statistic
estadística parcial, biased statistic
estadísticas, statistics, stats
estadístico[1], statistician
estadístico(a)[2], statistical
estado, state
estado financiero, bank statement
estándar, standard
no estándar, nonstandard
estandarización, standardization
estandarizar, standardize
estar de acuerdo, to agree
no estar de acuerdo, to disagree
estar en fase, be in phase

este, east
estereorradián, steradian
estimación, estimation
estimación lineal, linear estimation
estimación razonable, reasonable estimate
estimado, estimate, estimated
estimado aproximado, rough estimate
estimado estadístico del error, statistical estimate of error
estimado preliminar, rough estimate
estimador parcial, biased estimator
estimar, to estimate
estirar, to stretch
estrategia, strategy
estrategias para calcular aproximadamente, estimation strategies
estrategias para resolver los problemas, problem solving strategies
estratificado, stratified
estratificar, to stratify
estrecho, narrow
estructura, structure
estructurar, to structure
estudiar, to study
estudio, study
estudio empírico, empirical study
etapa, stage
en etapas, in stages, stratified

etcétera, etc. (et cetera)
etiqueta, label
etiquetar, label
    etiquetar el conjunto solución, label the solution set
Euclides, Euclid
euclidiano(a), Euclidean
evaluación, evaluation, assessment
evaluar, to evaluate, to assess, to analyze
    evaluar la eficiencia, evaluate efficiency
    evaluar una expresión algebraica, evaluate an algebraic expression
evento, event
    evento al azar, random event
    evento cierto, certain event
    evento compuesto, compound event
    evento favorable, favorable event
    evento imposible, impossible event
    evento independiente, independent event
    evento posible, possible event
    evento seguro, event that is certain
    evento simple, simple event
    evento singular, single event
    eventos complementarios, complementary events
    eventos compuestos, compound events
    eventos dependientes, dependent events
    eventos desligados, disjoint events
    eventos que se excluyen mutuamente, mutually exclusive events
evidencia, proof
evidente, evident
    evidente por sí mismo, self-evident
exactamente, exactly
exactitud, accuracy
exacto, correcto, exact
    exacto hasta el entero más cercano, correct to the nearest integer
    exacto hasta la décima más cercana, correct to the nearest tenth
examen, exam
    examen final, final exam
    examen parcial, mid-term exam
examinación, examination, review
examinar, to examine, to review, to scrutinize
exceder, to exceed, to out-pace
excelente, excellent
excentricidad, eccentricity
excéntrico, eccentric
excentros, excenters
excepción, exception
excepto, except
excepto cuando, unless

exceso, excess
excluir, to exclude
exclusive, exclusive
excluyente, exclusive
  mutuamente
  excluyente,
  mutually exclusive
éxito, success
  tener éxito,
  to succeed
exitoso, successful
expandir, to expand,
  to extend
  expandir un binomio,
  expand a binomial
expansión, expansion
  expansión binómica,
  binomial expansion
  expansión de un
  binomio, expansion
  of a binomial
expectativa, expectation
  expectativa númerica
  ampliada, expanded
  numeral expectation
expediente, file, record
experimental,
  experimental
experimentar,
  to experiment,
  to experience
experimento, experiment
  experimento
  controlado,
  controlled experiment
  experimento
  de Bernoulli,
  Bernoulli experiment
  experimento de
  evento singular,
  single-event
  experiment
  experimento único,
  single-event experi-
  ment
explicable, explicable
explicación, explanation
  explicación escrita,
  written explanation
  explicación verbal,
  verbal explanation
explicar, to explain,
  to account for
explícito, explicit
exploración, exploration
explorar, to explore
exponenciación,
  exponentiation
exponencial, exponential
exponente, exponent,
  power, index
  exponente cero,
  zero exponent
  exponente fraccional,
  fractional exponent
  exponente fracciona-
  rio, fractional exponent
  exponente integral,
  integral exponent
  exponente negativo,
  negative exponent
  exponente real,
  real exponent
expresar, to express
  expresar en forma
  radical simple,
  express in simplest
  radical form
  expresar en términos
  de, express in terms of
expresión, expression
  expresión abierta,
  open expression
  expresión algebraica,
  algebraic expression

expresión aritmética, arithmetic expression

expresión binómica, binomial expression

expresión cúbica perfecta, perfect cubic expression

expresión equivalente, equivalent expression

expresión exponencial, exponential expression

expresión fraccional, fractional expression

expresión general, general expression

expresión literal, literal expression

expresión numérica, numerical expression

expresión polinomial, polynomial expression

expresión racional, rational expression

expresión racional compleja, complex rational expression

expresión verbal, verbal expression

expresiones numéricas equivalentes, equivalent numerical expressions

extender, to extend, to spread, to stretch, expand

extender indefinidamente, extend indefinidamente

extender la línea númerica, extend the number line

extensión, extension, span, reach, spread

extensión finita, finite extension

extensión ilimitada, unlimited extent

extensión infinita, infinite extension

extenso, ample, broad

exterior, exterior, outside

el más exterior, outmost

más exterior, outer

externo(a), extraneous, external

el más externo, outmost

más externo, outer

extra, extra

extraer una raíz, extract a root

extraño, odd, strange, unusual, puzzling

extraordinario, unusual

extrapolación, extrapolation

extrapolar, to extrapolate

extremo[1], endpoint, extremum, extreme, edge

extremo lateral, lateral edge

extremos de una proporción, extremes of a proportion

extremo[2], extreme

fácil, easy
facilidad, ease
factible, feasible
fáctico, factual
factor, factor
    factor común,
    common factor
    factor común
    del monomio,
    common monomial
    factor
    factor común
    máximo, highest
    common factor
    factor común
    mayor, greatest
    common factor (GCF)
    factor común mayor
    del monomio, great-
    est monomial factor
    factor común míni-
    mo, least common
    factor
    factor constante,
    constant factor
    factor de conversión,
    conversion factor
    factor de crecimien-
    to, growth factor
    factor de repetición,
    repetend
    factor integral,
    integral factor
    factor primo,
    prime factor
    factor racionalizante,
    rationalizing factor
    ramificaciones

    de los factores,
    factor tree
factoreo, factoring
factorial, factorial
factorizable, factorable
factorización,
    factorization
    factorización prima,
    prime factorization
factorizar, to factor
    factorizar
    completamente,
    factor completely
    factorizar un
    polinomio,
    factor a polynomial
    factorizar un
    trinomio,
    factor a trinomial
factual, factual
fallar, to fail
falacia, fallacy
falsa, false
    falsa afirmación,
    false positive
    falsa negación,
    false negative
falso, false, untrue
    falso negativo,
    false negative
    falso positivo,
    false positive
faltante, missing
faltar, to miss
    faltar de hacer algo,
    to fail to do something
familia, family
fanega, bushel
fase, phase
fecha, date
fechar, to date
fenómeno, phenomena
    (sing. phenomenon)

fenómeno de la física, physical phenomena

fenómeno matemático, mathematical phenomena

fenómeno social, social phenomena

fiabilidad, reliability

fiable, dependable, reliable

no fiable, unreliable

ficha, chip

fidedigno, reliable

no fidedigno, unreliable

figura, figure, shape

figura abierta, open figure

figura cerrada, closed figure

figura circunscrita, circumscribed figure

figura de cuatro lados, four-sided figure

figura geométrica, geometric figure, geometric shape

figura inscrita, inscribed figure

figura simétrica, symmetrical figure

figura sólida, solid figure

figuras congruentes, congruent figures

figuras similares, similar figures

figuras geométricas planas, plane geometric figures

fijar, to set

fijo(a), fixed

fila, row

fila inicial, initial row

filoso, pointed, pointy, sharp

filtrar, to filter

filtro, filter

fin, end

al fin, at the end of

a fines de, towards the end of

sin fin, endless, never-ending

final, end, final

examen final, final exam

finitud, finiteness

finito, finite

fino, fine

física, physics

físico, physical

flecha, arrow

flexible, flexible, pliable

flexómetro, tape measure

flojo, loose

fluctuación de los datos, range of data

fluctuación de una función, range of a function

fluctuante, fluctuating

fluctuar, to fluctuate

fluir, to flow

flujo, flow, flux

flujograma, flow chart

foco, focus (pl. foci)

foco de una parábola, focus of a parabola

fondo, bottom

forma, form, shape

forma algebraica, algebraic form
forma binaria, binary form
forma corriente, standard form
forma estándar, standard form
forma exponencial, exponential form
forma gráfica de razonamiento, written form of reasoning
forma indefinida, indefinite form
forma indeterminada, indeterminate form
forma inversa, inverse form
forma irregular, irregular shape
forma lineal, linear form
forma logarítmica, logarithmic form
forma más simple, simplest form
forma normalizada, normalized form
forma pendiente intercepto, slope-intercept form
forma pendiente-punto de una línea, point-slope form of line
forma radical, radical form
forma radical más simple, simplest radical form

forma reducida, reduced form
forma regular de una ecuación cuadrática, standard form of a quadratic equation
formas equivalentes, equivalent forms
formado por una transversal, formed by a transversal
formalmente, formally
formar, to form, to shape
formato, format
formato horizontal, horizontal format
formato vertical, vertical format
fórmula, formula
fórmula cuadrática, quadratic formula
fórmula de diferencia para funciones trigonométricas, difference formula for trigonometric functions
fórmula de distancia, distance formula
fórmula de doble ángulo para una función trigonométrica, double angle formula for a trigonometric function
fórmula de Euler, Euler's formula
fórmula de Herón, Heron's formula
fórmula de interés compuesto, compound interest formula

fórmula de interés simple, simple interest formula

fórmula de medio ángulo para una función trigonométrica, half angle formula for a trigonometric function

fórmula de probabilidad binomial, binomial probability formula

fórmula de suma para funciones trigonométricas, sum formula for trigonometric functions

fórmula de Taylor, Taylor's Theorem

fórmula fundamental, fundamental formula

segunda fórmula de Green, second Green formula

formular, formulate, form

formular preguntas matemáticas, formulate mathematical questions

formular una conjetura, formulate a conjecture, form a conjecture

formular una pregunta, to ask a question

fortaleza, strength

forzar, to force, to make, to oblige

Fourier, Fourier

fracaso, failure

fracción, fraction

fracción algebraica, algebraic fraction

fracción aritmética, arithmetic fraction

fracción compuesta, complex fraction

fracción común, common fraction

fracción continua interminable, non-terminating continued fraction

fracción de términos simplificados, lowest terms fraction

fracción decimal, decimal fraction

fracción impropia, improper fraction

fracción mixta, mixed fraction

fracción periódica, periodic fraction

fracción propia, proper fraction

fracción racional, rational fraction

fracción reducible, reducible fraction, reduced fraction

fracción unitaria, unit fraction

fracciones equivalentes, equivalent fractions

fraccionación, fractionation

fraccionario, fractional

fractal, fractal

fragmentar, to fragment

fragmentario, fragmentary

fragmento, fragment

frase, sentence, phrase

frase abierta,
open sentence
frase aritmética,
arithmetic statement
frase cerrada,
closed sentence
frase matemática,
mathematical sentence
**frase universalmente
cuantificada,**
universally quantified
statement
**frases lógicamente
equivalentes,**
logically equivalent
statements
frecuencia, frequency
**frecuencia de una
función periódica,**
frequency of a periodic
function
**frecuencia esta-
dística,** statistical
frequency
**frecuencia relativa
acumulativa,** cumula-
tive relative frequency
frente, front
frontera, border
frontero, opposite, facing
fuera, outside, out
fuera de secuencia,
out of sequence,
out of order
fuera de uso,
obsolete
fuerte, strong
fuerza, force
fuerza resultante,
resultant force
función, function
función algebraica,
algebraic function

función asociada,
cofunction
función circular,
circular function
**función complemen-
taria,** complementary
function
**función comple-
tamente convexa,**
completely convex
function
función compuesta,
compound function
función conocida,
known function
función cosecante,
cosecant function
función coseno,
cosine function
función constante,
constant function
función cotangente,
cotangent function
función creciente,
increasing function
función cuadrática,
quadratic function
**función de escalón
generalizado,**
general step function
función de onda,
wave function
**función de uno
a uno,** one-to-one
function
**función de valor
absoluto,** absolute-
value function
función decreciente,
decreasing function
**función del entero
mayor,** greatest-inte-
ger function

función del seno, sine function

función escalonada, step function

función escalón unitario, unit step function

función explícita, explicit function

función exponencial, exponential function

función hiperbólica, hyperbolic function

función impar, odd function

función implícita, implicit function

función inversa, inverse function

función inversa de la tangente, inverse tangent function

función inversa del coseno, inverse cosine function

función inversa del seno, inverse sine function

función inversa en composición, inverse function under composition

función iterativa, iterative function

función lineal, linear function

función logarítmica, logarithmic function

función no periódica, non-periodic function

función numérica, numerical function

función periódica, periodic function

función polinómica, polynomial function

función racional, rational function

función secante, secant function

función tangente, tangent function

función trascendental, transcendental function

función trigonométrica, trigonometric function

función trigonométrica inversa, inverse trigonometric function

función trigonométrica recíproca, reciprocal trigonometric function

funcional, functional

funcionar, to function, to work

fundado, founded, supported, sound

fundamentado, supported

fundamental, fundamental

fundamentar, to support

fundamento, foundation

fundamento lógico, rationale

galón, gallon (gal.)

ganancias, earnings

ganancias netas, net earnings, profit

ganar, to earn, to win
    ganar neto,
    to net
gastar, to spend
gastos, expenses
Gaussiano, Gaussian
general, general
    en general,
    generally
generalización,
    generalization
generalizado, generalized
generalizar, to generalize
generalmente, generally
generar, to generate
geodésica, geodesic
geometría, geometry
    geometría analítica,
    analytic geometry,
    coordinate geometry
    geometría de
    coordenadas,
    coordinate geometry
    geometría de sólidos,
    solid geometry
    geometría diferen-
    cial, differential geom-
    etry
    geometría euclidiana,
    Euclidean geometry,
    plane geometry
    geometría hiperbóli-
    ca, hyperbolic geom-
    etry
    geometría no eucli-
    diana, non-Euclidean
    geometry
    geometría plana,
    plane geometry
    geometría sólida,
    solid geometry
    geometría transfor-
    macional, transforma-

tional geometry
geométrico(a), geometric
giga, giga
girando, pivoting
girar,
    to turn, to rotate,
    to revolve, to pivot
    girar alrededor
    del origen, turn
    about the origin
giro, whirl, turn
    de giro,
    pivoting
    giro de un cuarto,
    quarter-turn
    punto de giro,
    turning point
glosario, glossary
gota, drop
grabar, to record
gradiente,
    slope, gradient, grade
grado[1], degree
    cuarto grado,
    fourth degree
    de grado dos,
    second degree
    de grado tres,
    third degree
    de grado uno,
    first degree
    grado cero,
    zero degree
    grados de libertades,
    degrees of freedom
    grado de un ángulo,
    degree of an angle
    grado de un mono-
    mio, degree of a
    monomial
    grado de un poli-
    nomio, degree of a
    polynomial

grado de un término algebraico, degree of an algebraic term

grado de una ecuación, degree of an equation

grado de una expression algebraica, degree of an algebraic expresion

grado Fahrenheit, Fahrenheit (F)

grado más cercano, nearest degree

grado², grade

grado escolar, grade

graduación, graduation

graduado, graduated, graduate

gradual, gradual

gráfica, graph

gráfica circular, pie chart, circle graph

gráfica de barras, bar chart, bar graph

gráfica de bloque, block graph

gráfica de dibujos, picture graph

gráfica de líneas, line graph, line plot

gráfica de pastel, pie chart

gráfica lineal, line graph

gráficamente, graphically

graficar, to graph

graficar el conjunto, graph the set

graficar una desigualdad, graph an inequality

graficar una ecuación, graph an equation

graficar una ecuación cuadrática, graph a quadratic equation

gráfico¹, graph

gráfico de barras, bar graph

gráfico de barras dobles, double bar graph

gráfico de caja, box plot

gráfico de caja y bigotes, box and whisker diagram

gráfico de dispersión, scatter plot

gráfico de una ecuación en dos variables, graph of an equation in two variables

gráfico de una oración lineal abierta en dos variables, graph of a linear open sentence in two variables

gráfico escalonado, step graph

gráfico organizado, organized chart

gráficos de líneas dobles, double line graph

gráfico², graphic (graphical)

gramo, gram (g)

grande, large, big

el más grande, most, biggest, largest

gravedad, gravitation, gravity

gravitación, gravitation
griego, Greek
grosor, thickness
gruesa, gross
grueso, thick
grupo, group, cluster
    grupo abeliano,
    Abelian group
    grupo conmutativo,
    commutative group
    grupo finito,
    finite group
    grupos de conjuntos
    finitos, groups with
    finite sets
    grupos de conjuntos
    infinitos, groups with
    infinite sets
guía, guide
    guía de estudios,
    study guide
guiar, to guide

hacer, to do, to make
    hacer asociaciones,
    to match
    hacer concordancias,
    to match
    hacer esquina,
    to intersect
    hacer trampa,
    to cheat
    hacer un descuento,
    to discount
    hacer un dibujo,
    draw a picture
    hacer una lista,
    to make a list

    hacer una represen-
    tación del problema,
    act it out
hacia, towards
    hacia adentro,
    inward
    hacia afuera,
    outward
    hacia la derecha,
    to the right
    hacia la izquierda,
    to the left
halagar, to praise
halago, praise
hallar, to find
halo, halo
hecho, fact
    hecho aditivo,
    addition fact
    hecho aritmético,
    arithmetic fact
    hecho extendido,
    extended fact
    hecho geométrico,
    geometric fact
    hechos relacionados,
    related facts
hectárea, hectare
hélice, helix
hemisferio, hemisphere
heptágono, heptagon
hermítico(a), Hermitian
herramienta, tool
hexaedro, hexahedron
hexágono, hexagon
hexagrama, hexagram
hilo, string
hipérbola, hyperbola
    hipérbola rectan-
    gular, rectangular
    hyperbola
hiperbólico, hyperbolic
hipotenusa, hypotenuse

**hipotenusa con-
gruente,** hypotenuse
triangle congruence
hipótesis, hypothesis
(pl. hypotheses)
hipótesis alternativo,
alternative hypothesis
hipótesis nula,
null hypothesis
hipotético, hypothetical
histograma, histogram,
block graph
**histograma de fre-
cuencia acumulativa,**
cumulative frequency
histogram
hoja, sheet
hoja de cálculo,
spreadsheet
homogeneidad,
homogeneity
homogéneo, homogeneous
no homogéneo,
nonhomogenous
hora, hour
horizontal, horizontal
hoyo, hole
hueco, gap, hollow

I

icosaedro, icosahedron
icosaedro regular,
regular icosahedron
idea matemática,
mathematical idea
ideal, ideal
idealizar, to idealize
idéntico, identical, same
identidad, identity

**elemento de
identidad aditiva,**
identity element for
addition
identidad aditiva,
additive identity
identidad algebraica,
algebraic identity
**identidad de cocien-
te,** quotient identity
**identidad multipli-
cativa,** multiplicative
identity
identidad recíproca,
reciprocal identity
**identidad trigonomé-
trica,** trigonometric
identity
identificable, identifiable
no identificable,
unidentifiable
identificar, identify, label
**identificar los
pasos del trabajo,**
lable work,
show your work
idóneo, suitable
igual, equal, same, match
igual a,
equal to
igual distancia,
equidistance
igual suerte,
equal chance
no igual a,
not equal to
igualdad, equality
igualdad condicional,
conditional equality
ilógico, illogical
ilustración, illustration
ilustrar, to illustrate
imagen, image

imagen inversa, inverse image
imagen reflejada, reflected image
imaginario, imaginary
imán, magnet
impar, odd
imparcial, impartial, unbiased
impedir, to restrain
imperfección, flaw
imperfecto, imperfect
implicación, implication
implicar, to imply, to entail, to involve
implícito, implicit
imponerse, to assert
importancia, importance
   de poca importancia, minor
   sin importancia, unimportant
importante, important significant, major
importar, to matter, to import
imposible, impossible
impráctico, impractical
impreciso, imprecise, inaccurate, vague
impredecible, unpredictable
impreso, form
improbable, improbable
impropio, improper
imprudente, careless
impuesto, tax
   impuesto sobre el valor agregado (IVA), value added tax (VAT)
inadvertido, unobserved
inalámbrico, wireless
inalterable, unalterable

incalculable, incalculable
incertidumbre, uncertainty
incierto, uncertain
inclinación, inclination, slant, tilt
inclinado, askew, slanted
inclinar, to incline, to tilt, to slant
incluir, to include
   incluir en una lista, to list
inclusión, inclusion
inclusivo, inclusive
incógnito, unknown
incomparabilidad, incomparability
incomparable, incomparable
incompatibilidad, incompatibility, conflict
incompleto(a), incomplete
incomprensible, incomprehensible
inconcluyente, inconclusive
inconexo, unrelated, unconnected
incongruente, incongruent
inconsistencia, inconsistency
inconsistente, inconsistent
incorporar, to incorporate
incorrecto, wrong, incorrect
incrementar, to increase, to increment
incremento, increment
   incremento porcentual, percent increase

incuestionable,
unquestionable
incumplimiento, failure
incumplir, to fail
indefinidamente,
indefinitely
indefinido, indefinite
independencia,
independence
independencia lineal,
linear independence
independiente,
independent
indeterminado,
indeterminate
indexar, to index
indicar, to indicate,
to point
índice, index
índice de depre-
ciación, rate of
depreciation
índice de estadísti-
cas, index in statistics
índice de un radical,
index of a radical
índice racional,
rational index
indirecto, indirect
indistinguible,
indistinguishable
individual, individual
indivisible, indivisible
índole, nature
inducción, induction
inducción matemá-
tica, mathematical
induction
inducción por enu-
meración simple,
induction by simple
enumeration
inducir, to induce

inductivo, inductive
inercia, inertia, momentum
inesperado, unexpected
inexacto, inexact
inexplicable, inexplicable,
unexplainable
inexplorado, unexplored
inferencia, inference
inferencia de lo
inmediato, inference
of immediate
inferencia de
lo mediato,
inference of mediate
inferencia estadís-
tica, statistical inference
inferible, inferible
no inferible,
uninferible
inferior, lower
inferir, to infer
infinitamente, infinitely
infinitamente gran-
de, infinitely great
infinitamente mu-
cho, infinitely many
infinitesimal, infinitesimal
infinito, infinity, infinite
inflexible, inflexible
inflexión, inflection
información, information
información inapli-
cable, inapplicable
information
información inicial,
initial data
información
irrelevante,
irrelevant
information
información
relevante,

relevant information
información sin importancia, irrelevant information
informalmente, informally
informar, to inform
informática, computer science
informativo, informative
infrecuente, infrequent
infundado, unsound, unsupported
ingeniería, engineering
ingresos, earnings, revenue
   ingresos limpios, net earnings
   ingresos netos, net earnings
inhomogéneo, inhomogeneous
inicial, initial
injustificable, unjustifiable
inmenso, immense
inmensurable, immeasurable
innatural, unnatural
innecesario, unnecessary
innegable, undeniable
inobservable, unobservable
inquisitivo, inquisitive
inscribir, to inscribe, to enroll, to register
inscrito, inscribed
inseguro, unsure
inseparable, inseparable
inserción, insertion
insertar, to insert
insignificante, insignificant, negligible
insolucionabilidad, unsolvability
inspección, inspection

inspeccionar, to inspect, to check
instrucción, instruction
instruir, to instruct
instrumento, instrument
insuficiente, insufficient
intacto, intact, entire
integrabilidad, integrability
integración, integration
   integración numérica, numerical integration
   integración por partes, integration by parts
integral, integral
   integral de línea escalar orientada, scalar line integral oriented
   integral de Riemann, Riemann integral
   integral de superficie, surface integral
   integral de volumen, volume integral
   integral definida, definite integral
   integral doble, double integral
   integral impropia, improper integral
   integral indefinida, indefinite integral
   integral superior, upper integral
integrar, to integrate
intentar, try, attempt
intento, intent, try, trial, attempt
interacción, interaction
interactuar, to interact

intercambiable,
interchangeable
intercambiar, to exchange,
to interchange
interceptar, to intercept
intercepto, intercept
**intercepto de x
de una línea,**
x-intercept of a line
**intercepto de y
de una línea,**
y-intercept of a line
interconectar,
to interconnect
interconexión,
interconnection
interés, interest, yield
interés compuesto,
compound interest
**interés compuesto
anual,** interest com-
pounded annually
**interés compues-
to continuamente,**
interest compounded
continuously
**interés compuesto
semestral,**
interest compounded
semiannually
**interés compuesto
trimestral,**
interest compounded
quarterly
interés simple,
simple interest
interfaz, interface
interior, interior, inner
**interior de un ángu-
lo,** interior of an angle
intermedio, intermediate
interminable, endless,
neverending, unend-

ing, interminable
intermitente, intermittent
interno, inner
interpolación,
interpolation
**interpolación
inversa,** inverse
interpolation
**interpolación trigo-
nométrica,** trigono-
metric interpolation
interpolar, to interpolate
interpretación,
interpretation
interpretar, to interpret
interrumpido, interrupted,
discontinuous
interrumpir, to interrupt
intersección, intersection,
crossing point
**intersección de grá-
ficas,** intersection of
graphs
**intersección de
conjuntos,**
intersection of sets
**intersección de
punto geométricos,**
intersection of loci
intersectante, intersecting
intersectarse, to intersect
intervalo, interval, gap
intervalo abierto,
open interval
intervalo cerrado,
closed interval
intervalo de clase,
class interval
**intervalo de
confianza,**
confidence interval
intervalo de datos,
range of data

intervalo modal, modal interval
intervalos consecutivos, consecutive intervals
intransitivo, intransitive
introducción, introduction
introducir, to input, to introduce
intuición, intuition
intuir, to intuit
intuitivo, intuitive
inusual, unusual
inválido, void, invalid
invariabilidad orientacional, orientational invariance
invariable, invariable
invariante, invariant
invariedad, invariance
invención, invention
inventar, to invent
invento, invention
inventor, inventor
inverosímil, implausible, unbelievable
inverso(a), inverse, reverse
    inversa de un enunciado, inverse of a statement
    inverso aditivo, additive inverse
    inverso multiplicativo, multiplicative inverse
    inversos aditivos, additive inverses
invertibilidad, invertibility
invertir, to invert
    invertir el proceso, reverse the process
investigación, investigation, research

investigar, to investigate, to research
invierno, winter
involucrar, to involve
ir, to go
irracional, irrational, absurd
irreducible, irreducible
irreemplazable, irreplaceable
irreflexiva, irreflexive
irrefutable, irrefutable
irregular, irregular, patternless
irregularidad, irregularity
irrelevante, irrelevant, extraneous
irrestringido, unrestricted
irreversibilidad, irreversibility
irreversible, irreversible
isogonabilidad, isogonality
isogonal, isogonal
isometría, isometry
    isometría directa, direct isometry
    isometría opuesta, opposite isometry
isométrico(a), isometric
isomórfico, isomorphic
isósceles, isosceles
    triángulo isósceles, isosceles triangle
ítem, item
iteración, iteration
iterar, iterate
iterativo, iterative
IVA (impuesto sobre el valor agregado), VAT (value added tax)
izquierdo(a), left
    a la izquierda, to the left

J

jamás, never
ji cuadrada, chi square
joven, young
juego, set, game
    juego de cartas,
    deck of cards
    juego estándar de
    barajas, standard
    deck of cards
juntamente, jointly
juntar, to collect,
    to put together
junto, together
juntos, jointly
justificar, to justify
    justificar la
    afirmación,
    justify the
    statement
justo, fair
juzgar, to judge, juzgar
    igual, to match

K

Kelvin, Kelvin (K)
kilo, kilogram (kg), kilo
kilogramo, kilo, kilogram
kilolitro, kiloliter (kl)
kilómetro, kilometer (km)

L

laboratorio, laboratory
ladeado, lopsided, askew
ladear, to tilt
lado, edge, side, boundary,
    leg
    al lado de,
    next to, alongside,
    beside
    de lado opuesto,
    opposite side
    de un lado,
    one-sided
    del lado,
    neighboring
    lado común,
    common side
    lado contenido,
    included side
    lado correspondien-
    te, corresponding side
    lado inicial de un
    ángulo, initial side
    of an angle
    lado no adyacente,
    nonadjacent side
    lado no adyacente
    de un triángulo,
    nonadjacent side
    of a triangle
    lado opuesto,
    opposite side
    lado opuesto a un
    ángulo, side opposite
    an angle
    lado opuesto de un
    triángulo recto,
    opposite side in a
    right triangle

lado recto, latus rectum
lado terminal de un ángulo, terminal side of an angle
lados adyacentes, adjacent sides
lados congruentes, congruent sides
lados consecutivos, consecutive sides
laguna, gap, lagoon
lanzar, to throw
laplaciano de un campo escalar, Laplacian operator
laplaciano escalar, Laplacian operator
lapso, lapse, span
lapso de tiempo, time lapse
largo, length, long
el más largo, longest
más largo, longer
más largo que, longer than
lateral, sideways
latido, beat
latido del corazón, heart beat
latitud, latitude
lazo, loop
lejano, far
el más lejano, farthest
más lejano, farther
más lejano que, farther than
lejos, far
más lejos, farther
el más lejos, farthest
más lejos que, farther than
lema, lemma
lenguaje, language
lenguaje algebraico, algebraic language
lenguaje de la lógica, language of logic
lenguaje de programación, programming language
lenguaje escrito, written language
lenguaje gráfico, written language
lenguaje matemático apropiado, appropriate mathematical language
lenguaje verbal, verbal language
lente, lens
lento, slow
ley, law
ley de adición disyuntiva, law of disjunctive addition
ley asociativa, associative law
ley conmutativa, commutative law
ley de cancelación, cancellation law
ley de cancelación de la multiplicación, cancellation law of multiplication
ley de cancelación de la suma, cancellation law of addition

ley de cancelación derecha, right cancellation law

ley de conjunción, law of conjunction

ley de contradicción, law of contradiction

ley de contrapositivo, law of contrapositive

ley de cosenos, law of cosines

ley de De Morgan, De Morgan's law

ley de exponentes, law of exponents

ley de exponentes integrales positivos, law of positive integral exponents

ley de inferencia, law of inference

ley de inferencia disyuntiva, law of disjunctive inference

ley de la potencia de un cociente, power-of-quotient law

ley de la regla de cadena, law of chain rule

ley de logaritmos, law of logarithms

ley de los grandes números, law of large numbers

ley de Modus Tollens, law of Modus Tollens

ley de monotonía, monotonic law

ley de potencia de un producto, power-of-product law

ley de razonamiento, law of reasoning

ley de senos, law of sines

ley de simplificación, law of simplification

ley de sustitución, law of substitution

ley de tricotomía, trichotomy law

ley de la negación doble, law of double negation

ley del coseno, cosine law

ley del desprendimiento, detachment law, law of detachment

ley distributiva, distributive law

leyes de los exponentes, index laws

leyenda, key

leyenda del mapa, map legend

libra, pound (lb.)

libro, book

libro de ejercicios, workbook

libro de texto, textbook

ligar, to tie

limitación, limitation

limitado, bounded

limitante, limitation

limitar, to limit, to confine, to bind

límite, limit, boundary, border, bound

al límite, ad extremum

límite inferior,

lower limit, lower bound

límite infinito, infinite limit

límite superior, upper bound

límite superior de la suma, upper limit of summation

sin límite, limitless, boundless

limpiar, to clean

limpio, net, clean

línea, line

línea auxiliar, auxiliary line

línea cronológica, timeline

línea curva, curved line

línea de ajuste óptimo, least squares regression line

línea de campo, field line

línea de equidistancia, line of equidistance

línea de mejor ajuste, line of best fit

línea de números, number line

línea de puntos, dotted line

línea de reflección, line of reflection

línea de rumbo, trend line

línea de simetría, line of symmetry

línea de tendencia, trend line

línea de tiempo, timeline

línea entrecortada, dashed line

línea fija, fixed line

línea horizontal, horizontal line

línea horizontal de simetría, horizontal line symmetry

línea imaginaria, imaginary line

línea isogonal, isogonal line

línea numérica, number line

línea perpendicular, perpendicular line

línea polígonica, polygonal line

línea punteada, dotted line

línea recta, straight line

línea restante, remaining line

línea terminal, terminal line

línea vertical, vertical line

línea visual, line of sight

líneas concéntricas, concentric lines

líneas concurrentes, concurrent lines

líneas coplanares, coplanar lines

líneas equidistantes, equidistant lines

líneas imaginarias conjugadas, conjugate imaginary lines

líneas intersectantes, intersecting lines

líneas oblicuas, skew lines

líneas paralelas, parallel lines

líneas perpendiculares, perpendicular lines

lineal, linear

linealmente, linearly

linealmente dependiente, linearly dependent

linealmente independiente, linearly independent

lista, list

lista de presencia, roster form

literal, literal

litro, liter (l)

llamarse, to call

llave, brace, key

llenar, to fill, to shade

lleno, full

llevar, carry

llevar a cabo, to carry out, to conduct

llevar cuenta de, keep track of

llevar la cuenta, to tally

local, local

localizar, to locate, to localize

locus, locus (pl. loci)

locus compuesto, compound locus

locus de puntos, locus of points

logarítmicamente, logarithmically

logarítmico, logarithmic

logaritmo, log, logarithm

logaritmo común, common logarithm

logaritmo inverso, inverse logarithm

logaritmo natural, natural logarithm (natural log)

logaritmo neperiano, natural log, natural logarithm

lógica, logic, logical

lógica matemática, mathematical logic

lógicamente, logically

lógicamente equivalente, logically equivalent

lograr, to achieve, to succeed

logro, achievement, success

longitud, longitude, length

longitud de semicírculo, length of semicircle

longitud del arco, length of arc, arc length

lugar, location

en lugar de, instead of, place holder

en otros lugares, elsewhere

lugar decimal, decimal place

luz diurna, daylight

luz eléctrica, electricity

M

machote, template
magnético, magnetic
magnetismo, magnetism
magneto, magnet
magnitud, magnitude
   magnitud absoluta,
   absolute magnitude
   magnitud de campo,
   field quantity
   magnitud tensorial,
   tensor quantity
maleable, malleable
malformar, to misshape
maña, trick
mañana, tomorrow,
   morning
manecilla de las horas,
   hour hand
manecilla de los minutos,
   minute hand
manera, means
manipulación,
   manipulation
   manipulación al-
   gebraica, algebraic
   manipulation
manipular, to manipulate
mano, hand
   mano derecha,
   right-hand
   mano izquierda,
   left-hand
mantener, to support
mantisa, mantissa
mapa, map
   mapa del orden
   preservado,
   order-preserving map

mapear, to map
mapeo, mapping
maqueta, model
máquina, machine
marca, check mark
marcador, marker
   marcador de posi-
   ción, placeholder
marcar, to mark, to shade
marco, frame, framework
   marco de referencia,
   reference frame
   marco teórico,
   theoretical framework
más, plus, more
   a lo más,
   at most
   más de,
   more than
   más de las veces,
   mostly
   más que,
   more than
más alto, higher
   el más alto,
   highest
   más alto que,
   higher than
más bajo, shorter
   el más bajo,
   shortest
   más bajo que,
   shorter than
más cerca, nearer
   el más cerca,
   nearest
   más cerca que,
   nearer than
más cercano, nearer
   el más cercano,
   nearest
   más cercano que,
   nearer than

más corto, shorter
    el más corto,
    shortest
    más corto que,
    shorter than
más exterior, outer
    el más exterior,
    outmost
más externo, outer
    el más externo,
    outmost
más grande, bigger, larger
    el más grande,
    most, biggest, largest
    más grande que,
    bigger than,
    larger than
más largo, longer
    el más largo,
    longest
    más largo que,
    longer than
más lejano,
    farther
    el más lejano,
    farthest
    más lejano que,
    farther than
más lejos, farther
    el más lejos,
    farthest
    más lejos que,
    farther than
más ligero, lighter
    el más ligero,
    lightest
    más ligero que,
    lighter than
más liviano, lighter
    el más liviano,
    lightest
    más liviano que,
    lighter than

más pequeño, smaller
    el más pequeño,
    smallest
    más pequeño que,
    smaller than
más pesado, heavier
    el más pesado,
    heaviest
    más pesado que,
    heavier than
más próximo, nearer
    el más próximo,
    nearest
    más próximo que,
    nearer than
más que, more than
    más que suficiente,
    plenty
más rápido, faster
    el más rápido,
    fastest
    más rápido que,
    faster than
más reciente, latest
más simple, simpler
    el más simple,
    simplest
    más simple que,
    simpler than
más tarde,
    afterwards, later
    más tarde que,
    later than
masa, mass
**matemática del mundo
    real,** real world math
matemática integrada, integrated mathematics
matemáticas, mathematics
    matemáticas puras,
    pure math
matemático[1],
    mathematician

matemático²,
mathematical
materia, matter, subject,
course, class
materiales manipulativos,
manipulative materials
materiales prácticos,
manipulative materials
matriz,
matrix (pl. matrices)
matriz adjunta,
Hermitian conjugate
matrix
matriz columna,
column matrix
matriz cuadrada,
square matrix,
square array
**matriz definida
positiva,** positive
definite matrix
matriz diagonal,
diagonal matrix
matriz fila,
row matrix
matriz hermítica,
Hermitian matrix
matriz identidad,
identity matrix
matriz inversa,
inverse matrix
matriz invertible,
invertible matrix
matriz nula,
zero matrix
matriz recíproca,
inverse matrix
matriz regular,
regular matrix
matriz simétrica,
symmetric matrix
matriz singular,
singular matrix

matriz transpuesta,
transpose matrix
matriz unitaria,
identity matrix, unit
matrix, unitary matrix
maximizar, maximize
máximo(a), maximum,
maxima, max, highest,
maximal
máximo absoluto,
absolute maximum
**máximo común
denominador,**
greatest common divi-
sor (GCD)
**máximo común divi-
sor,** greatest common
factor (GCF), highest
common divisor
máximo global,
global maximum
máximo local,
local maximum
máximo parcial,
local maximum
mayor, major, greater,
older
el mayor,
greatest
mayor a,
above
mayor que,
greater than
mayormente, mostly
mayúscula, upper case
mecánica, mechanics
mecánica cuántica,
quantum mechanics
media, average, mean
a medias,
half
media aritmética,
arithmetic mean

media de trabajo, working mean
media geométrica, geometric mean
media hora, half-hour
media modelo, sample mean
media ponderada, weighted mean
media provisional, working mean
media vuelta alrededor del origen, half-turn
mediana, median
mediano, medium
mediante, by means of
mediatriz, perpendicular bisector
medible, measurable
medida, measure, measurement
medida de ángulo, angle measure
medida de ángulo central, measure of a central angle
medida de ángulo conservada, angle measure preserved
medida de la dispersión, measure of dispersion
medida de precisión, measure of precision, precision measurement
medida de radianes, measure of radians
medida de tendencia central, measure of central tendency
medida de variación, measure of variance
medida del radián, radian measure
medida directa, direct measurement
medida dirigida, direct measure
medida en grados, degree measure
medida estándar, standard measure
medida indirecta, indirect measurement
medida lineal, linear measure
medida lineal de un arco, linear measure of an arc
medidas no estándares, nonstandard measure
medio, medium (pl. media), half, middle, center, mid
en medio, in the middle, in half
en medio de, between
medio dólar, half-dollar
medio plano, half plane
medios de una proporción, means of a proportion
medio plano abierto, open half-plane
mediodía, noon
medir, to measure
medir la capacidad, measure capacity

mega, mega
(el, lo, la) mejor, best
    mejor aproximación,
    best approximation
mejorar, to improve, to get
    better
memoria, memory
menor, minor, less, below,
    lower, under, minus,
    fewer
    el menor,
    the least
    menor de,
    less than
    menor denominador
    común, lowest com-
    mon denominator
    (LCD)
    menor número de,
    fewest
    menor que,
    fewer than
menos, minus, fewer, least
    a menos que,
    unless
    al menos,
    at least
    menos de,
    less than, fewer than
    menos que,
    less than,
    fewer than
mensualmente, monthly
mensurabilidad,
    measurability
mensurable, measurable
mental, mental
mentir, to lie
mes, month
    meses del año,
    months of the year
meta, goal
meticuloso,

meticulous, careful
metódico, methodical
método, method
    método combinado,
    combined method
    método corto,
    short-out method
    método de aproxi-
    mación tangencial,
    tangential approxima-
    tion method
    método de aproxima-
    ciones, method of trial
    and error, trial and
    error method
    método de cance-
    lación, cancellation
    method
    método de elimi-
    nación, method of
    elimination
    método de extrapo-
    lación, extrapolation
    method
    método de factori-
    zación, factorization
    method
    método de inter-
    polación, method
    of interpolation
    método de la mitad,
    one-half method
    método de la raíz
    cuadrada,
    square root method
    método de los coefi-
    cientes indetermina-
    dos, method of suc-
    cessive substitution,
    method of undeter-
    mined coefficients
    método de Newton,
    Newton's method

método de prueba, method of proof

método de sustitución, substitution method

método deductivo, deductive method

método del agotamiento, method of exhaustion

método gráfico, graphical method

método operativo, operational method

método operacional, operational method

método pendiente intercepto, slope-intercept method

método sucesivo de eliminación, successive method of elimination

métrico, metric

metro, meter

metro cuadrado, square meter

metro cúbico, cubic meter

mezclado, mixed

mezclar, to mix

miembro, member

mil, thousand

mil millones, billion

milésimas, thousandths

milésimo, thousandth

mili, milli

miligramo, milligram (mg)

mililitro, milliliter (ml)

milímetro, millimeter (mm)

milla, mile (mi.)

milla cuadrada, square mile

milla marina, nautical mile

milla náutica, nautical mile

milla ordinaria, statute mile, land mile

milla terrestre, land mile, statute mile

millas por galón, miles per gallon (mpg)

millas por hora, miles per hour, mph

millar, thousand

millares, thousands, thousands place

millonésima, millionth

millón, million

millón de millones, trillion

minimizar, to minimize

mínimo(a), minima, minimum, lowest, minimal

mínimo absoluto, absolute minimum

mínimo común denominador, least common denominator (LCD), lowest common denominator (LCD)

mínimo común múltiplo, least common multiple (LCM), lowest common multiple

minuendo, minuend

minúsculo, minuscule, tiny, lower case

minuto, minute

mismo, same

mismo interior, co-interior

misterioso, puzzling

mitad, half (pl. halves)
   a la mitad,
   halfway, midway
   mitad de la circunferencia de un círculo,
   one-half the circumference of a circle
mixto, mixed
moda, mode
modal, modal
modelar, to model
modelo cuantitativo,
   quantitative model
modelo de regresión,
   regression model
modelo físico,
   physical model
modelo númerico,
   number model
modificar,
   to modify, to alter
modular, modular
módulo de un número complejo, modulus of
   a complex number
Modus Ponens,
   Modus Ponens
Modus Tollens,
   Modus Tollens
moneda, coin
   moneda de cinco centavos,
   nickel
monitor, monitor
monitorear, to monitor
monomio, monomial
   monomios semejantes, like monomials
monto, amount
mostrar,
   to show, to display
mover, to move
moverse, to move

movimiento,
   movement, motion
   movimiento ligero,
   rigid motion
   movimiento rectilíneo, rectilinear motion
   movimiento uniforme, uniform motion
mucho, many, plenty
muestra, sample
   muestra al azar,
   random sample
   muestra aleatoria,
   random sample
   muestra de datos,
   sample data
   muestra engañosa,
   biased sample
   muestra representativa, cross-section
muestrear, to sample
muestreo, sampling
multidimensional,
   multidimensional
multilateral, multilateral
multinomio, multinomial
multiplicación,
   multiplication
   multiplicación anidada, nested multiplication
   multiplicación cruzada, cross-multiplication
   multiplicación escalar, scalar multiplication
multiplicado por, times
multiplicador, multiplier
multiplicando,
   multiplicand
multiplicar,
   multiply, times

**multiplicar la pri-
mera fracción por la
inversa de la segun-
da,** to cross-multiply
**multiplicar por cua-
tro,** to quadruple
multiplicar por dos,
to double, doubling
multiplicativo,
multiplicative
multiplicidad, multiplicity
múltiplo, multiple
múltiplo común,
common multiple
mutuamente excluidos,
mutually exclusive
mutuamente excluyente,
mutually exclusive

N

nada, nothing, naught
natural, natural
naturaleza, nature
**naturaleza de
las raíces,** nature
of the roots
náutico, nautical
navegación, navigation
navegar, to navigate
necesario, necessary
negación, negation
falsa negación,
false negative
negar, to negate, to refuse
negativo, negative
falso negativo,
false negative
neto, net
ninguno, none

nivel, level
nivel de la vista,
eye level
nivel de precisión,
level of precision
**nivel de significan-
cia,** level of signifi-
cance
nivel del mar,
sea level
no adyacente, nonadjacent
no alineado, unaligned
no balanceado,
unbalanced, uneven
no cero, non-zero
no científico, unscientific
no claro, unclear
no clasificado, unclassified
no colineal, noncollinear
no complicado,
uncomplicated
no convencional,
non-conventional
no coplanar, non-coplanar
no degenerado,
non-degenerate
no denso, non-dense
no descubierto,
undiscovered
no equivalente a,
not equal to
no esencial, extraneous
no especificado,
unspecified
no estándar,
nonstandard
no estar de acuerdo,
to disagree
no fiable, unreliable
no fidedigno, unreliable
no homogéneo,
non-homogenous
no identificable,

unidentifiable
no igual a, not equal to
no inferible, uninferible
no original, unoriginal
no probado, unproven
no redondeado, unrounded
noche, evening, night
noción, notion
nódulo, node
nombrar, to name
nombre, name
   nombre del ángulo, angle name
nominal, nominal
non, odd
nonágono, nonagon
noreste, northeast
norma, norm, standard
normal, normal, standard
   normal principal, main normal
normalizar, to normalize, to standardize
noroeste, northwest
norte, north
nota, grade
notación, notation
   notación ampliada, expanded notation
   notación científica, scientific notation
   notación contraída, contracted notation
   notación de construcción de conjuntos, set-builder notation
   notación de la función, function notation
   notación decimal, decimal notation
   notación desarrollada, expanded form, expanded notation
   notación estándar, standard notation
   notación explícita, expanded form, expanded notation
   notación literal, literal notation
   notación por intervalos, interval notation
   notación sigma, sigma notation
noveno, ninth
nube de puntos, scattergram
nudo, knot (kt.)
nueve, nine
nuevo, new
   de nuevo, again
nulo, null, void
numeración, numeration
numerado, numbered
numerador, numerator
numeral, numeral
numéricamente, numerically
numérico(a), numerical, numeral
número, number, numeral, figure
   número al azar, random number
   número aproximado, approximate number
   número binario, binary number
   número cardinal, cardinal number
   número complejo, complex number

número compuesto, compound number, composite number

número cuadrado, square number

número cúbico, cubic number

número de cuenta, counting number,

número de dos dígitos, two-digit number

número de escala, scale number

número de golpes, number of strokes

número de Sterling, Sterling number

número de tres dígitos, three-digit number

número de un dígito, one-digit number

número decimal, decimal number

número del lado izquierdo, left-hand number

número desconocido, unknown number

número dirigido, directed number

número entero, whole number, integer

número entero impar, odd whole number

número entero par, even whole number

número escrito en palabras, number in words

número fraccionario, fractional number

número imaginario, imaginary number

número imaginario puro, pure imaginary number

número impar, odd number

número inconmesurable, incommensurable number

número inverso, inverse number

número irracional, irrational number

número mixto, mixed number

número natural, natural number

número negativo, negative number

número non, odd number

número opuesto, opposite number

número ordinal, ordinal number

número par, even number

número perfecto, perfect number

número positivo, positive number

número positivo real, positive real number

número prestado, borrowed number

número primo, prime number

número racional, rational number

número racional positivo, positive rational number

número real,
real number
número real negativo, negative real
number
número real puro,
pure real number
número redondeado,
rounded number
número romano,
Roman numeral
número sigma,
signed number
figura significativa,
significant figure
número sin signo,
unsigned number
número total de posibilidades, total
number of possibilities
número total de resultados, total
number of outcomes
número trascendental, transcendental
number
número triangular,
triangular number
números compatibles, compatible
numbers
números no negativos, non-negative
numbers
números no positivos, non-positive
numbers
números primos de Mersenne,
Mersenne primes
números semejantes,
like numbers
nunca, never

objetivo, objective
objeto, object
   objeto físico,
   physical object
   objeto justo e imparcial, fair and
   unbiased object
   objetos imparciales,
   unbiased objects
   objetos no polarizados, unbiased objects
oblicuo, oblique, askew
   triángulo oblicuo,
   oblique triangle
obligar,
   to constrain, to oblige,
   to make, to compel
oblongo, oblong
observación, observation
observar, to observe
obsoleto, obsolete
obstáculo,
   challenge, obstacle
obtener, obtain, get, elicit
obtuso, obtuse
   ángulo obtuso,
   obtuse angle
   triángulo obtuso,
   obtuse triangle
obvio, obvious
ocho, eight
octádico, octadic
octaedro, octahedron
octágono, octagon
octavo, eighth
ocurrencia, occurrence
   ocurrencia única,
   single event

ocurrir, to occur
oeste, west
oferta, sale, offer, supply
    oferta y demanda,
    supply and demand
ofrecer, to offer
omitir, omit
onda, wave
    onda de luz,
    light wave
    onda sinusoidal,
    sine wave
    onda sonora,
    sound wave
onza, ounce (oz.)
opción, choice, option
    opción múltiple,
    multiple-choice
opcional, optional
operación, operation
    operación aditiva,
    additive operation
    operación aritmética,
    arithmetic operation
    operación básica,
    base operation
    operación binaria,
    binary operation
    operación binaria bicondicional,
    biconditional binary operation
    operación con decimales, operation with decimals
    operación con fracciones, operation with fractions
    operación con monomio, operation with monomial
    operación con números elementales, fact, operation with basic numbers
    operación de conjunto, operation with set
    operación del lado izquierdo, left-hand operation
    operación inversa, inverse operation
    operación lógica, logical operation
    operación matemática, mathematical operation
    operaciones con números elementales relacionadas, related facts, fact family
    operaciones inversas, inverse operations
operador, operator
    operador nabla, nabla operator
oponer, to oppose, to go against
óptica, optics
óptimo, optimum
opuesto(a), opposite
oración, sentence
    oración abierta de primer grado con una variable, first-degree open sentence with one variable
    oración compuesta, compound sentence
    oración condicional, conditional sentence
    oración contrapositiva, contrapositive statement
    oración conversa, converse statement

oración equivalente, equivalent sentence
oración lineal abierta, linear open sentence
oración no matemática, non-mathematical sentence
oración numérica, number sentence, numerical sentence
oración verbal, verbal sentence
órbita, orbit
orbitar, to orbit
orden, order, ordering
    orden alfabético, alphabetical order
    orden ascendente, ascending order
    orden cíclico, cyclic order
    orden de magnitud, order of magnitude
    orden de operaciones, order of operations
    orden descendente, descending order
    orden inverso, reverse order
    orden lógico, logical order
    orden mantenido, order preserved
    orden numérico, numerical order
ordenado(a), ordinate, ordered
ordenador, computer
    ordenador análogo, analog computer
ordenamiento, arrangement
ordenamiento al azar, random arrangement
ordenamientos diferenciales, distinguishable arrangements
ordenamientos distintos, distinct arrangements
ordenar, to order, to arrange
ordinal, ordinal
ordinario, ordinary
organizar, to organize
orientación, orientation
    orientación del espacio, space orientation
    orientación opuesta, opposite orientation
orientado(a), oriented
orientar, to orient
oriente, east
origen, origin
original, original
ortocentro, orthocenter
ortogonal, orthogonal
ortonormal, orthonormal
oscilación, oscillation
oscilar, to oscillate
osciloscopio, oscilloscope
otoño, fall, autumn
otra vez, again
otro, another
óvalo, oval

pago inicial, down
payment
paliativo, remedial
palíndromo, palindrome
paloma, check mark
palomita, check mark
palomear, to mark correct
palpitación,
beat, palpitation
pantalla, display
papel, paper
**papel para hacer
dibujos isométricos,**
isometric graph paper
par, even, pair, couple
número par,
even number
par de factores,
pair of factors
par lineal,
linear pair
par lineal de ángulos,
linear pair of angles
par ordenado,
ordered pair
par primo,
prime pair
pares conjugados,
conjugate pairs
pares coordenados,
coordinate pairs
pares de ángulos,
angle pairs
parábola, parabola
parabólico, parabolic
paraboloide, paraboloid
paradoja, paradox
paradójico, paradoxical

paralelepípedo,
parallelepiped
**paralelepípedo
rectangular,** rectan-
gular parallelepiped
paralelismo, parallelism
**paralelismo man-
tenido,** parallelism
preserved
paralelo, parallel
**el paralelo postulado
de Euclides,** Euclid-
ean Parallel Postulate
paralelogramo,
parallelogram
paramétrico, parametric
parámetro, parameter
parcial, biased, prejudiced,
partial
parcialidad, bias
parecer, to resemble
parecido, alike, resembling
pareja, partner
parejo, even
paréntesis, parenthesis
(pl. parentheses)
paridad, parity
parte, part, piece
en todas partes,
everywhere
parte decimal,
decimal part
parte finita,
finite part
parte fraccionaria,
fractional part
parte inferior,
bottom
parte integral,
integral part
parte real,
real part
parte superior,

top
**partes correspon-
dientes,** correspond-
ing parts
partición, partition
particular, particular
pasar por un punto dado,
pass through a given
point
paso, step, pace, rate
paso a paso,
step-by-step
pasos sucesivos,
successive steps
patrón, pattern, model,
standard
patrón algebraico,
algebraic pattern
patrón de números,
pattern of numbers
patrón geométrico,
geometric pattern
patrón numérico,
numerical pattern
sin patrón,
patternless
peculiar, peculiar, unlike
pedazo, piece
en pedazos,
in pieces, piecewise
pedir, to ask, to request
pedir prestado,
to borrow
pegajoso, sticky, adhesive,
adherent
pegamento, paste, glue
pegar, to paste, to glue,
to stick together
pendiente, incline, slope
pendiente cero,
zero slope
**pendiente de
una línea,**

slope of a line
pendiente negativa,
negative slope
pendiente positiva,
positive slope
péndulo, pendulum
pensamiento,
thought, thinking
pensamiento crítico,
critical thinking
**pensamiento racio-
nal,** rational thought
pensar, to think
pentadecágono,
pentadecagon
pentágono, pentagon
penúltimo, next-to-last,
second-to-last
pequeño, little, tiny
el más pequeño,
smallest
más pequeño,
smaller
más pequeño que,
smaller than
percatarse, to realize,
to notice
perder, lose
pérdida, loss
perfecto, perfect
periférico, peripheral
perímetro, perimeter
periodicidad, periodicity
periódico, periodic
período, period
**período de un deci-
mal periódico,** period
of a repeating decimal
período recurrente,
recurring period
permutación, permutation
permutación alterna,
alternate permutation

permutación con repetición, permutation with repetition

perpendicular, perpendicular

perpendicular común, common perpendicular

perpendiculares recíprocas, mutually perpendicular

perpendicularidad, perpendicularity

perspectiva, perspective

perspicaz, perceptive

persuadir, to persuade

persuasivo, persuasive

pertenecer, to belong

pesar, to weigh

peso, weight

pi, pi

pictografía, pictograph

pictograma, pictogram

pie, foot (ft.)

pie cuadrado, square foot

pie cúbico, cubic foot

pies, feet (sing. foot)

pieza, piece, part

en piezas continuas, piecewise continuous

pila, stack, pile

pinta, pint (pt.)

pirámide, pyramid

pirámide recta, right pyramid

pirámide rectangular, rectangular pyramid

pirámide triangular, triangular pyramid

pivotar, to pivot

pivote, pivot

plan de estudios, syllabus

planar, planar

plano(a), plan, plane, plot, plotting

plano coordenado, coordinate plane

plano coordenado cartesiano, Cartesian coordinate plane

plano complejo, complex plane

plano de simetría, plane of symmetry

plano imaginario, imaginary plane

plano inclinado, inclined plane

plano osculador, osculating plane

plano tangente, tangent plane

planos coexistentes, concurrent planes

planos colineales, collinear planes

planos perpendiculares, perpendicular planes

plantilla, stencil, template

plática, discussion

platicar, to discuss

plausible, plausible

plazo, installment

plotear, to plot

población, population

poco, little

poco probable, unlikely

pocos, few

poder¹, can, to be able to
poder², power
> **sin poder,**
> powerless
> **poder pagar,**
> to afford

poderoso, powerful
polar, polar
polea, pulley
poliedro, polyhedron
polígono, polygon
> **polígono abierto,**
> open polygon
> **polígono circuns-
> crito,** circumscribed
> polygon
> **polígono circuns-
> crito a un círculo,**
> polygon circumscribed
> about a circle
> **polígono circunscri-
> to en un círculo,**
> polygon circumscribed
> in a circle
> **polígono cóncavo,**
> concave polygon
> **polígono convexo,**
> convex polygon
> **polígono de la
> frecuencia,**
> frequency polygon
> **polígono equiangular,**
> equiangular polygon
> **polígono equilátero,**
> equilateral polygon
> **polígono inscrito,**
> inscribed polygon
> **polígono irregular,**
> irregular polygon
> **polígono regular,**
> regular polygon
> **polígonos congruen-
> tes,** congruent

polygons
> **polígonos similares,**
> similar polygons

poliedro, polyhedron
> **poliedro circunscrito,**
> circumscribed polyhe-
> dron
> **poliedro cóncavo,**
> concave polyhedron
> **poliedro regular,**
> regular polyhedron

polinomio, polynomial
> **polinomio
> homogéneo,**
> homogenous
> polynomial
> **polinomio primo,**
> prime polynomial
> **polinomio reducible,**
> reducible polynomial

polo, pole
ponderado(a), weighted
poner, to place, to put
> **poner en grupos,**
> to group
> **poner en orden,**
> to order, to arrange,
> to sequence

ponerse, to become
poniente, west
por, per, times
> **por casualidad,**
> by chance
> **por ciento,**
> percent
> **por ciento de
> aumento,**
> percent increase
> **por ciento de
> disminución,**
> percent decrease
> **por ejemplo,**
> for example

por encima de,
above
por ende,
therefore
por lo general,
generally
por lo tanto,
therefore
por medio de,
by means of
porcentaje, percentage
**porcentaje de
disminución,**
percent of decrease
**porcentaje de
incremento,**
percent of increase
**porcentaje de
una cantidad,**
percent of a quantity
porcentual, percentile
porción debida, fair share
posibilidad, possibility,
chance
posible, possible
posiblemente, likely
posiblemente igual,
equally likely
posición, place, position
**posición de
las centenas,**
hundreds place
**posición de
las decenas,**
tens place
**posición de
las unidades,**
ones place
posición de mil,
thousands place
**posición de mil
millones,** billions
place value

posición de millar,
thousands place
posición de vector,
position vector
posición estándar,
standard position
posición normal,
standard position
posicionar, to position
positivo, positive
falso positivo,
false positive
post merídiem,
post meridian (p.m.)
postmeridiano (p.m.),
post meridian (p.m.)
postulacional,
postulational
postulado, postulate
**paralelo postulado
de Euclides,**
Euclidean Parallel
Postulate
**postulado de la
distancia,** distance
postulate
**postulado de la
partición,** partition
postulate
**postulado de la suma
de los ángulos,** angle
addition postulate
**postulado de trico-
tomía,** trichotomy
postulate
**postulado del pa-
ralelo de Euclides,**
parallel postulate
**postulado en la sus-
titución,** substitution
postulate
postulado reflexivo,
reflective postulate

postulado transitivo, transitive postulate
postulados de la igualdad, equality postulates
quinto postulado de Euclides, Euclid's Fifth Postulate
postular, to postulate
potencia, output, power, degree
  potencia de exponente negativo, negative exponent
  potencia de exponente positivo, positive exponent
  potencia de un término algebraico, degree of an algebraic term
  potencia de una expresión algebraica, degree of an algebraic expression
  potencia integral, integral power
  potencia positiva en base 10, positive power of 10
  potencias de i, powers of i
potencial, potential
  potencial vectorial, vector potential
práctica, practice
practicar, to practice
práctico, practical
precedencia, precedence
precedente[1], precedent
precedente[2], preceding
preceder, to precede, to go before
precio, price
precisión, accuracy, precision
preciso, accurate, precise
predecible, predictable
predecir, to predict
predicción, prediction
prefijo, prefix
pregunta, question
  preguntas aclaratorias, clarifying questions
preguntar, to question, to ask
preimagen, preimage
prejuicio, prejudice, bias
preliminar, rough
premisa, premise
preparar, to prepare, to get ready
prescribir, to prescribe
presentar, to present, to introduce
preservado(a), preserved
presión, pressure
  presión barométrica, barometric pressure
préstamo, loan
prestar, to lend, to loan
presupuestar, to budget
presupuesto, budget
prever, to foresee, to predict
previo, previous
previsto, predicted
prima rectangular, rectangular prism
primario, primary
primavera, spring
primer(a), first, lead
  primer cuartil, first quartile

primera fórmula de Green, first Green formula
primero, first
primeros auxilios, first aid
principal, primary, principal, main, lead
principio, principle
principio básico de conteo, Fundamental Counting Principle
principio de cuenta, counting principle
principio de dualidad, principle of duality
principio de sustitución, substitution principle
principio de sustitución de la igualdad, substitution property of equality
prisma, prism
prisma cuadrangular, rectangular prism
prisma recto, right prism
prisma regular, regular prism
prisma triangular, triangular prism
prisma truncado, truncated prism
prismático, prismatic
probabilidad, probability
probabilidad calculada, calculated probability
probabilidad con reemplazo, probability with replacement
probabilidad condi-
cional, conditional probability
probabilidad de un evento, probability of an event
probabilidad empírica, empirical probability
probabilidad experimental, experimental probability
probabilidad simple, simple probability
probabilidad sin reemplazo, probability without replacement
probabilidad teórica, theoretical probability
probabilidad uniforme, uniform probability
probable, probable, likely
probado, proven, proved
no probado, unproven
probar, to try, to test, to prove, to sample
problema, problem
problema algebraico, algebraic problem
problema escrito, word problem
problema modelo, model problem
problema númerico, numerical problem
problema verbal, word problem, verbal problem
problemas de móviles, motion problems
problemas del movimiento,

motion problems
problemático, problematic
procedimiento, procedure
procedimiento sistemático, step-by-step procedure
procesar, to process
proceso, process
proceso al azar, random process
proceso de eliminación, process of elimination
proceso deductivo, thought process
proceso irreversible, irreversible process
proceso reversible, reversible process
proceso verbal, verbal process
producción, yield
producir, to produce, to yield
producir un acarreo, to carry
producto, product
producto algebraico, algebraic product
producto cruzado de términos, cross-multiplication
producto de binomios, product of binomials
producto de la primera fracción por la inversa de la segunda, cross-multiplication
producto de punto, dot product
producto diádico, dyadic product

producto externo, vector product
producto hermítico, Hermitian product
producto interior, inner product
producto interno ponderado, weighted inner product
producto mixto, scalar triple product
producto tensorial, tensor product
producto transversal, cross product
producto transversal de dos vectores, cross product of two vectors
producto triple escalar, scalar triple product
producto vectorial, vector product
producto parcial, partial product
profundidad, depth
programa, program
programa de estudios, syllabus
programa informático de geometría dinámica, dynamic geometry software
programar, to program
progresión, progression
progresión aritmética, arithmetic progression
progresión geométrica, geometric progression

promediar, to average

promedio, average, GPA, grade point average

promoción escolar, grade

propiciar, elicit

propiedad, property, attribute, feature

  propiedad aditiva de la desigualdad, addition property of inequality

  propiedad aditiva de la igualdad, additive property of equality

  propiedad asociativa, associative property

  propiedad asociativa de multiplicación, associative property of multiplication

  propiedad asociativa de la suma, associative property of addition

  propiedad conmutativa, commutative property

  propiedad conmutativa de la multiplicación, commutative property of multiplication

  propiedad conmutativa de la suma, commutative property of addition

  propiedad de clausura, closure property

  propiedad de densidad, property of density

  propiedad de identidad, identity property

propiedad de inversa, inverse property

propiedad de la suma del cero, addition property of zero

propiedad de multiplicación de las proporciones, product property of proportions

propiedad de sustitución, substitution property

propiedad de tricotomía, trichotomy property

propiedad de una operación, property of an operation

propiedad del cero de la suma, zero property of addition

propiedad del orden, order property

propiedad del producto cero, zero product property

propiedad distributiva, distributive property

propiedad distributiva de la multiplicación respecto a la suma, distributive property of multiplication over addition

propiedad general asociativa, general associative property

propiedad general conmutativa, general commutative

property
propiedad inversa,
inverse property
propiedad multipli-
cativa de la desigual-
dad, multiplication
property of inequality
propiedad multi-
plicativa del cero,
multiplication proper-
ty of zero, zero prop-
erty of multiplication
propiedad neutro de
la multiplicación,
identity property of
multiplication
propiedad neutro
de la suma, identity
property of addition
propiedad reflexiva
de la congruencia,
reflexive property
of congruence
propiedad reflexiva
de la igualdad,
reflexive property
of equality
propiedad simétrica,
symmetrical property
propiedad simétri-
ca de la igualdad,
symmetric property
of equality
propiedad transitiva,
transitive property
propiedad transitiva
de las desigualdades,
transitive property
of inequality
propiedades angu-
lares de círculos,
angle properties
of circles

propiedades de los
ángulos en círculos,
angle properties of
circles
propiedades
mantenidas,
properties preserved
propina, gratuity
propio, proper
proponer, to propose
proporción,
proportion, ratio
proporción directa,
direct proportion
proporción inversa,
inverse proportion
proporción por
adición, proportion
by addition
proporción por
alternación,
proportion by
alternation
proporción por
resta, proportion
by subtraction
proporción simpli-
ficada, simplified
proportion
proporcional, proportional
proporcional media,
mean proportional
proporcionar, to provide,
to supply
proposición, proposal,
proposition
proposición abierta,
open sentence
proposición bicondi-
cionada, biconditional
statement,
proposición falsa,
false sentence

proposición hipotética, hypothetical proposition

proposición inversa, inverse proposition

proposición negativa, negative proposition

propuesta, proposal, proposition

propuestas contradictorias, contradictory prepositions

proveer, to provide, to supply

provisión, supply

próximo, next

el más próximo, nearest

más próximo, nearer

más próximo que, nearer than

proyección, projection

proyección de dirección preservada, sense-preserving mapping

proyección ortogonal, orthogonal projection

proyección paralela, parallel projection

proyectar, to project

proyecto, project

prudente, careful, prudent

prueba, proof, evidence, test, quiz, trial

prueba a dos columnas, two-column proof

prueba analítica, analytical proof

prueba de divisibilidad, divisibility test

prueba de dos colas, two-tailed test

prueba de hipótesis, hypothesis testing

prueba de la línea horizontal, horizontal-line test

prueba de la línea vertical para una función, vertical-line test for a function

prueba de la raíz, root test

prueba de párrafo, paragraph proof

prueba de transformación, transformational proof

prueba de una cola, one-tailed test

prueba deductiva, deductive proof

prueba directa, direct proof

prueba estadística, test statistic

prueba formal, formal proof

prueba independiente, independent trial

prueba indirecta, indirect proof

prueba indirecta informal, informal indirect proof

prueba lógica, logic proof

prueba por agotamiento de opciones, proof by exhaustion

prueba por contradicción, proof by contra-

diction
prueba por inducción, proof by induction
prueba t, t-test
prueba visual, visual proof
pruebas repetidas, repeated trials
pruebas sucesivas, successive trials
pseudoescalar, pseudo-scalar
pulgada, inch (in.)
pulgada cuadrada, square inch
pulgada cúbica, cubic inch
pulsación, beat, pulsation, pulse
puntaje, score
punto, dot, point
punto crítico, critical point
punto de concurrencia, point of concurrency
punto de contacto, point of contact, contact point
punto de esquina, corner point
punto de giro, turning point
punto de inflexión, inflection point, point of inflection
punto de intercepción, intercept point
punto de intersección, intersecting point, point of inter-

section
punto de porcentaje, percentage point
punto de reflexión, point of reflection
punto de simetría, point of symmetry
punto de tangencia, point of tangency
punto de trisección, trisection point
punto decimal, decimal point
punto en el infinito, point at infinity
punto externo, external point, endpoint
punto extremo, endpoint
punto fijo, fixed point
punto final, endpoint
punto focal, focal point, focus point
punto imagen, image point
punto imaginario, imaginary point
punto integral, integral point
punto interior, inner point, interior point
punto interno, inner point
punto lateral, lateral point
punto máximo, maximum point
punto medio, midpoint

punto medio conservado, midpoint preserved

punto mínimo, minimum point

punto modelo, sample point

punto opuesto, opposite point

punto radiante, radiant point

punto tendiente a cero, vanishing point

puntos cocíclicos, concyclic points

puntos colineales, collinear points

puntos coplanares, coplanar points

puntos distintos, distinct points

puntos equidistantes, equidistant marks

puntos igualmente espaciados, equally spaced points

puro, pure

puzle, puzzle

Q

quebrado, fraction

quebrado decimal, decimal fraction

quebrado impropio, improper fraction

quebrado propio, proper fraction

querer, to want, to wish

querer decir, to mean

quinto, fifth

quinto postulado de Euclides, Euclid's Fifth Postulate

quintuplicación, quintupling

quitar, to remove, to clear, take away

quitar los paréntesis, remove parentheses

R

racionabilidad, reasonableness

racionabilidad de una solución, reasonableness of a solution

racional, rational

racionalidad, rationality

racionalización, rationalization

racionalizar, to rationalize

racionalizar el denominador, rationalize the denominator

radián, radian

radiante, radiant

radical, radical

radicales diferentes, unlike radicals

radicales equivalentes, equivalent radicals

radicales semejantes, like radicals

radicando, radicand

radicando fraccionario, fractional radicand

radicando integral, integral radicand

radio, radius (pl. radii)

radio de un círculo, radius of a circle

radio de una esfera, radius of a sphere

radio del círculo circunscrito, radius of a circumscribed circle

radio del círculo inscrito, radius of an inscribed circle

raíz, root

raíces dobles, double roots

raíces múltiples, multiple roots

raíz compleja, complex root

raíz común, common root

raíz conjugada, conjugate root

raíz cuadrada, square root, radical

raíz cuadrada aproximada, approximate square root

raíz cuadrada de un número, square root of a number

raíz cuadrada de una fracción, square root of a fraction

raíz cuadrada del denominador, square root of the denominator

raíz cuadrada del numerador, square root of the numerator

raíz cuadrada monómica, monomial square root

raíz cuadrada principal, principal square root

raíz cuadrada real, real square root

raíz cúbica, cube root

raíz cúbica principal, principal cubic root

raíz de número integrales, integral root

raíz de un número cuadrado perfecto, root of a quadratic

raíz de una ecuación, root of an equation

raíz digital, digital root

raíz distinta, distinct root

raíz elevada a un exponente n, nth root

raíz extrínseca, extraneous root

raíz imaginaria, imaginary root

raíz indicada, indicated root

raíz irracional, irrational root

raíz principal, principal root

raíz principal enésima de (k), principal nth root of k

raíz racional, rational root

raíz repetida, repeated root

raíz sorda, surd root

raíz triple, triple root

rama, branch

ramificaciones de los factores, factor tree

rampa unitaria, unit ramp

rango, range, scale, rank

rango intercuartílico, interquartile range

rango percentil, percentile rank

ranura, groove

rapidez, speed

rápido, fast

rara vez, seldom

raro, strange, odd, unusual

rasgo, feature

rastro, trace

rayo, beam, ray

rayo inicial, initial ray

rayos opuestos, opposite rays

razón, ratio, reason

a razón de, in the amount of

razón continua, continued ratio

razón cosecante, cosecant ratio

razón cotangente, cotangent ratio

razón de la división, ratio of division

razón de la escala, scale ratio

razón de la igualdad, ratio of equality

razón de similtud, ratio of similitude

razón del coseno, cosine ratio

razón del seno, sine ratio

razón inversa, inverse ratio

razón parte-parte, part-to-part ratio

razón parte-todo, part-to-whole ratio

razón recíproca, reciprocal ratio

razón secante, secant ratio

razón tangencial, tangent ratio

razones equivalentes, equivalent ratios

razonable, reasonable

razonamiento, reasoning

razonamiento deductivo, deductive reasoning

razonamiento espacial, spatial reasoning

razonamiento inductivo, inductive reasoning

razonamiento lógico, logical reasoning

razonamiento proporcional, proportional reasoning

reaccción, response

reafirmación, reaffirmation

reafirmar, to reaffirm

reagrupación, regrouping
reagrupamiento,
    regrouping
reagrupar, to regroup
real, real, actual
realización de cálculos,
    performing computa-
    tion
realizar,
    to fulfill, to conduct, to
    perform, carry out
rebaja, discount
rebasar, to carry,
    to go beyond
rebatir,
    to counter, to refute,
    to rebut, to deduct a
    sum that should not
    have been included
rechazar, to reject
rechazo, rejection
recíprocamente desliga-
    dos, mutually disjoint
recíproco, reciprocal
    recíproco negativo,
    negative reciprocal
reclamación, claim
recoger, to collect,
    to gather, to pick up
recolectar, to collect
recomendar, to recom-
    mend, to suggest
reconocer, to acknowledge,
    to recognize
reconocimiento,
    acknowledgment,
    recognition
reconstitución, regrouping
reconstituir, to regroup
recordar, to remember
recta^1, straight line,
    straight path
    rectas inclinadas,

    inclined lines
    rectas oblicuas,
    skewed lines
    semirecta,
    half-line, ray
recta^2, straight, stretch
    línea recta,
    straight line
    pirámide recta,
    right pyramid
rectangular, rectangular
rectángulo, rectangle
    rectángulo áureo,
    golden rectangle
    rectángulo dorado,
    golden rectangle
rectilinealidad,
    rectilinearity
rectilíneo, rectilinear
recto, straight, right
    ángulo recto,
    right angle
    cilindro recto,
    right cylinder
    cono circular recto,
    right circular cone
    cono recto,
    right cone
    prisma recto,
    right prism
    triángulo recto,
    right triangle
recuperación, retrieval
recuperar, to retrieve,
    to recuperate
recursivo, recursive
recusable,
    open to challenge
recusación, challenge
recusar, to challenge
red, net, network
    red de puntos,
    lattice points

redacción técnica, technical writing

redondeado, rounded

no redondeado, unrounded

redondear, to round, round off

redondear hasta el decimal más cercano, round off to the nearest tenth

redondeo, rounding

redondez, roundness

redondo, round

reducción sucesiva, successive reduction

reducibilidad, reducibility

reducible, reducible

reducir, to reduce

reducir a los términos mínimos, reduce to lowest terms

redundante, redundant

reemplazar, to replace

reemplazo, replacement

con reemplazo, with replacement

conjunto de reemplazo, replacement set

sin reemplazo, without replacement

referencias personales de capacidad, personal references for capacity

referencias personales de unidades de masa, personal references for units of mass

referir, to refer

reflejar, to mirror, to reflect

reflejo, reflection, reflex

reflexibilidad, reflexivity

reflexión, reflection

reflexión de puntos, point reflection

reflexión en una línea, reflection in a line

reflexión por deslizamiento, glide reflection

reflexivo, reflexive

reformular, to rewrite, to rephrase

reforzar, to reinforce

refracción, refraction

refutable, refutable

refutar, to disprove, to refute

región, region

región abierta, open region

región circular, circular region

región crítica, critical region

región exterior, exterior region

región exterior de un círculo, exterior region of a circle

región interior, interior region

región interior de un círculo, interior region of a circle

región sombreada, shaded region

regla, rule, norm, standard

regla de cálculo, slide rule

regla de concatenación, Chain Rule

regla de Cramer, Cramer's Rule
regla de eliminación, rule of elimination
regla de función, function rule
regla de L'Hôpital, L'Hôpital's Rule
reglamento, rule
reglón, straight edge
regresar, to go back, to return
regresión, regression
regresión lineal, linear regression
regular, regular
rehusar, to refuse
relación, relation, relationship
relación algebraica, algebraic relationship
relación asimétrica, asymmetric relation, non-symmetric relation
relación binaria, binary relation
relación de conmutación, commutation relation
relación de equivalencia, equivalence relation, relation of equivalence
relación de identidad, relation of identity, identity relation
relación de orden, order relation
relación especial, spatial relationship
relación funcional, functional relation

relación fundamental, fundamental relationship
relación geométrica, geometric relationship
relación idéntica, identical relation
relación inversa, inverse relation
relación irreflexiva, irreflexive relation
relación lineal, linear relationship
relación no reflexiva, non-reflexive relation
relación no transitiva, non-transitive relation
relación parte-parte, part-to-part ratio
relación parte-todo, part-to-whole ratio
relación recíproca, reciprocal relation
relación reversible, reversible relation
relación simétrica, symmetrical relation
relación transitiva, transitive relation
relaciones matemáticas, mathematical relationships
relacionar, to relate
relatividad, relativity
relativo, relative
reloj, clock, watch
en sentido contra las manecillas del reloj, counterclockwise
en sentido de las manecillas del reloj, clockwise

rotación contraria a las agujas del reloj, counterclockwise rotation

rotación similar al reloj, clockwise rotation

reloj analógico, analog clock

reloj digital, digital clock

remanente, remainder

remediador, remedial

remover, to remove

rendimiento, yield

rendir, to perform, to yield

renombrar, to rename

renta, profits, rent

reordenamiento, rearrangement

reordenar, to rearrange

repetición, repetition

    con repetición, with repetition

    repeticiones sucesivas de la curva, successive repetitions of the curve

    sin repetición, without repetition

repetido, repeating, repeated

repetir, to repeat

    repetir un año, to be held back a year

repetirse, to recur

réplica, replication

replicar, to replicate

representación, representation

    representación algebraica, algebraic representation

    representación estándar, standard representation

    representación gráfica, graphical representation, plot

    representación matemática, mathematical representation

    representación pictórica, pictorial representation

    representaciones concretas, concrete representations

    representaciones gráficas, written representations

    representaciones múltiples, multiple representations

    representaciones no estándares, nonstandard representations

    representaciones orales, oral representations

representar, to represent, to stand for

reprobar, to fail

reproducción, replication

reproducible, replicable

reproducir, to replicate

reproducirse, to recur

requerir, to require

requisito, requirement

    reunir los requisitos, to meet requirements, to be elegible

reseña, outline

reserva, constraint

residuo, remainder, residue, residual

resoluble, solvable
resolución, solution
resolver, to resolve,
to solve
resolver gráficamente, solve graphically
resolver un problema, solve a problem
resolver una ecuación, solve an equation
resolver una ecuación cuadrática, solve a quadratic equation
resolver una ecuación fraccional, solve a fractional equation
resolver una variable, to solve for a variable
resorte, spring
respaldar, to support, to back up
respaldo, support, back-up
respectivamente, respectively
respecto, respect
responder, to answer
respuesta, answer, outcome, response
respuesta exacta, exact answer
resta, subtraction, difference
resta repetida, repeated subtraction
sumas y restas, addition and subtraction
restante[1], remainder
restante[2], remaining
restar, to subtract, to minus, to deduct
resto, remainder, rest
restricción, restriction, constraint
restringir, to restrict, to confine
resultado, outcome, score, result
resultado específico, specific result
resultado imposible, impossible outcome
resultado posible, possible outcome, resultant
resultados experimentales, experimental results
resultado favorable, favorable outcome
resultante[1], resultant
resultante[2], resulting
resumen, summary
resumen estadístco de cinco datos, five-number statistical summary
resumir, to summarize
retar, to challenge
retención, retention, deduction
retener, to retain, to hold, to hold back, to withhold, to deduct
reto, challenge
retraso de fase, phase lag
retroceder, to go back, to go backwards
reunir los requisitos, to meet requirements, to be elegible
revelar, to reveal
reversibilidad, reversibility
reversible, reversible
reverso[1], back side, back page

reverso², reverse
revés, backside
al revés,
reverse, backwards
revisar, to review,
to go over
revisión, review
revolución, revolution
revoluciones
por minuto,
revolutions per
minute (rpm)
rezago, lag, gap
rígido, rigid
rincón, corner
ritmo, pace, rate
rodar, to roll
rodeante, surrounding
rodear, to surround,
to go around
rombo, rhombus
romboedro, rhombohedron
romboide, rhomboid
rompecabezas, puzzle
romper, to break
rotación, rotation, spin
rotación contraria a
las agujas del reloj,
counterclockwise
rotation
rotación similar
al reloj, clockwise
rotation
rotacional, rotational, curl
rotulado, lettered
rotura, break
regla recta, straightedge,
straight edge
ruleta, spinner
rumbo, direction, bearing,
course
rumbo a,
towards

ruta, route
rutina, routine

sacar, take out
sacar conclusiones,
draw conclusions
saldo, balance, sale
saldo de una cuenta,
balance an account
salida, output
saliente, salient
salir, to leave, to go out
saltar, to jump, to skip
satisfacer, to satisfy
secante, secant
secante a un círculo,
secant to a circle
secante de un círcu-
lo, secant of a circle
sección, section,
cross-section
cónica central,
central conic
cónica no centrada,
non-centered conic
sección cónica,
conic section
sección paralela,
parallel section
sección planar,
plane section
sección recta,
cross-section
sección sin centro,
conic without a center
sector, sector
sector circular,
circular sector

sector de un círculo, sector of a circle
secuencia, sequence
secuencia aritmética, arithmetic sequence
secuencia armónica, harmonic sequence
secuencia creciente, increasing sequence
secuencia de Fibonacci, Fibonacci sequence
secuencia de intervalos, sequence of intervals
secuencia de números abiertos, open number sequence
secuencia de pasos, key sequence
secuencia de puntos, sequence of points
secuencia decreciente, decreasing sequence
secuencia geométrica, geometric sequence
secuencia lógica, logical sequence
secuencia opuesta, opposite sequence
secuenciar, sequencing
secundario, secondary
segmentar, to segment
segmento, segment, piece
segmento de línea congruentes, congruent line segments
segmento de línea recta, straight line segment

segmento de recta, straight line segment
segmentos de rectas paralelas, parallel line segments
segmento de tangente, tangent segment
segmento de un círculo, segment of a circle
segmento de una línea, line segment
segmento externo de una secante, external segment of a secant
segmento inicial, initial segment
segmento mayor, major segment
segmento menor, minor segment
segmento perpendicular, perpendicular segment
segmento secante, secant segment
segmento unitario, unit segment
segmentos de líneas proporcionale, proportional line segments
seguimiento, tracking, follow-up
seguir, to follow, to go after, to go behind, to track
seguir un patrón, to pattern
según, according to
segunda derivada, second derivative

segunda fórmula de Green, second Green formula

segundo, second

seguro, certain, dependable, sure

seis, six

selección, selection, choice

    selección al azar, random selection

    selección múltiple, multiple choice

seleccionar, to select, to choose

semana, week

semanalmente, weekly

semejante, similar, like

semicircular, semicircular

semicírculo, semicircle

semirecta, half-line, ray

semivida, half-life

señalar, to indicate, to mark, to point

sencillo, simple

sendero, path

seno, sine

sensato, sensible

sentido¹, direction

    en sentido contra las manecillas del reloj, counterclockwise

    en sentido de las manecillas del reloj, clockwise

sentido², sense, meaning

    sentido de orientación, sense of orientation

    sentido de reversión, sense-reversing

    sentido de rotación, sense of rotation

    sentido de una línea, sense of a line

sin sentido, senseless, meaningless

separado, separate

separar, to separate

séptimo, seventh

seriado, serial

serial, serial

seriar, to seriate

serie, series, string

    serie alterna, alternating series

    serie aritmética, arithmetic series

    serie armónica, harmonic series

    serie convergente, convergent series

    serie creciente, increasing series

    serie de Fourier, Fourier series

    serie de números naturales, series of natural numbers

    serie de potencias, power series

    serie de potencias crecientes, series of increasing powers

    serie de términos positivos, series of positive terms

    serie divergente, divergent series

    serie geométrica, geometric series

    series trigonométricas, trigonometric series

sextos, sixths

si, if, whether

    si y solamente si,

iff, if and only if
siempre, always, forever
    siempre y cuando,
    whenever, as long as
siete, seven
sigla, acronym
siglo, century
sigma, sigma
significado, meaning
significar, to mean
significativo,
    significant,
    meaningful
signo, sign
    signo de adición,
    addition sign
    símbolo de ángulo,
    angle symbol
    signo de desigualdad,
    inequality sign
    signo de división,
    division sign
    signo de extracción
    radical,
    radical sign
    signo de igual,
    equal sign
    signo de igualdad,
    equal sign
    signo de mayor
    o igual, greater
    or equal to sign
    signo de mayor que,
    greater than sign
    signo de menor
    o igual, less than or
    equal to sign
    signo de menor que,
    less than sign
    signo de multiplica-
    ción, multiplication
    sign
    signo de paralelismo,

parallel symbol
signo de resta,
subtraction sign
signo de semejanza,
similarity symbol
signo de suma,
addition sign,
summation sign
signo de sustracción,
minus sign
signo menos,
minus sign
signo negativo,
negative sign
signo positivo,
positive sign
signo radical,
radical sign
siguiente, next, following
silogismo, syllogism
simbólicamente,
    symbolically
simbólico, symbolic
simbolismo, symbolism
simbolizar, to symbolize
símbolo, symbol
    símbolo de agrupa-
    ción, grouping symbol
    símbolo de con-
    gruencia, congru-
    ence symbol
    símbolo de desigual-
    dad, inequality symbol
    símbolo de identidad,
    identity symbol
    símbolo de relación,
    relation symbol
    símbolo matemático,
    mathematical symbol
    símbolo numérico,
    numerical symbol
    símbolo operativo,
    operative symbol

símbolo para agrupar, grouping symbol
símbolo para operación, symbol for operation
símbolo escrito, symbol in written form
símbolo gráfico, symbol in written form, written symbols
símbolo monetario, currency symbol
símbolo radica, radical symbol
símbolo verbal, symbol in verbal form, verbal symbol
simetría, symmetry
  simetría axial, symmetry with respect to a line
  simetría central, central symmetry
  simetría con respecto a un plano, symmetry with respect to a plane
  simetría con respecto a un punto, symmetry with respect to a point
  simetría con respecto a una recta, symmetry with respect to a line
  simetría oblicua, skew symmetry
  simetría rotacional, rotational symmetry
  simetría translacional, translational symmetry
  simetría vertical, vertical symmetry
simétrico(a), symmetric, symmetrical
similar, similar, analogous, same
similaridad, similarity
similitud, similitude
simplex, simplex
simplificación, simplification
simplificado(a), simplified
simplificar, to simplify
  simplificar el resultado, simplify a result
  simplificar la expresión, simplify an expression
  simplificar una expresión algebraica, simplify an algebraic expression
  simplificar una fracción, simplify a fraction
simulacro, simulation
  simulacro de incendio, fire drill
simular, to simulate
simultáneo, simultaneous, concurrent
sin, without
  sin patrón, patternless
  sin reemplazo, without replacement
  sin sentido, senseless, meaningless
  sin unión, disjoint
singular, unique
singularidad, singularity, uniqueness

singularidad de orden, uniqueness of order

singularidad de solución, uniqueness of solution

sinusoide, sinusoid

sistema[1], system

sistema algebraico, algebraic system

sistema anglosajón de medidas, customary measurement system

sistema cerrado, closed system

sistema completo, complete system

sistema coordenado tridimensional, three dimensional coordinate system

sistema cuadrático lineal, linear-quadratic system

sistema de conos, system of conics

sistema de conteo, counting system

sistema de coordenadas cartesianas, Cartesian coordinate system

sistema de coordenadas, coordinate system

sistema de desigualdades, system of inequalities

sistema de ecuación cuadrático-lineal, quadratic-linear equation system

sistema de ecuaciones, system of equations

sistema de ecuaciones con dos variables, system of equations with two variables

sistema de ecuaciones dependientes, system of dependent equations

sistema de ecuaciones lineales, system of linear equations

sistema de frases, system of sentences

sistema de desigualdades lineales, system of linear inequalities

sistema de medición, measurement system

sistema de módulo, mod system, module system

sistema de numeración binaria, binary number system

sistema de numeración decimal, base ten number system

sistema de reloj, clock system

sistema internacional, SI, System International

sistema lógico, logical system

sistema matemático, mathematical system

sistema métrico, metric system

sistema númerico, number system

sistema númerico binario, binary number system

sistema númerico decimal, decimal number system

sistema octal, octal system

sistema postulacional, postulational system

sistema rectangular de coordenadas, rectangular coordinate system

sistema², means

sistemático, systematic

situación del mundo real, real world situation

situación modelo, model situation

sobrante, remainder, left-over

sobre, on, over, above, concerning, onto

sobrepasar, to outpace

sobresaliente, outstanding

sofisticación, sophistication

sofisticado, sophisticated

solicitar, to apply

solicitud, application

solidez, compactness, solidity

sólido, solid

sólido geométrico, geometric solid

sólido rectangular, rectangular solid

sólido truncado, frustum

solubilidad, solubility

solución, solution

sin solución, unsolvable

solución algebraica, algebraic solution

solución alterna, alternate solution

solución aproximada, approximate solution

solución de problemas, problem solving

solución de una oración, solution of the sentence

solución finita, finite solution

solución gráfica, graphic solution

solución inicial, initial solution

solución mínima, minimum solution

solución numérica, numerical solution

solución principal, principal solution

solución real, real solution

solución simplificada, simplified solution

solución única, unique solution

solución exacta, exact solution

sombra, shadow, shade

sombreado, shading

sombrear, to shade

sondear, survey

sondeo, survey

sonido, sound

sopesar, to weigh, to consider

soportar, to tolerate, to put up with, to support

soporte, support

soslayo, askew, slanted

sostener, to support, to sustain, to hold up

sostenido, supported

subconjunto, subset

    subconjunto propio, proper subset

subdivisión, subdivision

subespacio, subspace

subgrupo, subgroup

subíndice, subscript

subir, to rise, to raise, to go up

subjetivo, subjective

sublevar, to raise

subpuesto, subtended

subrayar, underline

subsidiaria, subsidiary

subtender, subtend

    subtender un ángulo, subtend an angle

sucediente, succeeding

sucesión, sequence, succession

    sucesión de Fibonacci, Fibonacci sequence

sucesivamente, successively

sucesivo, successive

sucesor, successor

sudeste, southeast

sudoeste, southwest

suficiente, sufficient, adequate

    más que suficiente, plenty

sufijo, suffix

sugerir, to suggest, to recommend

sujeto, fastened

sujeto a, subject to

suma, addition, summation, sum, amount

    suma algebraica, algebraic sum

    suma como operación binaria, addition as a binary operation

    suma de dos cubos, sum of two cubes

    suma de una serie aritmética, sum of an arithmetic series

    suma de una serie geométrica, sum of a geometric series

    suma digital, digital sum

    suma repetida, repeated addition

    sumas y restas, addition and subtraction

sumabilidad, summability

sumando, addend, summand

    sumandos, summed numbers

sumar, to add, to total

sumatoria, partial summation

    sumatoria de series, summation of series

suministrar, to supply

suministro, supply

superpotencia, super power

superficie, surface

    superficie cerrada, closed surface

superficie cilíndrica, cylinder surface, cylindrical surface

superficie lateral, lateral surface

superficie mínima, minimal surface

superficie orientada, oriented surface

superficie piramidal, pyramidal surface

superficie totalmente plana, completely flat surface

superfluo, extraneous, superfluous

superíndice, superscript

superior, higher, upper

suplementario, supplementary

ángulos suplementarios, supplementary angles

suplemento, supplement

suponer, to suppose, to assume, to entail

suposición, assumption

sur, south

surco, groove

suscrito, subscript

sustancia, substance, matter

sustancial, substantial

sustentado, supported

sustentar, to support

sustitución, substitution

sustitución idéntica, identical substitution

sustitución sucesiva, successive substitution

sustituir, to substitute, to replace

sustracción, subtraction

sustraendo, subtrahend

sustraer, subtract, take away

tabla, table, chart

tabla de distribución de frecuencias, frequency distribution table

tabla de distribución de frecuencias acumuladas, cumulative frequency distribution table

tabla de entradas y salidas, intput/output table

tabla de frecuencia, frequency table

tabla de frecuencia de datos, data frequency table

tabla de información, data table

tabla de madera, board

tabla de multiplicación, multiplication table

tabla de tasas de cambio, exchange rate table

tabla de verdad, truth table

tabla isométrica, isometric chart

tabla numérica, numerical table

tabulación, tabulation
tachar, to cross out,
    to mark wrong
tamaño, size, scale
tangencial, tangential
tangente, tangent
    tangente común,
    common tangent
    tangente común
    externa, common
    external tangent
    tangente común
    interna, common
    internal tangent
    tangente de un
    círculo, tangent
    of a circle
    tangente externa,
    external tangent
    tangente interna,
    internal tangent
    tangentes conjuga-
    das, conjugate tan-
    gents
    tangentes consecu-
    tivas, consecutive
    tangents
tangible, tangible
tangrama, tangram
tanteo, score
tarde, afternoon, tardy, late
    más tarde,
    afterwards
tarea, homework,
    assignment
tarifa unitaria, unit rate
tasa, rate
    tasa de cambio,
    rate of change,
    exchange rate
    tasa de interés,
    interest rate
    tasa de interés anual,

    APR, annual percent-
    age rate
    tasa por unidad,
    per-unit rate
tautología, tautology
taza, cup
técnica, technique
    técnica de facto-
    rización inversa,
    reverse factoring
    técnicas de conteo,
    counting techniques
    técnicas de modelaje,
    sampling techniques
técnico, technical
tecnología, technology
    tecnología de la
    información,
    IT, information
    technology
telescopio, telescope
    telescopio dióptico,
    refracting telescope
    telescopio reflector,
    reflecting telescope
tema, subject
temperatura,
    temperature
tendencia, trend
    tendencia central,
    central tendency
tender a, converge to
tener, to have, to possess
    tener cuidado,
    to be careful
    tener en cuenta,
    to take into account,
    to keep in mind
    tener éxito,
    to succeed
    tener los medios,
    to afford
tensor, tensor

tensor antisimétrico, antisymmetric tensor

tensor de Kronecker, Kronecker tensor

tensor de segundo orden, tensor of the second order

tensor simétrico, symmetrical tensor, symmetric tensor

tensorial, tensor

teorema, theorem

teorema central del límite, central limit theorem

teorema converso, converse theorem

teorema de Ampère-Stokes, circulation theorem, Stokes theorem

teorema de binomio, binomial theorem

teorema de la circulación, circulation theorem, Stokes theorem

teorema de la divergencia, divergence theorem

teorema de Pitágoras, Pythagorean identity

teorema de raíces racionales, rational root theorem

teorema de Rolle, Rolle's Theorem

teorema de semejanza SAS, SAS Similarity Theorem

teorema de Taylor, Taylor's Theorem

teorema de valor medio, Mean Value Theorem

teorema del binomio, binomial theorem

teorema del campo, field theorem

teorema del límite central, central limit theorem

teorema fundamental, fundamental theorem

teorema fundamental de la aritmética, Fundamental Theorem of Arithmetic

teorema fundamental del álgebra, Fundamental Theorem of Algebra

teorema fundamental del cálculo, Fundamental Theorem of Calculus

teorema inverso, inverse theorem

teorema de grupo, group theorem

último teorema de Fermat, Fermat's last theorem

teoría, theory

teoría de la probabilidad, probability theory

teoría de la relatividad, theory of relativity

teoría de números, number theory

teoría numérica, number theory

teórico, theoretical

tercer, third
    tercer cuartil,
    third quartile
tercera, third
    tercera parte,
    third part
tercero, third
tercio, third
termal, thermal
térmico, thermal
terminable, terminating
terminal, terminal
terminar, terminate, finish
término, term
    término absoluto,
    absolute term
    término constante,
    constant term
    término desconocido,
    unknown term
    **término elevado a
    un exponente n,**
    nth term
    término exterior,
    outer term
    término indefinido,
    undefined term
    término inicial,
    initial term
    término interno,
    inner term
    término medio,
    middle term
    términos definidos,
    defined terms
    términos diferentes,
    unlike terms
    términos medios,
    mean terms
    **términos medios
    de una proporción,**
    mean terms of
    proportion

    términos mínimos,
    lowest terms
    términos semejantes,
    like terms
    términos similares,
    similar terms, like
    terms
    términos sucesivos,
    successive terms
    términos superiores,
    higher terms
terminología, terminology
termómetro, thermometer
terna, triple
teselado, tessellation
tetraedro, tetrahedron
tiempo, time
tieso, stiff
típico, typical, standard
tipo, type, class
    tipo de cambio,
    exchange rate
    **tipo de cambio de
    divisas,** foreign
    exchange rate
tira, strip
tirar, throw, throw away
    tirar dados,
    to roll dice
    tirar monedas,
    to flip coins
tocando, touching
tocar, to touch
todo(a), all, every, any
    todos juntos,
    all together
    **todos los posibles
    resultados,** all pos-
    sible outcomes
    todos y cada uno,
    each and every
tolerable, tolerable
tolerancia, tolerance

tolerar, to tolerate
tomar, to take
tonelada, ton (T)
topología, topology
topológico, topological
torcido, crooked, askew
total, total
totalizar, to total
trabajar, to work
    trabajar de atrás
    para adelante,
    work backwards
trabajo, work
tradicional, traditional
trama, plot
trampa, trick
transformación,
    transformation
    transformación de
    coordenadas, coordi-
    nate transformation
    transformación de
    Fourier, Fourier
    transformation
    transformación
    idéntica, identical
    transformation
    transformación
    inversa, inverse
    transformation
    transformación
    isogonal, isogonal
    transformation
    transformación
    lineal, linear
    transformation
    transformación
    opuesta, opposite
    transformation
    transformación
    reversible, reversible
    transformation
transformacional,
    transformational
transformada de Fourier,
    Fourier transform
transformado,
    transformed
transformar, to transform
    transformar la fór-
    mula, transform the
    formula
transitividad, transitivity
transitivo(a), transitive
translación, translation
transmisión, transmission
transmitir, to transmit
transparente, clear
transponer, to transpose
transportador, protractor
transporte paso a paso,
    step-by-step carry
transporte total,
    complete carrying
transposición,
    transposition
transversal, transversal
transverso(a), transverse
trapecio, trapezoid,
    trapezium
    trapecio isósceles,
    isosceles trapezoid
trapezoide, trapezoid
    trapezoide isósceles,
    isosceles trapezoid
trascendental,
    transcendental
trasfondo, background
traslación, translation
trasladar, to translate
traslado del origen,
    shift of origin
traslado paralelo,
    parallel shift
traslapar, to overlap
traslape, overlap,

intersection
**trasunto de calificacio-
nes,** transcript
trayectoria,
    path, trajectory
trazado, trace
trazar, to trace
    trazar puntos,
    to plot
trazo, trace
tres, three
triangulación,
    triangulation
triangular, triangular
triángulo, triangle
    triángulo agudo,
    acute triangle
    **triángulo circuns-
    crito,** circumscribed
    triangle
    **triángulo semejante
    AA,** AA triangle simi-
    larity
    **triángulo semejan-
    te AAA,** AAA triangle
    similarity
    **triángulo congruente
    AAS,** AAS triangle con-
    gruence
    **triángulo congruente
    ASA,** ASA triangle con-
    gruence
    **triángulo congruen-
    te SAS,** SAS triangle
    congruence
    **triángulo congruen-
    te SSS,** SSS triangle
    congruence
    triángulo de Pascal,
    Pascal's triangle
    **triángulo de vecto-
    res,** vector triangle
    triángulo equian-

gular, equiangular
triangle
    triángulo equilátero,
    equilateral triangle
    triángulo escaleno,
    scalene triangle
    triángulo esférico,
    spherical triangle
    triángulo isósceles,
    isosceles triangle
    triángulo oblicuo,
    oblique triangle
    triángulo obtuso,
    obtuse triangle
    triángulo primitivo,
    primitive triangle
    triángulo recto,
    right triangle
    **triángulos congruen-
    tes,** congruent trian-
    gles
    **triángulos interca-
    lados,** overlapping
    triangles
    triángulos similares,
    similar triangles
tricotomía, trichotomy
tridimensional,
    three-dimensional
triédrico, trihedral
triedro, trihedron
    triedro directo,
    right-handed trihedron
    triedro inverso,
    left-handed trihedron
trigonometría,
    trig, trigonometry
    **trigonometría de un
    triángulo recto,**
    right triangle trigo-
    nometry
trigonométrico,
    trigonometric

un ciclo de una función trigonométrica, one cycle of a trigonometric function

trillón, trillion

trinomial, trinomial

trinomio, trinomial

trinomio cuadrado perfecto, perfect square trinomial

trinomio cuadrático, quadratic trinomial

triple, triple

triple pitagórico, Pythagorean triple

triplete, triad

triplicar, to triple

trisección, trisection

trisección de un ángulo, trisection of an angle

trisectriz, trisectrix

trivial, trivial

tronco, frustum

truco, trick

truncamiento, truncation

truncar, to truncate

tubo de ensayo, test tube

U

ubicación, location

ubicar, locate, plot

último(a), last

última conjetura de Fermat, Fermat's last theorem

último teorema de Fermat, Fermat's last theorem

último término, last term

una vuelta completa, around in a full rotation

unario, unary

único, unique, sole, only

unidad[1], unit

unidad apropiada, appropriate unit

unidad correspondiente, corresponding unit

unidad cuadrada, square unit

unidad cúbica, cubic unit

unidad de billón, billions place value

unidad de centésima, hundredth

unidad de medida, unit measure

unidad entera, whole unit

unidad estándar, standard unit

unidad imaginaria, imaginary unit

unidad lineal, linear unit

unidad métrica de medida, metric unit

unidad métrica de medición, metric unit

unidad normal, unit normal

unidades, ones, ones place

unidades de capaci-

dad anglosajonas, customary units of capacity

unidades equivalentes de capacidad anglosajonas, equivalent customary units of capacity

unidades de masa anglosajonas, customary units of mass

unidades de mil, thousands, thousands place

unidades de millar, thousands, thousands place

unidades de millión, millions, millions place

unidades no estándares, nonstandard units

unidimensional, one-dimensional

uniforme, uniform

uniformemente distribuido, evenly distributed

uniformidad, uniformity

unión, union, binding

    unión de conjuntos, union of sets

    unión de gráficos, union of the graphs

    unión desajustada, mismatch

    sin unión, disjoint

unir, to unite, to join

    unir mal, to mismatch

univariado, univariate

universal, universal

universidad, university

universo, universe

uno, one

    de uno a uno, one at a time

    de uno en uno, one-by-one

    función de uno a uno, one-to-one function

    uno a la vez, one at a time

    uno sí, otro no, every other

usual, usual, customary

usuario, user

útil, useful

utilidad, usefulness

    utilidades, profits

utilizar, to utilize, to use

vacío, vacuum, void, empty

vago, vague

validez, validity

    validez universal, universal validity

válido, valid

valor, value

    valor absoluto, absolute value

    valor absoluto de un número, absolute-value of a number

    valor aproximado, approximate value

    valor atípico, outlier

valor correspondiente de, corresponding value for

valor de una expresión algebraica, value of an algebraic expression

valor de una función, value of a function

valor de una variable, value of a variable

valor de verdad, truth value

valor de verdad incierto, uncertain truth value

valor del espacio, place value

valor designado, designated value

valor exacto, exact value

valor extremo, outlier, extreme value

valor fijo, fixed value

valor inajustable, unsuitable value

valor inicial, initial value

valor intermedio, intermediate value

valor máximo, at most, maximum value

valor medio, mean value

valor medio armónico, harmonic mean value

valor medio asumido, assumed mean

valor mínimo, minimum value

valor nominal, nominal value

valor númerico de base, base numeral value

valor posicional, place value

valor propio, eigenvalue

valor racional aproximado, approximate rational value

valor trigonométrico, trigonometric value

valor verdadero, truth value

valores de entrada, input values

valores de ingreso, income values

variable, variable

de varias variables, multiple variables

variable dependiente, dependent variable

variable independiente, independent variable

variable principal, leading variable

variable real, real variable

variable suscrito, subscripted variable

variación, variance, variation

variación combinada, combined variation

variación conjunta, joint variation

variación de una

función, range of a function
variación directa, direct variation
variación inversa, inverse variation
varianza, variance
    análisis de varianza, ANOVA, analysis of variance
variar, to vary
varias veces, several times
varios, several
vector, vector
    cantidad del vector, vector quantity
    vector axial, axial vector
    vector fila, row vector
    vector polar, polar vector
    vector propio, eigenvector
    vector radial, radius vector
    vector unitario, unit vector
vectorial, vector
velocidad, velocity, speed, rate,
    velocidad angular, angular velocity
ver, to see, to observe
verano, summer
veraz, true
verbal, verbal
verbalmente, verbally
verdad, truth
verdadero, true
verificación, verification
    verificación de una hipótesis, hypothesis testing
verificado, verified
verificar, to verify, to check, to prove
    verificar afirmaciones de otros, verify the claims of others
    verificar los resultados, verify results
verosímil, credible, believable, plausible
verosimilitud, plausibility
vertical, vertical
vértice, vertex (pl. vertices), cusp, apex
    vértice común, common vertex
    vértice de un cono, vertex of a cone
    vértice opuesto, opposite vertex
    vértices cíclicos de un cuadrilátero, cyclic vertices of a quadrilateral
    vértices consecutivos, consecutive vertices
vestigio, trace
vez (pl. veces), time, turn
    algunas veces, sometimes
    cada vez, every time
    de vez en cuando, occasionally, sometimes, from time to time
    dos veces, twice
    otra vez, again

rara vez, seldom

una vez, once

uno a la vez, one at a time

varias veces, several times

viajar, to travel

viaje de ida y vuelta, round trip

viaje redondo, round trip

vida media, half-life

vincular, to link, to bind, to bound

vínculo, link

vista, view

vista de un lado, side view

visual, visual

visual matemático, mathematical visual

visualización, visualization

visualizar, to visualize

voltear, to flip, to turn, to rotate

volumen, volume

integral de volumen, volume integral

volumen de un cono, volume of a cone

volumen de un sólido, volume of a solid

volumen de una figura sólida, volume of a solid figure

volver, to return, to do again,

volver a calcular, to recalculate

volver hacia atrás, to go backwards

volverse, to become

vuelta, turn

yacer, to lie

yacer sobre el gráfico, lie on the graph of

yacer sobre la línea, lie on the line

yarda, yard (yd.)

yarda cuadrada, square yard

zona, zone

zona crítica, critical region

zurdo, left-handed

Section II
English - Spanish

AA triangle similarity,
triángulo semejante
AA
AAA triangle similarity,
triángulo semejante
AAA
AAS triangle congruence,
triángulo congruente
AAS
abacus, ábaco
abbreviate, abreviar
abbreviation, abreviación,
abreviatura
Abelian group,
grupo abeliano
aberration, aberración
abnormal, anormal
about, acerca de,
aproximadamente
above, arriba de, sobre, por
encima de, mayor a
above zero,
encima de cero
abscissa, abscisa
absent, ausente
absolute, absoluto
absolute deviation,
desviación absoluta
absolute inequality,
desigualdad absoluta
absolute magnitude,
magnitud absoluta
absolute maximum,
máximo absoluto
absolute minimum,
mínimo absoluto
absolute scale,
escala absoluta

absolute term,
término absoluto
absolute value,
valor absoluto
**absolute value
inequality,**
desigualdad de
valor absoluto
**absolute value
equation,** ecuación
de valor absoluto
**absolute value
function,** función
de valor absoluto
**absolute-value
of a number,**
valor absoluto de
un número
abstraction, abstracción
absurd, absurdo, irracional
abundance, abundancia,
plenitud
abundant, abundante
academic, académico
academy, academia
accelerate, acelerar
acceleration, aceleración
accept, aceptar
access[1], acceder, accesar
access[2], acceso
accompany, acompañar
accompanying diagram,
diagrama acompa-
ñante
accordance, acuerdo,
conformidad
in accordance with,
de acuerdo con
according, conforme
according to,
según
account[1], computar
to account for,

explicar
account², cuenta
   to take into account,
   tener en cuenta
accrue, acumularse
accumulate, acumular
accumulated capital,
   capital acumulado
accumulation,
   acumulación
accumulator, acumulador
accuracy, exactitud,
   precisión
accurate, preciso
achievable, alcanzable
achieve, lograr
achievement, logro
acknowledge, reconocer
acknowledgment,
   reconocimiento
acre, acre
acronym, siglas
act it out,
   hacer una representa-
   ción del problema
activate, activar
activation, activación
active, activo
activity, actividad
actual, efectivo, real
acute, agudo
   acute angle,
   ángulo agudo
   acute triangle,
   triángulo agudo
ad extremum, al límite
adapt, adaptar
add, sumar, agregar,
   añadir
addend, sumando
addition, adición, suma
   addition and subtrac-
   tion, sumas y restas

**addition as a binary
operation,** suma como
operación binaria
addition fact,
hecho aditivo
**addition property
of inequality,**
propiedad aditiva
de la desigualdad
**addition property
of zero,** propiedad
de la suma del cero
addition sentence,
ecuación de suma
addition sign,
signo de suma
repeated addition,
suma repetida
additional, adicional
additive, aditivo
   additive identity,
   identidad aditiva
   additive inverse,
   inverso aditivo
   additive operation,
   operación aditiva
   **additive property
   of equality,**
   propiedad aditiva
   de la igualdad
adequate, adecuado,
suficiente
adhere, adherirse, pegarse
adherent, adherente,
pegajoso
adhesion, adhesión
adhesive, adhesivo,
pegajoso, pegamento
adjacency, adyacencia
adjacent, adyacente,
colindante, contiguo
   adjacent angles,
   ángulos adyacentes

adjacent sides, lados adyacentes
adjoint, adjunto
adjust, ajustar
adjustable, ajustable
adjustment, ajuste
advance[1], avanzar
advance[2], adelanto, avance
advanced, avanzado
aerodynamic, aerodinámico
affect, afectar
affirm, afirmar
affirmation, afirmación
afford, poder pagar, tener los medios, costear
after, después, después de
afternoon, tarde
afterwards, después, más tarde
again, de nuevo
aggregate, agregado
agree, estar de acuerdo, acordarse
aid[1], ayudar, auxiliar
aid[2], ayuda, auxilio
airplane, avión, aeronave
algebra, álgebra
   algebra of logic, álgebra de lógica
   Boolean algebra, álgebra de Boole
   linear algebra, álgebra lineal
   matrix algebra, álgebra matricial
algebraic, algebraico
   algebraic analysis, análisis algebraico
   algebraic application, aplicación algebraica
   algebraic curve, curva algebraica

   algebraic equation, ecuación algebraica
   algebraic expression, expresión algebraica
   algebraic form, forma algebraica
   algebraic fraction, fracción algebraica
   algebraic function, función algebraica
   algebraic identity, identidad algebraica
   algebraic language, lenguaje algebraico
   algebraic manipulation, manipulación algebraica
   algebraic pattern, patrón algebraico
   algebraic problem, problema algebraico
   algebraic product, producto algebraico
   algebraic relationship, relación algebraica
   algebraic representation, representación algebraica
   algebraic solution, solución algebraica
   algebraic sum, suma algebraica
   algebraic system, sistema algebraico
algebraically, algebraicamente
   algebraically equivalent, algebraicamente equivalente
   algebraically independent, algebraicamente independiente

algebraically independent basis, base algebraicamente independiente

algorithm, algoritmo

division algorithm, algoritimo de la división

Euclid's algorithm, algoritmo de Euclides

square-root algorithm, algoritmo de la raíz cuadrada

standard algorithm, algoritmo estándar

align, alinear

aligned, alineado

alike, parecido

all, todo(a)

all possible outcomes, todos los posibles resultados

all together, todos juntos

almost, casi

alongside, al costado de, al lado de

alphabet, abecedario, alfabeto

alphabetical order, orden alfabético

alter, cambiar, modificar

alteration, alteración

alternate[1], alternar

alternate[2], alterno

alternate angle, ángulo alterno

alternate approach, enfoque alternativo, aproximación alternativa

alternate exterior angle, ángulo alterno externo

alternate interior angle, ángulo alterno interno

alternate permutation, permutación alterna

alternate solution, solución alterna

alternating, alternante

alternating series, serie alterna

alternation, alternancia

alternative, alternativo

altimeter, altímetro

altitude, altitud, altura

always, siempre

ambiguous, ambiguo

ambition, ambición

ambitious, ambicioso

amount, cantidad, suma, monto

in the amount of, a razón de

amp (ampere), ampere

ampere, ampere

ample, abundante, amplio, extenso

amplification, amplificación

amplify, amplificar

amplitude, amplitud

analog, análogo

analog clock, reloj analógico

analog computer, computadora analógica

analogous, análogo, similar, comparable

analogy, analogía

analysis, análisis
  algebraic analysis,
  análisis algebraico
  analysis of variance,
  análisis de varianza
  **ANOVA (analysis of
  variance),** análisis
  de varianza
  Fourier analysis,
  análisis de Fourier
  **mathematical
  analysis,** análisis
  matemático
  **nonstandard
  analysis,** análisis
  no estándar
analytic, analítico
  analytic geometry,
  geometría analítica
analytical proof,
  prueba analítica
analyze, analizar, evaluar
angle, ángulo
  acute angle,
  ángulo agudo
  alternate angle,
  ángulo alterno
  **alternate exterior
  angle,** ángulo alterno
  externo
  **alternate interior
  angle,** ángulo alterno
  interno
  **angle addition postu-
  late,** postulado de la
  suma de los ángulos
  angle bisector,
  ángulo bisector
  **angle in a standard
  position,** ángulo en
  posición normal
  **angle inscribed in a
  circle,** ángulo inscrito

en un círculo
  **angle inscribed in
  a semicircle,**
  ángulo inscrito en
  un semi-círculo
  angle measure,
  medida de ángulo
  **angle measure pre-
  served,** medida de
  ángulo conservada
  angle name,
  nombre del ángulo
  **angle of a circular
  segment,** ángulo de
  un segmento circular
  **angle of circumfer-
  ence,** ángulo de la
  circunferencia
  **angle of contin-
  gence,** ángulo de
  contingencia
  angle of depression,
  ángulo de depresión
  angle of elevation,
  ángulo de elevación
  angle of incidence,
  ángulo de incidencia
  angle of reflection,
  ángulo de refracción
  angle pairs,
  pares de ángulos
  **angle properties
  of circles,**
  propiedades de los
  ángulos en círculos,
  propiedades angulares
  de círculos
  angle symbol,
  símbolo de ángulo
  base angle,
  ángulo de la base
  central angle,
  ángulo central

**central angle of
a regular polygon,**
ángulo central de
un polígono regular
**complementary
angles,** ángulos
complementarios
concave angle,
ángulo cóncavo
congruent angle,
ángulo congruente
conjugate angles,
ángulos conjugados
consecutive angles,
ángulos consecutivos
convex angle,
ángulo convexo
**corresponding
angles,** ángulos
correspondientes
coterminal angles,
ángulos coterminales
dihedral angle,
ángulo diedro
directed angle,
ángulo dirigido
exterior angle,
ángulo exterior
**exterior angle
of a triangle,**
ángulo exterior
de un triángulo
first-quadrant angle,
ángulo del primer
cuadrante
flat angle,
ángulo plano
**fourth-quadrant
angle,** ángulo del
cuarto cuadrante
**half angle formula for
a trigonometric func-
tion,** fórmula de me-

dio ángulo para una
función trigonométrica
included angle,
ángulo contenido
inscribed angle,
ángulo inscrito
interior angle,
ángulo interior
**interior angle
of a triangle,**
ángulo interior
de un triángulo
nonadjacent angles,
ángulos no adyacentes
obtuse angle,
ángulo obtuso
opposite angles,
ángulos opuestos
orientation angle,
ángulo de orientación
phase angle,
ángulo de fase
position angle,
ángulo de posición
principal angle,
ángulo principal
quadrantal angle,
ángulo cuadrantal
reference angle,
ángulo de referencia
reflex angle,
ángulo de reflexión,
ángulo reflexivo
**remote interior
angles,** ángulos
interiores remotos
right angle,
ángulo recto
**second-quadrant
angle,** ángulo del
segundo cuadrante
solid angle,
ángulo sólido

spherical angle, ángulo esférico

straight angle, ángulo llano

subtended angle, ángulo subpuesto

superior angle, ángulo superior

supplementary angles, ángulos suplementarios

third-quadrant angle, ángulo del tercer cuadrante

trihedral angle, ángulo triedro

vertex angle, ángulo del vértice

vertical angles, ángulos verticales

z-angle, ángulo z

angular, angular

angular velocity, velocidad angular

annual, anual

annual percentage rate (APR), tasa de interés anual

annually, anualmente

annulus, ánulo, anillo, dona, corona circular

another, otro

ANOVA (analysis of variance), análisis de varianza

answer[1], contestar, responder

answer[2], respuesta

exact answer, respuesta exacta

ante meridian (a.m.), ante merídiem, ante-meridiano (a.m.)

antecedent, antecedente

antiderivative, antiderivada

antidifferentiation, antidiferenciación

antilog, antilogaritmo

antilogarithm, antilogaritmo

antinomy, antinomia

antiprism, antiprisma

antisymmetric, antisimétrico

antisymmetric tensor, tensor antisimétrico

any, cualquier, todo

apex, vértice, ápice, cima

apothem, apotema

appear, aparece

appendix, apéndice

applicable, aplicable

application, aplicación, solicitud

algebraic application, aplicación algebraica

apply, aplicar, solicitar

apply a variety of strategies, aplicar diversas estrategias

appraisal, apreciación

approach[1], aproximarse, acercarse

approach[2], acercamiento, acceso

approaching, acercamiento

appropriate, apropiado, adecuado

appropriate mathematical language, lenguaje matemático apropiado

appropriate unit,

unidad apropiada
approximability, aproximabilidad
approximate[1], aproximarse
approximate[2], aproximado
   approximate calculation, cálculo aproximado
   approximate construction, construcción aproximada
   approximate number, número aproximado
   approximate rational value, valor racional aproximado
   approximate solution, solución aproximada
   approximate square root, raíz cuadrada aproximada
   approximate value, valor aproximado
approximately, aproximadamente
   approximately equal to, casi igual a
approximation, aproximación
   approximation of 1st degree, aproximación de primer grado
   approximation of root, aproximación de raíz
   approximation of the average, aproximación al promedio
   best approximation, mejor aproximación
   optimal approximation, aproximación óptima
   successive approximation, aproximación sucesiva
   tangential approximation method, método de aproximación tangencial
   trigonometric approximation, aproximación trigonométrica
APR (annual percentage rate), tasa de interés anual
arbitrary, arbitrario
   arbitrary constant, constante arbitraria
arc, arco
   arc length, longitud del arco
   arc subtended by a chord, arco sujeto por una cuerda
   arccos, arcocoseno
   arcsin, arcoseno
   arctan, arcotangente
   circular arc, arco circular
   closed arc, arco cerrado
   congruent arc, arco congruente
   intercepted arc, arco interceptado
   major arc, arco mayor

minor arc,
arco menor
open arc,
arco abierto
segmental arc,
arco segmental
superior arc,
arco superior
arccos, arcocoseno
arch¹, arquear
arch², arco
arched, arqueado
arcsin, arcoseno
arctan, arcotangente
area, área
   area of a circle,
   área de un círculo
   area of a rectangle,
   área de un rectágulo
   lateral area of a cone,
   área lateral del cono
   lateral surface area,
   área de superficie
   lateral
   surface area,
   área de la superficie
argument, argumento
   logical argument,
   argumento lógico
arithmetic, aritmético(a)
   arithmetic expres-
   sion, expresión
   aritmética, expresión
   númerica
   arithmetic fact,
   hecho aritmético
   arithmetic fraction,
   fracción aritmética
   arithmetic mean,
   media aritmética
   arithmetic operation,
   operación aritmética
   arithmetic

   progression,
   progresión aritmética
   arithmetic sequence,
   secuencia aritmética
   arithmetic series,
   serie aritmética
   arithmetic
   statement,
   frase aritmética
   binary arithmetic,
   aritmética binaria
around, alrededor, cerca
de, aproximadamente
   around in a full
   rotation, una vuelta
   completa
arrange, ordenar, arreglar,
poner en orden o
secuencia, agrupar
arrangement, arreglo,
ordenamiento
   random arrangement,
   ordenamiento al azar
array, arreglo
arrow, flecha
as long as,
siempre y cuando
ASA triangle congruence,
triángulo congruente
ASA
ascend, ascender, subir
ascending,
creciente, ascenden-
te, que asciende, que
incrementa, que sube
   ascending order,
   orden ascendente
ask, preguntar, formular
una pregunta, pedir
askew,
inclinado, torcido,
ladeado, oblicuo,
soslayo

assert, afirmar, declarar,
imponerse

assess, evaluar, calificar

assessment, evaluación

assign, asignar

   assign values,
asignar valores

assignment,
tarea, asignación

associate, asociar

association, asociación

associative, asociativo

   associative law,
ley asociativa

   associative property,
propiedad asociativa

   **associative property
of addition,**
propiedad asociativa
de la suma

   **associative property
of multiplication,**
propiedad asociativa
de multiplicación

associativity,
asociabilidad

assume, suponer, asumir

assumed mean,
valor medio asumido

assumption, suposición

asterisk, asterisco

asymmetric, asimétrico

   asymmetric relation,
relación asimétrica

asymmetrical, asimétrica

   **asymmetrical
relation,** relación
asimétrica

asymmetry, asimetría

asymptote, asíntota

at, en

   at least,
al menos

   at most,
a lo más

atmosphere, atmósfera

attach, adjuntar, asignar

attached, adjunto

attempt[1], intentar

attempt[2], intento

attribute[1], atribuir

attribute[2], atribuir, característica, propiedad

atypical, atípico

augment, aumentar

authentic, auténtico

autonomous, autónomo

autonomy, autonomía

autumn, otoño

auxiliary, auxiliar

   auxiliary line,
línea auxiliar

availability,
disponibilidad

average[1], promediar

average[2], promedio, media

   average error,
error promedio

   **GPA (grade point
average),**
promedio

average[3], medio

axial vector, vector axial

axiom, axioma

   **Closure Axiom
of Addition,**
axioma de clausura
de adición, axioma de
clausura de la suma

   **Closure Axiom of
Multiplication,**
axioma de clausura de
multiplicación, axioma de clausura de la
multiplicación

axis (pl. axes), eje

axis of a conic section, eje de una sección cónica
axis of a cylinder, eje de un cilindro
axis of abscissas, eje de las abscisas
axis of imaginaries, eje imaginario
axis of ordinates, eje de ordenadas
axis of quadric, eje cuádrico
axis of rotation, eje de rotación
axis of symmetry, eje de simetría
coordinate axes, ejes de coordenadas
horizontal axis, eje horizontal
imaginary axis, eje imaginario
longitudinal axis, eje longitudinal
major axis, eje mayor
minor axis, eje menor
number axis, eje numérico
real axis, eje real
real number axis, eje de los números reales
rotation axis, eje de rotación
transverse axis, eje transverso
vertical axis, eje vertical
x-axis, eje de las x, eje x
y-axis, eje de las y, eje y

back page, reverso
back[1], parte de atrás, espalda, dorso, reverso
back[2], de atrás, trasero
back[3], atrás, hacia atrás, de vuelta
back up, respaldar
background, trasfondo
backup, respaldo
backside, revés
backwards, al revés
balance[1], balancear, equilibrar
  balance an account, saldo de una cuenta
balance[2], báscula, balanza, equilibrio, saldo
  pan balance, balanza de platillos
balanced, balanceado
ball, bola
band, banda, cinta
bank statement, estado financiero
bar, barra
  bar chart, gráfica de barras
  bar graph, gráfica de barras
  double bar graph, gráfico de barras dobles
barometer, barómetro
barometric, barométrico

barometric pressure,
presión barométrica
barrel, barril
barycenter,
baricentro
barycentric coordinates,
coordenadas baricén-
tricas
base, base
base angle,
ángulo de la base
base cosine curve,
curva básica del
coseno
base numeral value,
valor númerico
de base
base of a cylinder,
base del cilindro
base of a figure,
base de una figura
base of a logarithm,
base de un logaritmo
base of a power,
base de una potencia
**base of an exponen-
tial function,**
base de una función
exponencial
base operation,
operación básica
base ten,
base diez
**base ten number
system,** sistema de
numeración decimal
common base,
base común
lower base,
base inferior
orthonormal base,
base ortonormal
upper base,

base superior
basic, básico
bead, abalorio
beam, barra, rayo
bearing,
ángulo de orientación
o de posición, rumbo
beat, pulsación, palpitación, golpe, latido
heart beat,
latido del corazón
become, convertirse en,
volverse, ponerse
before, antes
behavior, conducta,
comportamiento
behind[1], atrasado
behind[2], detrás de
belief, creencia
believable,
creíble, verosímil
believe, creer
bell curve, curva en forma
de campana, campana
de Gauss, curva de
distribución normal
belong, pertenecer
below, abajo, debajo de,
menor
below zero,
bajo cero
bend, encorvar, doblar
benefit, beneficio
bent, encorvado, doblado
Bernoulli experiment,
experimento de
Bernoulli
beside, al lado de
best, (el, lo, la) mejor
best approximation,
mejor aproximación
between, entre,
en medio de

bias

bias, parcialidad, prejuicio
biased, parcial
  biased estimator, estimador parcial
  biased sample, muestra engañosa
  biased statistic, estadística parcial
  unbiased, imparcial
biconditional, bicondicional
  biconditional binary operation, operación binaria bicondicional
  biconditional statement, proposición bicondicionada
big, grande
bigger, más grande
  bigger than, más grande que
biggest, el más grande
bijection, aplicación biyectiva
bilateral, bilateral
bilingual education, educación bilingüe
billion, mil millones, millardo
billions place value, posición de mil millones, unidad de billón
bimodal, bimodal
binary, binario
  binary arithmetic, artimética binaria
  binary digit, dígito binario
  binary form, forma binaria
  binary number, número binario
  binary number system, sistema de numeración binaria
  binary operation, operación binaria
  binary relation, relación binaria
bind, unir, enlazar, vincular, limitar
binding, encuentro, unión
binomial, binomio
  binomial coefficient, coeficiente binomial
  binomial curve, curva binómica
  binomial expansion, expansión binómica
  binomial expression, expresión binómica
  binomial probability formula, fórmula de probabilidad binomial
  binomial theorem, teorema de binomio
binormal, binormal
biquadratic, bicuadrada
bisect, bisecar
bisecting each other, bisecarse entre sí
bisecting line, bisectriz
bisector, bisectriz, bisector
  angle bisector, ángulo bisector
  bisector of a segment, bisector de un segmento
  external bisector, bisector externo
  internal bisector, bisector interno
  perpendicular bisector, mediatriz, bisector

perpendicular
bit, bit
bivariate data,
datos bivariados
block, bloque
block graph,
gráfica de bloque,
histograma
board, tabla de madera
body, cuerpo
body of rotation,
elemento de rotación
book, libro
Boolean algebra,
álgebra de Boole
border, borde, límite,
frontera
bordering, delimitante,
contiguo, que compar-
te lados o bordes
borrow, pedir prestado
borrowed number,
número prestado
bottom, parte inferior,
fondo
bound[1], vincular, limitar
bound[2], límite
lower bound,
límite inferior
upper bound,
límite superior
boundary, lado, límite
boundary line,
ámbito
bounded, limitado, acotado
boundless, sin límite
box and whisker diagram,
gráfico de caja y
bigotes
box plot, gráfico de caja,
gráfica de caja
box-and-whisker plot,
diagrama de caja y

bigotes
brace, llave
bracket, corchete
round bracket,
corchete circular
square bracket,
corchete, corchete
cuadrado
branch, rama
breadth, ancho, anchura,
de ancho
break[1], romper
break[2], rotura
break down, descomponer
break into, descomponer
breakdown,
descomposición
brief, breve
broad, extenso
budget[1], calcular el presupuesto, presupuestar
budget[2], presupuesto
build, construir
built, construido
bushel, fanega
buy, comprar
by means of, mediante,
por medio de
byte, byte

calculability,
calculabilidad
calculable, calculable
calculate, calcular
**calculate the
volume of,**
cubicar, calcular
el volumen de

calculated probability,
probabilidad calculada
calculation, cálculo
calculator, calculadora
    graphing calculator,
    calculadora gráfica
    **programmable cal-
culator,** calculadora
programable
    scientific calculator,
    calculadora científica
calculus, cálculo
    differential calculus,
    cálculo diferencial
    **Fundamental
Theorem of Calculus,**
teorema fundamental
del cálculo
    integral calculus,
    cálculo integral
calendar, calendario,
almanaque
caliper, calibrador
cancel, cancelar
cancellation, cancelación
    cancellation law,
    ley de cancelación
    **cancellation law of
addition,** ley de can-
celación de la suma
    **cancellation law of
multiplication,**
ley de cancelación de
la multiplicación
    cancellation method,
    método de cancelación
canonical, canónico(a)
capacity, capacidad
card, carta
    deck of cards,
    juego de cartas
cardinal, cardinal
    cardinal number,

número cardinal
care, cuidado
careful, cuidadoso,
meticuloso, prudente
    be careful,
    tener cuidado
careless, descuidado,
imprudente
carry, rebasar, producir un
acarreo, cargar, llevar
    carry out,
    llevar a cabo,
efectuar, realizar
Cartesian, cartesiano
    **Cartesian coordinate
plane,** plano coorde-
nado cartesiano
    **Cartesian coordinate
system,** sistema de
coordenadas cartesia-
nas
    **Cartesian coordi-
nates,** coordenadas
cartesianas
case, caso
cash, dinero en efectivo
categorize, clasificar
catenary, catenaria
causation, causalidad
cause[1], causar
cause[2], causa
cavity, cavidad
cease, dejar de, cesar
cell, celda, casilla
Celsius (C), Celsio, Celsius,
centígrado
census, censo
cent, centavo
center[1], centrar
center[2], centro
    barycenter,
    baricentro
    center of a circle,

centro de un círculo
center of a conic section, centro de una sección cónica
center of a dilation, centro de dilatación
center of a regular polygon, centro de un polígono regular
center of a rotation, centro de rotación
center of a sphere, centro de una esfera
center of gravity, centro de gravedad
center of mass, centro de masas
center of symmetry, centro de simetría
center-radius equation of a circle, ecuación centro-radial de un círculo
inner center, centro interno, centro interior
orthocenter, ortocentro
centered, centrado
centigrade, centígrado
centiliter, centilitro
centimeter (cm), centímetro
cubic centimeter (cc or cm³), centímetro cúbico
central, central
central angle, ángulo central
central angle of a regular polygon, ángulo central de un polígono regular
central conic,

cónica central
central limit theorem, el teorema central del límite
central symmetry, simetría central
central tendency, tendencia central
centrifugal, centrífugo
centripetal, centrípeto
centroid, centroide de un triángulo
century, siglo
certain, cierto, seguro
certain case, caso cierto
certain event, evento cierto
certainty, certeza
chain, cadena
Chain Rule, regla de concatenación
challenge¹, desafiar, retar, recusar
challenge², desafío, reto, obstáculo, recusación
chance¹, posibilidad, probabilidad
chance², por casualidad
change¹, cambiar
change², cambio, alteración
percentage change, cambio percentil
rate of change, tasa de cambio
volume change, cambio de volumen
chaos, caos
chaotic, caótico
characteristic, característica
charge¹, cobrar
charge², carga

chart, tabla, cuadro
    bar chart,
    gráfica de barras
    flow chart,
    flujograma
    isometric chart,
    tabla isométrica
    pie chart, gráfica de
    pastel, gráfica circular
cheap, barato
cheat, hacer trampa,
    copiar, engañar
check, inspeccionar,
    averiguar, comprobar,
    verificar, checar
    check by factoring,
    comprobar por
    factoración
check mark, paloma,
    palomita, marca
chi square, ji cuadrada
chi-squared distribution,
    distribución de
    chi-cuadrada
chip, ficha
choice, elección, selección,
    opción
choose, escoger, elegir
chord, cuerda, acorde
    chord at contract,
    cuerda de contacto
    chord of curvature,
    cuerda de curvatura
    common chord,
    cuerda común
chronological, cronológico
circle[1], circular
circle[2], círculo
    circle circumscribed
    about a polygon,
    círculo circunscrito a
    un polígono
    circle graph,

gráfica circular
circle inscribed in
a polygon, círculo
inscrito en un polígono
circle inscribed in a
triangle, círculo inscrito en un triángulo
circumcircle,
circuncírculo
circumscribed circle,
círculo circunscrito
concentric circles,
círculos concéntricos
congruent circles,
círculos congruentes
Euler circles,
círculos de Euler
great circle,
círculo mayor
imaginary circle,
círculo imaginario
inscribed circle,
círculo inscrito
internally tangent
circles, círculos de
tangencia interna
isometric circle,
círculo isométrico
null circle,
círculo nulo
open circle,
círculo abierto
quarter-circle,
cuarto de círculo
semicircle,
semicírculo
unit circle,
círculo unitario
circuit, circuito
    closed circuit,
    circuito cerrado
    shortcircuit,
    cortocircuito

circular, circular
   circular arc,
   arco circular
   circular cone,
   cono circular
   circular curve,
   curva circular
   circular cylinder,
   cilindro circular
   circular function,
   función circular
   circular region,
   región circular
circulate, circular
circulation theorem,
   teorema de la circu-
   lación, teorema de
   Ampère-Stokes
circumcenter,
   circuncentro
circumcircle, circuncírculo
circumference,
   circunferencia
   circumference of a
   circle, circunferencia
   de un círculo
circumscribe, circunscribir
circumscribed,
   circunscrito
   circumscribed about,
   circunscrito a
   circumscribed circle,
   círculo circunscrito
   circumscribed cone,
   cono circunscrito
   circumscribed figure,
   figura circunscrita
   circumscribed
   polygon, polígono
   circunscrito
   circumscribed
   polyhedron,
   poliedro circunscrito

   circumscribed
   sphere, esfera
   circunscrita
   circumscribed
   triangle, triángulo
   circunscrito
circumsphere,
   esfera circunscrita
cisoid, cisoide
claim, reclamación
clarify, aclarar, clarificar
clarifying questions,
   preguntas aclaratorias
class, clase, tipo
   class interval,
   intervalo de clase
classification, clasificación
   classification of tri-
   angles, clasificación
   de triángulos
classified, clasificado
classify, clasificar
classifying angles by
   quadrant, clasificación de ángulos de
   acuerdo al cuadrante
clean[1], limpiar
clean[2], limpio
clear[1], despejar, quitar
clear[2], claro, transparente
climb, subir, ascender,
   escalar
clock system,
   sistema de reloj
clockwise, en sentido de
   las manecillas del reloj
   clockwise direction,
   en la dirección de las
   manecillas del reloj
   clockwise rotation,
   rotación similar al
   reloj
close[1], cerrar

close², casi, cerca, cercano
closed, cerrado
    closed arc,
    arco cerrado
    closed circuit,
    circuito cerrado
    closed curve,
    curva cerrada
    closed figure,
    figura cerrada
    closed interval,
    intervalo cerrado
    closed path,
    contorno cerrado
    closed sentence,
    frase cerrada
    closed surface,
    superficie cerrada
    closed system,
    sistema cerrado
closest, más cercano
closure, clausura
    Closure Axiom of Addition, axioma de clausura de adición, axioma de clausura de la suma
    Closure Axiom of Multiplication, axioma de clausura de multiplicación, axioma de clausura de la multiplicación
    closure property, propiedad de clausura
cluster¹, agruparse
cluster², grupo, agrupación
cm (centimeter), centímetro
code, código
codify, codificar
codomain, codominio
coefficient, coeficiente

binomial coefficient, coeficiente binomial
coefficient of a product, coeficiente de un producto
constant coefficient, coeficiente constante
correlation coefficient, coeficiente de correlación
indeterminate coefficient, coeficiente indeterminado
integral coefficient, coeficiente integral
integer coefficient, coeficiente entero
lead coefficient, coeficiente principal
leading coefficient, coeficiente conductor
literal coefficient, coeficiente literal
multinomial coefficient, coeficiente multinómico
numerical coefficient, coeficiente numérico
rational coefficient, coeficiente racional
regression coefficient, coeficiente de regresión
undetermined coefficient, coeficiente indeterminado
cofunction, cofunción, función asociada
    trigonometric cofunctions, cofunciones trigono-

métricas
coherent, coherente
    coherent whole,
    coherente total
coin¹, acuñar
coin², moneda
coincide, coincidir
coincident, coincidente
co-interior, mismo interior,
    co-interior
collaborate, colaborar
collaboration, colaboración
collect, recoger, recolectar,
    juntar, cobrar, colectar
collection, colección
    collection of data,
    colección de datos
collinear, colineal
    collinear planes,
    planos colineales
    collinear points,
    puntos colineales
collinearity, colinealidad
    collinearity pre-
    served, colinealidad
    preservada
cologarithm, cologaritmo
color, color
column, columna
    column matrix,
    matriz columna
    initial column,
    columna inicial
combination, combinación
    combination with
    repetition, combina-
    ción con repetición
    combination without
    repetition, combina-
    ción sin repetición
combine, combinar
    combine like radi-
    cals, combinar los

radicales semejantes
combine like terms,
    combinar los términos
    semejantes
combine the radicals,
    combinar los radicales
combined method,
    método combinado
combined variation,
    variación combinada
come out even,
    dividir exactamente,
    dividir sin resto,
    dividir residuo
commission, comisión
common,
    común, en común
    common base,
    base común
    common chord,
    cuerda común
    common denomina-
    tor, denominador
    común
    common difference,
    diferencia común
    common divisor,
    divisor común
    common external
    tangent, tangente
    común externa
    common factor,
    factor común
    common fraction,
    fracción común
    common internal
    tangent, tangente
    común interna
    common logarithm,
    logaritmo común
    common monomial
    factor, factor común
    del monomio

common multiple, múltiplo común

common perpendicular, perpendicular común

common root, raíz común

common side, lado común

common tangent, tangente común

common vertex, vértice común

commutation relation, relación de conmutación

commutative, conmutativo

commutative group, grupo conmutativo

commutative law, ley conmutativa

commutative property, propiedad conmutativa

commutative property of addition, propiedad conmutativa de la suma

commutative property of multiplication, propiedad conmutativa de la multiplicación

commutativity, conmutatividad

commute, conmutar

compact, compacto

compactness, compactación, compacto, densidad, solidez

compare, comparar

comparison, comparación

compass, brújula, compás

compatible numbers, números compatibles

compel, compeler, persuadir, obligar, forzar

compelling, convincente, persuasivo, contundente

compensation, compensación

compete, competir

competence, competencia

competent, competente

competition, competencia, concurso

competitive, competitivo

competitor, competidor

complement^1, complementar

complement^2, complemento

complementary, complementario

complementary angles, ángulos complementarios

complementary divisor, divisor complementario

complementary events, eventos complementarios

complementary function, función complementaria

complete^1, completar

complete the square, completar el cuadrado

complete^2, completo

complete carrying, transporte total

complete system, sistema completo

completely convex func-

tion, función completamente convexa
completely flat surface, superficie totalmente plana
complex, complejo, complicado
  complex closed curve, curva compleja cerrada
  complex conjugate, conjugado complejo
  complex curve, curva compleja
  complex fraction, fracción compuesta
  complex number, número complejo
  complex plane, plano complejo
  complex rational expression, expresión racional compleja
  complex root, raíz compleja
complicate, complicar
complicated, complicado
complication, complicación
component, componente
  imaginary component, componente imaginario
compose, componer
composed, compuesto
composite, compósito, compuesto
  composite number, número compuesto
composition, composición
  composition of func-

  tions, composición de las funciones
  composition of transformations, composición de las transformaciones
compound, compuesto
  compound events, eventos compuestos
  compound function, función compuesta
  compound interest, interés compuesto
  compound interest formula, fórmula de interés compuesto
  compound locus, locus compuesto
  compound number, número compuesto
  compound sentence, oración compuesta
  compound statement, enunciado compuesto
comprehend, comprender
comprehensible, comprensible
comprehension, comprensión
computacional, computacional
computation, cómputo
  performing computation, realización de cálculos
compute, calcular, computar
computer, computadora, ordenador
  analog computer, computadora análoga, ordenador análogo

computer science,
informática, computa-
ción, ciencias compu-
tacionales
concave, cóncavo
concave angle,
ángulo cóncavo
concave curve,
curva cóncava
concave polygon,
polígono cóncavo
concave polyhedron,
poliedro cóncavo
concavity, concavidad
concentric, concéntrico
concentric circles,
círculos concéntricos
concentric lines,
líneas concéntricas
concept, concepto
conceptualize,
conceptualizar
concerning, sobre, acerca
de, con respecto a
conclude, concluir
conclusion, conclusión
draw conclusions,
sacar conclusiones
logical conclusion,
conclusión lógica
conclusive, concluyente,
contundente
concrete, concreto
**concrete representa-
tions,** representacio-
nes concretas
concur, concurrir
concurrence, concurrencia
concurrent, simultáneo,
concurrente
**concurrent altitudes
of a triangle,**
alturas coexistentes

de un triángulo
**concurrent angle
of a triangle,**
ángulo coexistente
de un triángulo
concurrent lines,
líneas concurrentes
concurrent planes,
planos coexistentes
concyclic points,
puntos cocíclicos
condition, condición
initial condition,
condición inicial
**necessary and suf-
ficient condition,**
condición necesaria y
suficiente
**necessary but not
sufficient condition,**
condición necesaria
pero no suficiente
necessary condition,
condición necesaria
sufficient condition,
condición suficiente
conditional, condicional
conditional equality,
igualdad condicional
conditional equation,
ecuación condicional
**conditional inequal-
ity,** desigualdad con-
dicional
**conditional prob-
ability,** probabilidad
condicional
conditional sentence,
oración condicional
**conditional state-
ment,** enunciado
condicional
hidden conditional,

condicional oculta
conduct[1],
llevar a cabo, realizar,
conducir
conduct[2], conducta,
comportamiento
conductor, conductor
cone, cono
circular cone,
cono circular
circumscribed cone,
cono circunscrito
cone of revolution,
cono de revolución
right circular cone,
cono circular recto
right cone,
cono recto
confidence, confianza
confidence interval,
intervalo de confianza
confine, limitar, restringir
confirm, confirmar
confirmed, confirmado
conflict[1], contradecir
conflict[2], conflicto,
incompatibilidad
conflicting, contradictorio
confuse, confundir
confused, confundido
confusing, confuso
congruence, congruencia
congruence symbol,
símbolo de congruen-
cia
congruency, congruencia
congruent, congruente,
conforme
congruent angle,
ángulo congruente
congruent arc,
arco congruente
congruent circles,

círculos congruentes
congruent figures,
figuras congruentes
**congruent line
segments,**
segmento de línea
congruentes
congruent polygons,
polígonos congruentes
congruent sides,
lados congruentes
congruent triangles,
triángulos congruentes
conic, cónico
central conic,
cónica central
conic section,
sección cónica
**conic without a
center,** sección
sin centro
self-conjugate conic,
cono autoconjugado
conjecture[1], conjeturar
conjecture[2], conjetura
form a conjecture,
formular una
conjetura
**Goldbach's conjec-
ture,** conjetura de
Goldbach
**mathematical conjec-
ture,** conjetura mate-
mática
conjugacy, composición
conjugate, conjugado(a)
complex conjugate,
conjugado complejo
conjugate angles,
ángulos conjugados
**conjugate imaginary
lines,** líneas imagina-
rias conjugadas

conjugate of a complex number, conjugado de un número complejo
conjugate pairs, pares conjugados
conjugate root, raíz conjugada
conjugate tangents, tangentes conjugadas
conjunction, conjunción
connect, conectar
connection, conexión
consecutive, consecutivo
consecutive angles, ángulos consecutivos
consecutive even integers, enteros pares consecutivos
consecutive integers, enteros consecutivos
consecutive intervals, intervalos consecutivos
consecutive odd integers, enteros impares consecutivos
consecutive sides, lados consecutivos
consecutive tangents, tangentes consecutivas
consecutive vertices, vértices consecutivos
consequent, consiguiente
conservation, conservación
conserve, conservar
consider, considerar
consist, consistir
consistence, coherencia
consistence of equations, consistencia de ecuaciones

consistency, consistencia
consistency of axioms, consistencia de axiomas
consistent, consistente
consistent equations, ecuaciones consistentes
consistent with, conforme a
consolidate, consolidar
constant, constante
arbitrary constant, constante arbitraria
constant coefficient, coeficiente constante
constant factor, factor constante
constant function, función constante
constant of dilation, constante de dilatación
constant of proportionality, constante de proporcionalidad
constant term, término constante
literal constant, constante literal
numerical constant, constante numérica
physical constant, constante física
constitute, constituir
constrain, obligar, restringir
constraint, restricción, reserva
construct, construir
construction, construcción
geometric construction, construcción

geométrica
contact, contacto
contact point,
punto de contacto
contain, contener
container, contenedor
contest, concurso
context, contexto
continuation,
continuación
continued ratio,
razón continua
continuity, continuidad
continuous, continuo
piecewise continuous, continuidad por
piezas, continuidad en
piezas continuas
contracted notation,
notación contraída
contradict, contradecir
contradiction,
contradicción
contradictory,
contradictorio
contradictory prepositions,
propuestas
contradictorias
contrapositive,
contrapositivo
contrapositive statement, oración
contrapositiva
contrast[1], contrastar
contrast[2], contraste
contrasting, contrastante
contribute,
contribuir, aportar
contribution, contribución
controlled experiment,
experimento controlado

convenient, conveniente
convention, convención
conventional,
convencional
converge, convergir
converge to,
tender a
convergence,
convergencia
convergent, convergente
convergent series,
serie convergente
converging, convergente
converse, converso
converse of a statement, converso de
una frase
converse statement,
oración conversa
converse theorem,
teorema converso
conversion, conversión
conversion factor,
factor de conversión
convert, convertir
convert measures,
convertir las medidas
convex, convexo
convex angle,
ángulo convexo
convex body,
elemento convexo
convex polygon,
polígono convexo
convexity, convexidad
convince, convencer
convincing, convincente,
contundente
coordinate[1], coordinar
coordinate[2], coordenada
barycentric coordinates, coordenadas
baricéntricas

Cartesian coordinate plane, plano coordenado cartesiano

coordinate axes, ejes de coordenadas

coordinate curve, curva analítica, curva de coordenadas

coordinate geometry, geometría analítica, geometria de coordenada

coordinate grid, cuadrilla de coordenadas

coordinate pairs, pares coordenados

coordinate plane, plano coordenado

coordinate system, sistema de coordenadas

coordinate transformation, transformación de coordenadas

linear coordinates, coordenades lineales

rectangular coordinate system, sistema rectangular de coordenadas

three dimensional coordinate system, sistema coordenado tridimensional

x-coordinate, coordenada x

y-coordinate, coordenada y

coplanar, coplanar

coplanar lines, líneas coplanares

coplanar points, puntos coplanares

copy, copiar

corner, esquina, rincón

corner point, esquina, punto de esquina

corollary, corolario

correct[1], corregir

correct[2], correcto, exacto

correct to the nearest integer, exacto hasta el entero más cercano

correct to the nearest tenth, exacto hasta la décima más cercana

correlate, correlacionar

correlation, correlación

correlation coefficient, coeficiente de correlación

inverse correlation, correlación inversa

negative correlation, correlación negativa

positive correlation, correlación positiva

correspond, corresponder

corresponding unit, unidad correspondiente

correspondence, correspondencia

isometric correspondence, correspondencia isométrica

one-to-many correspondence, correspondencia de uno a muchos

one-to-one correspondence,

correspondencia de uno a uno, correspondencia biunívoca

many-to-one correspondence, correspondencia de muchos a uno

corresponding, correspondiente

corresponding angle, ángulo correspondiente

corresponding parts, partes correspondientes

corresponding side, lado correspondiente

corresponding value for, el valor correspondiente de

cosecant, cosecante

cosecant function, función cosecante

cosecant ratio, razón cosecante

cosine, coseno

cosine function, función coseno

cosine law, ley del coseno

cosine ratio, razón del coseno

inverse cosine function, función inversa del coseno

cost[1], costar

cost[2], costo

cotangent, cotangente

cotangent function, función cotangente

cotangent ratio, razón cotangente

coterminal angles, ángulos coterminales

count[1], contar

count back, contar en forma regresiva

count backwards, contar en forma regresiva

count by, contar por

skip count, contar por múltiplos de un número

count[2], conteo, cómputo, cuenta

countable, contable

counter[1], rebatir

counter[2], contador

counterclockwise, en sentido contra las manecillas del reloj

counterclockwise direction, en dirrección contraria al reloj

counterclockwise rotation, rotación contraria a las agujas del reloj

counterexample, ejemplo contrario

counterfactual, contra los hechos

counterintuitive, contra la intuición, contraintuitivo

counting, conteo

counting number, número de cuenta

counting principle, principio de cuenta

counting system, sistema de conteo

counting techniques, técnicas de conteo

couple, un par de, pareja

course, clase, asignatura, materia, rumbo

covariance, covarianza

cover, cubrir

Cramer's Rule, regla de Cramer

create, crear

credible, verosímil

credit, crédito

criteria (sing. criterion), criterios

critical, crítico

   critical point, punto crítico

   critical region, región crítica, zona crítica

   critical thinking, pensamiento crítico

criticism, crítica

criticize, criticar

critique[1], criticar

critique[2], crítica

crooked, torcido

cross, cruzar

   cross out, tachar

cross product, producto transversal

   cross product of two vectors, producto transversal de dos vectores

crossing, cruce

   crossing point, intersección

cross-multiplication, multiplicación cruzada, producto cruzado de términos, producto de la primera fracción por la inversa de la segunda

cross-multiply, usar la multiplicación cruzada, multiplicar la primera fracción por la inversa de la segunda

cross-section, sección recta, muestra representativa

crucial, crucial, decisivo

cube[1], elevar al cubo

   cube both sides, elevar ambos lados al cubo

cube[2], cubo, cúbico(a)

   cube root, raíz cúbica

cubed, elevado al cubo

cubic (cu.), cúbico

   cubic centimeter (cc or cm³), centímetro cúbico

   cubic equation, ecuación cúbica

   cubic foot, pie cúbico

   cubic inch, pulgada cúbica

   cubic meter, metro cúbico

   cubic number, número cúbico

   cubic unit, unidad cúbica

cuboid, cuboide

cumulative, acumulado

   cumulative frequency distribution table, tabla de distribución de frecuencias acumuladas

cumulative frequency histogram, histograma de frecuencia acumulativa

cumulative relative frequency, frecuencia relativa acumulativa

cup, taza

curl, rotacional

currency symbol, símbolo monetario

current[1], corriente

electric current, corriente eléctrica

current[2], actual

curvature, curvatura

curve[1], encorvar

curve[2], curva

algebraic curve, curva algebraica

base cosine curve, curva básica del coseno

bell curve, curva en forma de campana, campana de Gauss, curva de distribución normal

binomial curve, curva binómica

circular curve, curva circular

closed curve, curva cerrada

complex closed curve, curva compleja cerrada

complex curve, curva compleja

concave curve, curva cóncava

coordinate curve, curva analítica, curva coordenada

curve of pursuit, curva de seguimiento

curved line, línea curva

degenerative curve, curva degenerativa

frequency curve, curva de la frecuencia

inverse curve, curva inversa

normal curve, curva normal

open curve, curva abierta

oriented curve, curva orientada

parametric curve, curva paramétrica

periodic curve, curva periódica

quadratic curve, curva cuadrática

reciprocal logarithmic curve, curva logarítmica recíproca

ruled curve, curva reglada

secant curve, curva secante

sharp curve, curva cerrada

simple closed curve, curva simple cerrada, curva cerrada simple

smooth curve, curva continua

space curve, curva espacial

step curve, curva escalonada

symmetrical curve, curva simétrica

tangent curve,
curva tangente
**transcendental
curve,** curva
trascendental
unsmoothed curve,
curva áspera
curved, curva
curved line,
línea curva
curvilinear, curvilíneo
cusp, vértice
customary,
usual, acostumbrado
**customary measure-
ment system,** sistema
anglosajón de medidas
**customary units of
capacity,** unidades
de capacidad
anglosajonas
**customary units of
mass,** unidades de
masa anglosajonas
cut, cortar
cycle^1, ciclar
cycle^2, ciclo
cyclic, cíclico
cyclic order,
orden cíclico
**cyclic vertices of a
quadrilateral,**
vértices cíclicos de un
cuadrilátero
cyclical, cíclico
cylinder, cilindro
circular cylinder,
cilindro circular
**cylinder of revolu-
tion,** cilindro de revo-
lución
cylinder surface,
superficie cilíndrica

**right circular cylin-
der,** cilindro circular
recto
right cylinder,
cilindro recto
cylindrical, cilíndrico
cylindrical surface,
superficie cilíndrica

D

daily, diario
dashed line,
línea entrecortada
data (sing. datum), datos
bivariate data,
datos bivariados
data frequency table,
tabla de frecuencia de
datos
data table,
tabla de información
grouped data,
datos agrupados
initial data,
información inicial
raw data,
datos base, datos
de fundamento,
datos crudos,
datos originales
sample data,
muestra de datos
univariate data,
datos univariados
database, base de datos
datum, dato
date^1, fechar
date^2, fecha
day, día

daylight, luz diurna
De Morgan's law,
  ley de De Morgan
debit, débito
decade, década
decagon, decágono
decahedron, decaedro
decay exponentially, decaer exponencialmente
decelerate, desacelerar
deceleration, deceleración
decidable, decidible, que
  no puede ser decidido
decide, decidir
deciliter, decilitro
decimal, decimal
  decimal fraction,
  fracción decimal,
  quebrado decimal
  decimal notation,
  notación decimal
  decimal number,
  número decimal
  **decimal number
  system,** sistema
  númerico decimal
  decimal part,
  parte decimal
  decimal place,
  lugar decimal
  decimal point,
  punto decimal
  equivalent decimals,
  decimales equivalentes
  finite decimal,
  decimal finito
  infinite decimal,
  decimal infinito
  mixed decimal,
  decimal mixto
  **non-repeating
  decimal,** decimal
  no periódico

  **non-terminating
  decimal,**
  decimal infinito
  periodic decimals,
  decimales periódicos
  recurring decimal,
  decimal recurrente
  repeating decimal,
  decimal periódico
  terminating decimal,
  decimal finito, decimal
  terminal
  unlimited decimal,
  decimal ilimitado
decimeter, decímetro
decision, decisión
deck of cards,
  juego de cartas
declination, declive
decline, declinar
decode, descodificar,
  decodificar, descifrar
decoding, decodificación
decompose, descomponer
decomposition,
  descomposición
decrease, disminuir
decreasing, decreciente
  decreasing function,
  función decreciente
  decreasing sequence,
  secuencia decreciente
deduce, deducir
deduced statement,
  afirmación deducida
deduct, restar, deducir,
  retener
deductible, deducible
deduction, deducción,
  retención
deductive, deductivo
  deductive method,
  método deductivo

deductive proof,
prueba deductiva
deductive reasoning, razonamiento
deductivo
defend, defender
define, definir
defined terms,
términos definidos
definite, definitivo
definite integral,
integral definida
definition, definición
deform, deformar
degenerative curve,
curva degenerativa
degree, grado
degree measure,
medida en grados
degree of a monomial, grado de un monomio
degree of a polynomial, grado de un
polinomio
degree of an algebraic term, grado de
un término algebraico,
potencia de un término algebraico
degree of an angle,
grado de un ángulo
degree of an equation, grado
de una ecuación
degree of an algebraic expression,
grado de una expresión algebraica, potencia de una expresión
algebraica
degrees of freedom,
grados de libertades

first degree,
de grado uno
first-degree equation,
ecuación de primer
grado
fourth degree,
cuarto grado
nearest degree,
grado más cercano
second degree,
de grado dos
**second-degree
equation,** ecuación
de segundo grado
third degree,
de grado tres
zero degree,
grado cero
delete, anular
deltahedron, deltaedro
deltoid, deltoide
demand, demanda
supply and demand,
oferta y demanda
demonstrate, demostrar
denominator,
denominador
common denominator, denominador
común
**least common
denominator (LCD),**
mínimo común denominador, menor
denominador común
**lowest common
denominator (LCD),**
mínimo común divisor, mínimo común
denominador, menor
denominador común
like denominators,
denominadores seme-

jantes, denominadores comunes
denote, denotar
denoted by, denotado por
dense, denso
   dense domain, dominio denso
density, densidad
denumerable, contable
depend on, depender de
dependable, fiable, seguro
dependent, dependiente
   dependent equations, ecuaciones dependientes
   dependent events, eventos dependientes
   dependent linear equations, ecuaciones lineales dependientes
   dependent variable, variable dependiente
deplete, agotar
depletion, agotamiento
depreciate, depreciar
depreciation, depreciación, amortización
depress, deprimir
depression, depresión
depth, profundidad
derangement, degradación
derivation, derivación
derivative, derivada
   antiderivative, antiderivada
   higher-order derivative, derivada de orden superior
   second derivative, segunda derivada
   partial derivative, derivada parcial
derive, derivar

derived equation, ecuación derivada
descend, descender
descending, descendente
   descending order, orden descendente
design¹, diseñar
design², diseño
   experimental design, diseño experimental
designate, designar
designated value, valor designado
designation, designación
detachment law, ley del desprendimiento
detail¹, detallar
detail², detalle
determinant, determinante
determine, determinar
develop, desarrollar, elaborar
development, desarrollo
deviate, desviar
deviation, desviación
   absolute deviation, desviación absoluta
   mean absolute deviation, desviación absoluta media
   standard deviation, desviación estándar, desviación típica, desviación normal
diagonal, diagonal
   diagonal matrix, matriz diagonal
   leading diagonal, diagonal principal
   main diagonal, diagonal principal
   principal diagonal, diagonal principal

diagonalization of a matrix, diagonalización de una matriz
diagram, diagrama
  accompanying diagram, diagrama acompañante
  box and whisker diagram, gráfico de caja y bigotes
  flow diagram, diagrama de flujo
  frequency diagram, diagrama de frecuencia
  tree diagram, diagrama de árbol, diagrama ramificado
  Venn diagram, diagrama de Venn
diameter, diámetro
  diameter of a circle, diámetro de un círculo
  diameter of a sphere, diámetro de una esfera
diamond, diamante
dice (sing. die), dados
dichotomy, dicotomía
dictionary, diccionario
die (pl. dice), dado
difference, diferencia, resta
  common difference, diferencia común
  difference formula for trigonometric functions, fórmula de diferencia para funciones trigonométricas
  difference of two cubes, diferencia entre dos cubos
  difference of two perfect squares, diferencia de dos cuadrados perfectos
  difference of two squares, diferencia de dos cuadrados
  difference set, conjunto de diferencia
different, diferente
differentiable, diferenciable
differential, diferencial
  differential calculus, cálculo diferencial
  differential equation, ecuación diferencial
  differential geometry, geometría diferencial
differentiate, diferenciar, distinguir
differentiation, diferenciación
  antidifferentiation, antidiferenciación
  implicit differentiation, diferenciación implícita
difficult, difícil
digit, cifra, dígito
  binary digit, dígito binario
  significant digit, dígito significativo
digital, digital
  digital clock, reloj digital
  digital root, raíz digital
  digital sum, suma digital
dihedral angle, ángulo diedro
dilate, dilatar

dimension, dimensión
  dimensions of a rectangle, dimensiones de un rectángulo
dimensional, dimensional
  multidimensional, multidimensional
  one-dimensional, unidimensional, de una dimensión
  three-dimensional, tridimensional, de tres dimensiones
  two-dimensional, de dos dimensiones
dimensionality, dimensionalidad
Diophantine, diofántico
  diophantine equation, ecuación diofantina, ecuación diofántica
Dirac function, distribución de Dirac
direct¹, dirigirse
direct², directo, dirigir
  direct isometry, isometría directa
  direct measure, medida dirigida
  direct measurement, medida directa
  direct proof, prueba directa
  direct proportion, proporción directa
  direct variation, variación directa
directed, dirigido
  directed angle, ángulo dirigido
  directed number, número dirigido

direction, dirección, sentido
directory of a parabola, directriz de una parábola
directrix, directriz
disagree, no estar de acuerdo, no coincidir, discrepar, contrariar
disc, disco
discard, descartar
disconnect, desconectar
disconnected, desconectado
disconnection, desconexión
discontinuous, discontinuo, interrumpido
discount¹, descartar, descontar, hacer u ofrecer un descuento
discount², descuento, rebaja
discover, descubrir
discovered, descubierto
discovery, descubrimiento
discrete, discreto
discriminant, discriminante
discriminate, discriminar
discuss, platicar
discussion, plática
disjoint¹, sin unión, disyuntivo , desligado
  disjoint elements, elementos disyuntivos
  disjoint events, eventos desligados
  disjoint sets, conjuntos disyuntivos
  mutually disjoint, recíprocamente desligados

disjoint², desunir
disjunction, disyunción
disjunctive, disyuntivo
disk, disco
disoriented, desorientado
disperse, dispersar
dispersion, dispersión
displace, desplazar
displacement,
    desplazamiento
    phase displacement,
    desplazamiento de
    fase
    simultaneous
    displacement,
    desplazamiento
    simultáneo
    successive
    displacements,
    deplazamientos
    sucesivos
display¹, mostrar
display², pantalla
disproportionate,
    desproporcionado
disprove, refutar
dissimilar, distinto
distance, distancia
    distance between a
    point and a line,
    distancia entre un
    punto y una recta
    distance between
    two parallel lines,
    distancia entre dos
    rectas paralelas
    distance between
    two points, distancia
    entre dos puntos
    distance formula,
    fórmula de distancia
    distance from a fixed
    point, distancia desde

un punto fijo
    distance postulate,
    postulado de la
    distancia
    distance preserved,
    distancia preservada
    Euclidean distance,
    distancia euclidiana
    horizontal distance,
    distancia horizontal
    sum formula for trig-
    onometric functions,
    fórmula de suma para
    funciones trigonomé-
    tricas
distant, distante
distinct, distinto
    distinct arrange-
    ments, ordenamientos
    distintos
    distinct points,
    puntos distintos
    distinct root,
    raíz distinta
distinction, distinción
distinguish, distinguir
distinguishable,
    distinguible
    distinguishable
    arrangements,
    ordenamientos
    diferenciales
distort, distorsionar
distortion, distorsión
distribute, distribuir
distribution, distribución
    chi-squared distribu-
    tion, distribución de
    chi-cuadrada
    frequency distribu-
    tion, distribución
    de frecuencias
    normal distribution,

distribución normal
Poisson distribution, distribución de Poisson
standard normal distribution, distribución normal estándar
t-distribution, distribución de t
distributive, distributivo
distributive law, ley distributiva
distributive property, propiedad distributiva
distributive property of multiplication over addition, propiedad distributiva de la multiplicación respecto a la suma
distributivity, distributividad
divergence, divergencia
divergence theorem, teorema de la divergencia
divergent, divergente
divergent series, serie divergente
divide, dividir
divide in half, dividir por la mitad
divide into n evenly, dividir en n partes iguales
dividend, dividendo
divisibility, divisibilidad
divisibility test, prueba de divisibilidad
divisible, divisible
divisible by, divisible por
division, división

division algorithm, algoritimo de la división
division of a line segment, división de un segmento de recta
division sign, signo de división
divisor, divisor
common divisor, divisor común
complementary divisor, divisor complementario
greatest common divisor (GCD), máximo común denominador
highest common divisor, máximo común divisor
lowest common denominator (LCD), mínimo común divisor, mínimo común denominador, menor denominador común
null divisor, divisor nulo
trial divisor, divisor de prueba
zero divisor, divisor cero
do, hacer
dodecagon, dodecágono
dodecahedron, dodecaedro
dollar, dólar
domain, dominio
dense domain, dominio denso
domain of a function, dominio de una función

real domain,
dominio real
restricted domain,
dominio restringido
domino, dominó
dot, punto
dot product,
producto de punto
dotted line, línea de puntos, línea punteada
double[1], duplicar,
multiplicar por dos
double[2], doble
double angle formula for a trigonometric function,
fórmula de doble ángulo para una función trigonométrica
double bar graph,
gráfico de barras dobles
double integral,
integral doble
double line graph,
gráficos de líneas dobles
double roots,
raíces dobles
doubling,
duplicar, doblar,
multiplicar por dos
doubtful, dudoso
down, abajo
down payment,
pago inicial
downhill, cuesta abajo
doz. (dozen), docena
dozen (doz.), docena
draft, borrador
rough draft,
borrador
draw[1], dibujar

draw a picture,
hacer un dibujo,
dibujar una imagen
draw the figure,
dibujar la figura
draw the graph of,
dibujar el gráfico de
draw[2], escoger al azar
draw at random,
elegir al azar
draw conclusions,
sacar conclusiones
drawing, dibujo
drop a class, retirarse
de una materia
drop[1], dejar caer,
soltar, bajar
drop[2], bajada, gota
duplicate[1], duplicar
duplicate[2], duplicado
dyadic product,
producto diádico
dynamic, dinámico
dynamic geometry software, programa
informático de geometría dinámica

each, cada
each and every,
todos y cada uno
earn, ganar
earnings, ganancias,
ingresos
net earnings,
ingresos limpios,
ingresos netos
ease, facilidad

east, este, oriente
easy, fácil
eccentric, excéntrico
eccentricity, excentricidad
edge, borde, lado, extremo
    lateral edge,
    extremo lateral,
    borde lateral
    straight edge,
    reglón, herramienta
    para dibujar líneas
    rectas, regla recta
    straightedge,
    reglón, herramienta
    para dibujar líneas
    rectas, regla recta
education, educación
    bilingual education,
    educación bilingüe
    special education,
    educación especial
effect, efecto
eigenvalue, valor propio
eigenvector, vector propio
eight, ocho
eighth, octavo
electric, eléctrico
    electric current,
    corriente eléctrica
    electric field,
    campo eléctrico
electricity, electricidad,
    luz eléctrica
electromagnetic,
    electromagnético
    **electromagnetic
    field,** campo
    electromagnético
elegible, elegible
element, elemento
    disjoint elements,
    elementos disyuntivos
    element in a set, ele-

mento de un conjunto
    finite element,
    elemento finito
    identity element,
    elemento de identidad
    inverse element,
    elemento inverso
    leading element,
    elemento guía
    neutral element,
    elemento neutro
    null element,
    elemento nulo
    scalar line element,
    elemento escalar
    de línea
    **self-corresponding
    element,** elemento
    autocorrespondiente
    unit element,
    elemento de unidad
    vector line element,
    elemento vectorial
    de línea
    vector path element,
    elemento vectorial
    de arco
    **vector surface
    element,** elemento
    vectorial de superficie
    volume element,
    elemento de volumen
elementary, elemental
    elementary school,
    escuela primaria
elevate, elevar
elevation, elevación
elicit, obtener, propiciar
eligible, elegible
    be elegible,
    reunir los requisitos
eliminate, eliminar
elimination, eliminación

elimination of irrelevant factors, eliminación de factores irrelevantes

elimination of substitution, eliminación por sustitución

elimination of unknowns, eliminación de variables desconocidos

method of elimination, método de eliminación

process of elimination, proceso de eliminación

successive elimination, eliminación sucesiva

ellipse, elipse

ellipsoid, elipsoide

elliptic, elíptico

elliptical, elíptico

elongate, alargar

elsewhere, en otros lugares

emphasis, énfasis

emphasize, enfatizar

empirical, empírico

empirical probability, probabilidad empírica

empirical study, estudio empírico

empty, vacío

empty set, conjunto vacío, conjunto nulo

encircle, circular

enclose, encerrar

encode, codificar

encounter, encuentro

end, final, fin

at the end of, al fin

endless, interminable, sin fin

endpoint, punto extremo, punto final, extremo

energy, energía

engineering, ingeniería

enlarge, agrandar

enlargement, agrandamiento

entail, implicar, suponer, acarrear

enter (a table or graph), entrar (una tabla o gráfica)

entire, entero, intacto

entity, entidad

enumerate, enumerar

enumeration, enumeración

induction by simple enumeration, inducción por enumeración simple

epicycle, epiciclo

epicycloid, epicicloide

equal¹, ser igual a

not equal to, no igual a, no equivalente a, distinto de

equal², igual

equal chance, igual suerte

equal sign, signo de igual, signo de igualdad

equality, igualdad

conditional equality, igualdad condicional

equality postulates, postulados de la igualdad

equality test of

fractions, prueba de
igualdad de fracciones
equalize, emparejar
equally likely,
posiblemente igual
equally spaced points,
puntos igualmente
espaciados
equation, ecuación
  **absolute value
equation,** ecuación
de valor absoluto
  algebraic equation,
ecuación algebraica
  conditional equation,
ecuación condicional
  consistent equations,
ecuaciones consis-
tentes
  cubic equation,
ecuación cúbica
  **diophantine equa-
tion,** ecuación dio-
fantina, ecuación
diofántica
  **equation contain-
ing parentheses,**
ecuación que contiene
paréntesis
  equation of a line,
ecuación de la recta
  first-degree equation,
ecuación de primer
grado
  **first-degree equation
with one variable,**
ecuación de primer
grado con una variable
  **inconsistent equa-
tions,** ecuaciones
inconsistentes
  indefinite equation,
ecuación indefinida

  **indeterminate equa-
tion,** ecuación indeter-
minada
  inverse equation,
ecuación inversa
  linear equation,
ecuación lineal
  **linear equation
in one variable,**
ecuación lineal
de una variable
  literal equation,
ecuación literal
  quadratic equation,
ecuación cuadrática
  polynomial equation,
ecuación polinomial
  system of equations,
sistema de ecuaciones
  tangential equation,
ecuación tangencial
equiangular, equiangular
  equiangular polygon,
polígono equiangular
  equiangular triangle,
triángulo equiangular
equidistance,
igual distancia
equidistant,
equidistante
  equidistant lines,
líneas equidistantes
  equidistant marks,
puntos equidistantes
equilateral, equilátero
  equilateral polygon,
polígono equilátero
  equilateral triangle,
triángulo equilátero
equipotential,
equipotencial
equivalence,
equivalencia

equivalence relation, relación de equivalencia

equivalent, equivalente

algebraically equivalent, algebraicamente equivalente

equivalent customary units of capacity, unidades equivalentes de capacidad anglosajonas

equivalent decimals, decimales equivalentes

equivalent equations, ecuaciones equivalentes

equivalent expression, expresión equivalente

equivalent forms, formas equivalentes

equivalent fractions, fracciones equivalentes

equivalent inequality, desigualdad equivalente

equivalent numerical expressions, expresiones numéricas equivalentes

equivalent radicals, radicales equivalentes

equivalent ratios, razones equivalentes

equivalent sentence, oración equivalente

equivalent sets, conjuntos equivalentes

logical equivalent, equivalente lógico

erase, borrar

eraser, borrador

Eratosthenes' sieve, criba de Eratóstenes

err, errar

erratic, errático

erroneous, erróneo

error, error

average error, error promedio

percentage error, error de porcentaje

relative error, error relativo

rounding error, error de redondeamiento

sampling error, error de muestreo

statistical estimate of error, estimado estadístico del error

trial and error, ensayo y error

truncation error, error de truncamiento

type I error, error tipo I

type II error, error tipo II

essential, esencial

establish, establecer

estimate[1], estimar, calcular aproximadamente

estimate[2], estimado

reasonable estimate, estimación razonable

rough estimate, estimado aproximado, estimado preliminar, cálculo aproximado

statistical estimate of error, estimado estadístico del error

estimated, estimado
estimation, estimación
    estimation strategies, estrategias para calcular aproximadamente
    front-end estimation, cálculo aproximado a partir de los primeros dígitos
    linear estimation, estimación lineal
etc. (et cetera), etcétera
Euclid, Euclides
    Euclid's algorithm, algoritmo de Euclides
    Euclid's Fifth Postulate, quinto postulado de Euclides
Euclidean, euclidiano(a)
    Euclidean distance, distancia euclidiana
    Euclidean geometry, geometría euclidiana
    Euclidean Parallel Postulate, paralelo postulado de Euclides
    Euclidean space, espacio euclidiano
Euler circles, círculos de Euler
Euler's formula, fórmula de Euler
evaluate, evaluar
    evaluate an algebraic expression, evaluar una expresión algebraica
    evaluate efficiency, evaluar la eficiencia
evaluation, evaluación
even, par, parejo
    even integer, entero par
    even number, número par
    even whole number, número entero par
evening, noche
evenly, uniformemente, equitativamente
    evenly distributed, uniformemente distribuido
event, evento
    compound event, evento compuesto
    complementary events, eventos complementarios
    compound events, eventos compuestos
    dependent events, eventos dependientes
    disjoint events, eventos desligados
    event that is certain, un evento seguro
    favorable event, evento favorable
    impossible event, evento imposible
    independent event, evento independiente
    mutually exclusive events, eventos que se excluyen mutuamente
    possible event, evento posible
    random event, evento al azar
    simple event, evento simple
    single event, evento singular, ocurrencia única

single-event experiment, experimento de evento singular, experimento único

every, cada, todo

every other, uno sí, otro no

everyday, cotidiano

everywhere, en todas partes

evident, evidente

exact, exacto

exact answer, respuesta exacta

exact solution, solución exacta

exact value, valor exacto

exactly, exactamente

exam, examen

final exam, examen final

mid-term exam, examen parcial

examine, examinar

example, ejemplo

counterexample, ejemplo contrario

for example, por ejemplo

exceed, exceder

excellent, excelente

excenters, excentros

except, excepto

exception, excepción

excess, exceso

exchange, canjear, intercambiar

exchange rate, tipo de cambio, tasa de cambio

exchange rate table, tabla de tasas de cambio

exclude, excluir

exclusive, exclusivo

exercise, ejercicio

exhaust, agotar

exhaustion, agotamiento

existential qualifier, cuantificador existencial

expand, expandir, desarrollar, extender

expand a binomial, expandir un binomio

expanded form, notación desarrollada, notación explícita

expanded notation, notación ampliada

expanded numeral expectation, expectativa númerica ampliada

expansion, expansión

binomial expansion, expansión binómica

expansion of a binomial, expansión de un binomio

expect, esperar

expectation, expectativa

expenses, gastos

expensive, caro

experiment¹, experimentar

experiment², experimento

Bernoulli experiment, experimento de Bernoulli

controlled experiment, experimento controlado

single-event experi-

ment, experimento de evento singular, experimento único
experimental, experimental
experimental design, diseño experimental
experimental probability, probabilidad experimental
experimental results, resultados experimentales
explain, explicar
explanation, explicación
explicable, explicable
explicit, explícito
explicit definition, definición explícita
explicit function, función explícita
exploration, exploración
explore, explorar
exponent, exponente
fractional exponent, exponente fraccional
integral exponent, exponente integral
negative exponent, potencia de exponente negativo
positive exponent, potencia de exponente positivo
real exponent, exponente real
zero exponent, exponente cero
exponential, exponencial
exponential decay, decrecimiento exponencial

exponential equation, ecuación exponencial
exponential expression, expresión exponencial
exponential form, forma exponencial
exponential function, función exponencial
exponential growth, crecimiento exponencial
exponential increase, crecimiento exponencial
exponentiation, exponenciación
express, expresar
express in simplest radical form, expresar en forma radical simple
express in terms of, expresar en términos de
expression, expresión
algebraic expression, expresión algebraica
arithmetic expression, expresión aritmética, expresión númerica
binomial expression, expresión binómica
complex rational expression, expresión racional compleja
equivalent expression, expresión equivalente
fractional expression, expresión fraccional

general expression, expresión general

literal expression, expresión literal

numerical expression, expresión numérica

open expression, expresión abierta

perfect cubic expression, expresión cúbica perfecta

polynomial expression, expresión polinomial

rational expression, expresión racional

verbal expression, expresión verbal

extend, extender, expandir

extend indefinitely, extender indefinidamente

extend the number line, extender la línea númerica

extended fact, hecho extendido

extension, extensión

finite extension, extensión finita

infinite extension, extensión infinita

exterior, exterior

exterior angle, ángulo exterior

exterior angle of a triangle, ángulo exterior de un triángulo

exterior region, región exterior

exterior region of a circle, región exterior de un círculo

external, externo(a)

external bisector, bisector externo

external point, punto externo

external segment of a secant, segmento externo de una secante

external tangent, tangente externa

externally tangent circles, círculos externamente tangentes

extra, extra, adicional

extract a root, extraer una raíz

extraneous, irrelevante, superfluo, externo

extraneous root, raíz extrínseca

extrapolate, extrapolar

extrapolation, extrapolación

extrapolation method, método de extrapolación

extreme, extremo

extreme value, valor extremo

extremes of a proportion, extremos de una proporción

extremum, extremo

eye level, altura de los ojos, nivel de la vista

F (Fahrenheit),
grado Fahrenheit
face, cara
face of a polyhedron,
cara de un poliedro
facing, frontero
fact¹, hecho
addition fact,
hecho aditivo
arithmetic fact,
hecho aritmético
extended fact,
hecho extendido
geometric fact,
hecho geométrico
related facts,
operaciones con
números elementales
relacionadas, hechos
relacionados
fact², operación con números elementales
fact family,
operaciones con nú-
meros elementales
relacionados
factor¹, calcular los factores, factorizar
factor a number,
calcular los factores
factor a polynomial,
factorizar un polino-
mio
factor a trinomial,
factorizar un trinomio
factor completely,
factorizar completa-
mente

factor², factor
common factor,
factor común
**common monomial
factor,** factor común
del monomio
constant factor,
factor constante
conversion factor,
factor de conversión
factor tree, ramificaciones de los factores
**greatest common
factor (GCF),**
factor común mayor,
máximo común divisor
**greatest monomial
factor,** factor común
mayor del monomio
growth factor,
factor de crecimiento
**highest common
factor,** factor común
máximo
integral factor,
factor integral
least common factor,
factor común mínimo
prime factor,
factor primo
rationalizing factor,
factor racionalizante
factorable, factorizable
factorial, factorial
factoring, la descomposición en factores,
el factoreo
factorization, factorización
**factorization meth-
od,** método de factori-
zación
prime factorization,
factorización prima

factual, factual, fáctico, basado en hechos

Fahrenheit (F), grado Fahrenheit

fail, incumplir, fallar, faltar de hacer algo, reprobar, desaprobar

failure, incumplimiento, fracaso, fallo

fair, justo
>   **fair and unbiased object,** objeto justo e imparcial
>   **fair share,** porción debida

fall[1], caerse

fall[2], caída, otoño

fallacy, falacia

false, falso(a)
>   **false negative,** falsa negación, falso negativo
>   **false positive,** falsa afirmación, falso positivo
>   **false sentence,** proposición falsa

family, familia
>   **fact family,** operaciones con números elementales relacionados

far, lejano, lejos

farther, más lejos, más lejano

farthest, el más lejos, el más lejano

fast, rápido

faster, más rápido
>   **faster than,** más rápido que

fastest, el mas rápido

favorable event, evento favorable

favorable outcome, resultado favorable

feasible, factible

feature, atributo, característica, propiedad, rasgo

feet (sing. foot), pies

fence, cerca

Fermat's Last Theorem, último teorema de Fermat, última conjetura de Fermat

few, pocos

fewer, menos, menor
>   **fewer than,** menos de, menos que, menor que

fewest, menor número de

Fibonacci sequence, secuencia de Fibonacci

field, área, campo, cancha
>   **electric field,** campo eléctrico
>   **electromagnetic field,** campo electromagnético
>   **field line,** línea de campo
>   **field quantity,** magnitud de campo
>   **field theorem,** teorema del campo
>   **finite field,** campo finito
>   **irrotational field,** campo irrotacional
>   **magnetic field,** campo magnético
>   **ordered field,** campo ordenado
>   **scalar field,** campo escalar
>   **solenoidal field,**

campo solenoidal,
campo de flujo conser-
vativo
tensor field,
campo tensorial
vector field,
campo vectorial
zero-divergence field,
campo solenoidal,
campo de flujo conser-
vativo
fifth, quinto
figure, cifra, número,
figura
   circumscribed figure,
   figura circunscrita
   closed figure,
   figura cerrada
   congruent figures,
   figuras congruentes
   geometric figure,
   figura geométrica
   inscribed figure,
   figura inscrita
   open figure,
   figura abierta
   similar figures,
   figuras similares
   significant figure,
   figura significativa
   solid figure,
   figura sólida
   symmetrical figure,
   figura simétrica
figure out, averiguar
file[1], archivar, limar, lijar
file[2], archivo, expediente,
lima, lija
fill, llenar
filter[1], filtrar
filter[2], filtro
final, final
   final exam,

examen final
find, encontrar, hallar
   **find the circumfer-
   ence of,** encontrar la
   circunferencia de un
   círculo
   find the solution set,
   encontrar la solución
   del conjunto
   find the value of,
   encontrar el valor de
fine, fino
finish, terminar
finite, finito
   finite decimal,
   decimal finito
   finite element,
   elemento finito
   finite extension,
   extensión finita
   finite field,
   campo finito
   finite group,
   grupo finito
   finite part,
   parte finita
   finite sample space,
   espacio muestral finito
   finite set,
   conjunto finito
   finite solution,
   solución finita
finiteness, finitud
fire, incendio
   fire drill,
   simulacro
   de incendio
first, primer(a), primero
first aid, primeros auxilios
first degree, de grado uno
   first-degree equation,
   ecuación de primer
   grado

first-degree equation with one variable, ecuación de primer grado con una variable

first-degree inequality, desigualdad de primer grado

first-degree open sentence with one variable, oración abierta de primer grado con una variable

first-quadrant angle, ángulo del primer cuadrante

first Green formula, primera fórmula de Green

first quartile, primer cuartil

fit, encajar

five, cinco

five-number statistical summary, resumen estadístico de cinco datos

fix, arreglar, fijar

fixed, fijo(a)
fixed distance, distancia fija
fixed line, línea fija
fixed point, punto fijo
fixed value, valor fijo

flat, plano
flat angle, ángulo plano

flaw, defecto, imperfección, desperfecto

flawed, defectuoso

flexible, flexible

flip, voltear
flip coins, tirar monedas

flow[1], fluir

flow[2], flujo
flow chart, flujograma
flow diagram, diagrama de flujo

fluctuate, fluctuar

fluctuating, fluctuante

flux, flujo

focal point, punto focal

focus[1], enfocar

focus[2], enfoque, foco
focus of a parabola, foco de una parábola
focus point, punto focal

follow, seguir, adherirse, derivar de

following, siguiente, a continuación

foot (ft.), pie
cubic foot, pie cúbico
square foot, pie cuadrado

force, fuerza

foreign exchange rate, tipo de cambio de divisas

foresee, prever

forever, siempre

form[1], formar, formular
form a conjecture, formular una conjetura

form[2], forma
algebraic form, forma algebraica
binary form, forma binaria

indefinite form, forma indefinida
indeterminate form, forma indeterminada
inverse form, forma inversa
linear form, forma lineal
logarithmic form, forma logarítmica
normalized form, forma normalizada
point-slope form of line, ecuación pendiente-punto de una línea
radical form, forma radical
reduced form, forma reducida
standard form forma estándar, forma corriente
form³, impreso
roster form, lista de presencia
formal proof, prueba formal
formally, formalmente
format, formato
horizontal format, formato horizontal
vertical format, formato vertical
formed by a transversal, formado por una transversal
formula, fórmula
binomial probability formula, fórmula de probabilidad binomial
compound interest formula, fórmula de interés compuesto
difference formula for trigonometric functions, fórmula de diferencia para funciones trigonométricas
distance formula, fórmula de distancia
double angle formula for a trigonometric function, fórmula de doble ángulo para una función trigonométrica
Euler's formula, fórmula de Euler
first Green formula, primera fórmula de Green
fundamental formula, fórmula fundamental
half angle formula for a trigonometric function, fórmula de medio ángulo para una función trigonométrica
Heron's formula, fórmula de Herón
quadratic formula, fórmula cuadrática
second Green formula, segunda fórmula de Green
simple interest formula, fórmula de interés simple
sum formula for trigonometric functions, fórmula de suma para funciones trigonométricas
formulate, formular

**formulate a conjec-
ture,** formular una
conjetura
**formulate math-
ematical questions,**
formular preguntas
matemáticas
foundation, fundamento
founded, fundado, basado
four, cuatro
four-sided figure,
figura de cuatro lados
Fourier, Fourier
Fourier analysis,
análisis de Fourier
Fourier series,
serie de Fourier
Fourier transform,
transformada de
Fourier
**Fourier transforma-
tion,** transformación
de Fourier
fourth, cuarto(a)
fourth degree,
cuarto grado
**fourth-quadrant
angle,** ángulo del
cuarto cuadrante
fractal, el fractal
fraction, quebrado,
fracción
algebraic fraction,
fracción algebraica
arithmetic fraction,
fracción aritmética
common fraction,
fracción común
complex fraction,
fracción compuesta
decimal fraction,
fracción decimal,
quebrado decimal

equivalent fractions,
fracciones equiva-
lentes
improper fraction,
fracción impropia,
quebrado impropio
**lowest terms frac-
tion,** fracción de tér-
minos simplificados
mixed fraction,
fracción mixta
**non-terminating
continued fraction,**
fracción continua
interminable
periodic fraction,
fracción periódica
proper fraction,
fracción propia,
quebrado propio
rational fraction,
fracción racional
reduced fraction,
fracción reducida
reducible fraction,
fracción reducible
unit fraction,
fracción unitaria
fractional, fraccionario
fractional equation,
ecuación fraccionaria
fractional exponent,
exponente fraccionario
fractional expression,
expresión fraccional
fractional number,
número fraccionario
fractional part,
parte fraccionaria
fractional radicand,
radicando fraccionario
fractionation,
fraccionación

fragment¹, fragmentar
fragment², fragmento
fragmentary, fragmentario
frame¹, enmarcar
frame², marco, armazón
   reference frame,
   marco de referencia
framework, marco
   theoretical frame-
   work, marco teórico
frequency, frecuencia
   frequency curve,
   curva de la frecuencia
   frequency diagram,
   diagrama de frecuencia
   frequency distribu-
   tion, distribución
   de la frecuencia
   frequency distribu-
   tion table, tabla de
   distribución de fre-
   cuencias
   frequency of a
   periodic function,
   frecuencia de una
   función periódica
   frequency polygon,
   polígono de la fre-
   cuencia
   frequency table,
   tabla de frecuencia
front¹, frente,
   parte delantera
front², delantero, anterior
   in front,
   por delante
   in front of,
   delante, enfrente de
front-end estimation,
   cálculo aproximado a
   partir de los primeros
   dígitos

front page, anverso
frustum,
   cono truncado, sólido
   truncado, tronco
ft. (foot), pie
fulfill, realizar, cumplir
full, completo, lleno
function¹, funcionar
function², función
   absolute value
   function, función
   de valor absoluto
   algebraic function,
   función algebraica
   circular function,
   función circular
   compound function,
   función compuesta
   complementary func-
   tion, función complementaria
   completely
   convex function,
   función completamen-
   te convexa
   constant function,
   función constante
   cosecant function,
   función cosecante
   cosine function,
   función coseno
   cotangent function,
   función cotangente
   decreasing function,
   función decreciente
   Dirac function,
   distribución de Dirac
   explicit function,
   función explícita
   exponential function,
   función exponencial
   function notation,
   notación de la función

function rule,
regla de función
general step function, función de escalón generalizado
greatest-integer function, función del entero mayor
hyperbolic function, función hiperbólica
implicit function, función implícita
increasing function, función creciente
inverse cosine function, función inversa del coseno
inverse function, función inversa
inverse function under composition, función inversa en composición
inverse sine function, función inversa del seno
inverse tangent function, función inversa de la tangente
inverse trigonometric function, función trigonométrica inversa
iterative function, función iterativa
linear function, función lineal
logarithm function, función logarítmica
non-periodic function, función no periódica
numerical function,

función numérica
odd function,
función impar
one-to-one function,
función de uno a uno
periodic function,
función periódica
polynomial function,
función polinómica
quadratic function,
función cuadrática
rational function,
función racional
secant function,
función secante
sine function,
función del seno
step function,
función escalonada
tangent function,
función tangente
transcendental function, función trascendental
trigonometric function, función trigonométrica
unit step function, función escalón unitario
wave function, función de onda
functional, funcional
functional relation, relación funcional
fundamental, fundamental
Fundamental Counting Principle, principio básico de conteo
fundamental formula, fórmula fundamental
fundamental

relationship, relación fundamental
fundamental theorem, teorema fundamental
Fundamental Theorem of Algebra, teorema fundamental del álgebra
Fundamental Theorem of Arithmetic, teorema fundamental de la aritmética
Fundamental Theorem of Calculus, teorema fundamental del cálculo

g. (gram), gramo
gallon (gal.), galón
game, juego
gap, espacio, hueco, intervalo, distancia, espacio en blanco, laguna, rezago
gather, recoger
Gaussian, Gaussiano
general, general
general associative property, propiedad general asociativa
general case, caso general
general commutative property, propiedad general conmutativa
general expression, expresión general

general step function, función de escalón generalizado
generalization, generalización
generalize, generalizar
generalized, generalizado
generally, generalmente, en general, por lo general
generate, generar
geodesic, geodésica
geometric, geométrico(a)
geometric construction, construcción geométrica
geometric fact, hecho geométrico
geometric figure, figura geométrica
geometric mean, media geométrica
geometric pattern, patrón geométrico
geometric progression, progresión geométrica
geometric relationship, relación geométrica
geometric sequence, secuencia geométrica
geometric series, serie geométrica
geometric shape, figura geométrica
geometric solid, sólido geométrico
geometric statement, declaración geométrica
geometry, geometría
analytic geometry, geometría analítica

coordinate geometry, geometría analítica, geometria de coordenada

differential geometry, geometría diferencial

Euclidean geometry, geometría euclidiana

hyperbolic geometry, geometría hiperbólica

non-Euclidean geometry, geometría no euclidiana

plane geometry, geometría plana, geometría euclidiana

solid geometry, geometría sólida

transformational geometry, geometría transformacional

get, obtener, conseguir

get behind, quedar atrás, atrasarse

get better, mejorar

get ready, preparar

giga, giga

give to, dar a

given, dado(a)

glide reflection, reflexión por deslizamiento

global maximum, máximo global

glossary, glosario

glue, pegamento

go, ir

go after, seguir

go against, contradecir, oponerse

go ahead, adelantar

go along, continuar

go along with, acompañar

go away, marcharse, irse

go back, retroceder, regresar

go backwards, retroceder, volver hacia atrás

go before, preceder, ir delante

go behind, seguir, ir detrás

go between, ir en medio de

go beyond, rebasar, ir más allá

go down, bajar, descender

go forward, ir adelante

go in, entrar

go near, acercarse

go out, salir

go over, pasar por arriba, revisar, estudiar

go under, ir por debajo, ir por abajo

go up, subir

goal, meta

Goldbach's conjecture, conjetura de Goldbach

golden rectangle, rectángulo áureo, rectángulo dorado

goodness of fit, bondad de ajuste

GPA (grade point average), promedio

grade¹, calificar

grade², gradiente, calificación, nota, grado escolar, promoción escolar

grade point average, promedio

gradient, gradiente

gradual, gradual

graduated, graduado

graduation, graduación

gram (g), gramo

graph¹, graficar

graph an equation, graficar una ecuación

graph an inequality, graficar una desigualdad

graph the set, graficar el conjunto

graph², gráfico(a)

bar graph, gráfica de barras

block graph, gráfica de bloque, histograma

circle graph, gráfica circular

double bar graph, gráfico de barras dobles

double line graph, gráficos de líneas dobles

graph a quadratic equation, graficar una ecuación cuadrática

graph of an equation in two variables, gráfico de una ecuación en dos variables

graph of a linear open sentence in two variables, gráfico de una oración lineal abierta en dos variables

line graph, gráfica de líneas

pictograph, pictografía

picture graph, gráfica de dibujos

step graph, gráfico escalonado

graphic (graphical), gráfico(a)

graphic calculator, calculadora de gráficos

graphic solution, solución gráfica

graphical method, método gráfico

graphical representation, representación gráfica

graphically, gráficamente

graphing calculator, calculadora gráfica

gratuity, propina

gravitation, gravedad, gravitación

gravity, gravedad

center of gravity, centro de gravedad

great circle, círculo mayor
greater, más grande, mayor
   greater than, mayor que
   greater or equal to symbol, signo de mayor o igual
   greater than symbol, signo de mayor que
greatest common divisor (GCD), máximo común denominador
greatest common factor (GCF), factor común mayor, máximo común divisor
greatest monomial factor, factor común mayor del monomio
greatest-integer function, función del entero mayor
Greek, griego
grid, cuadrícula
   coordinate grid, cuadrilla de coordenadas
groove, ranura, surco
gross, gruesa, bruto, doce docenas
group¹, agrupar, poner en grupos
group², grupo, conjunto
   Abelian group, grupo abeliano
   commutative group, grupo conmutativo
   finite group, grupo finito
   group theorem, teorema de grupo
   groups with finite sets, grupos de conjuntos finitos
   groups with infinite sets, grupos de conjuntos infinitos
grouped, agrupado
   grouped data, datos agrupados
   grouped frequency distributions, distribuciones de frecuencias grupales
grouping, agrupación
   grouping symbol, símbolo para agrupar, símbolo de agrupación
grow, crecer
growing, creciente
growth, crecimiento
   exponential growth, crecimiento exponencial
   growth factor, factor de crecimiento
   linear growth, crecimiento lineal
guess¹, adivinar
   guess correctly, acertar
guess², adivinanza, conjetura
guide¹, guiar
guide², guía
   study guide, guía de estudios

half¹ (pl. halves), mitad
half², medio
 half angle formula
 for a trigonometric
 function,
 fórmula de medio án-
 gulo para una función
 trigonométrica
 half-dollar,
 medio dólar
 half-hour,
 media hora
 half-life,
 semivida,
 vida media
 half-line,
 semirecta
 half-plane,
 medio plano
 half-turn,
 media vuelta
 alrededor del origen
half³, a medias
halfway, a la mitad
halo, halo
halve, dividir en mitades,
 dividir por la mitad
halving, dividir en mitades,
 dividir por la mitad
hard, duro, difícil
harmonic, armónico
 harmonic mean
 value, valor medio
 armónico
 harmonic sequence,
 secuencia armónica
 harmonic series,
 serie armónica

head (of a coin),
 cara (de una moneda)
heading, encabezado
heart beat,
 latido del corazón
heavier, más pesado
 heavier than,
 más pesado que
heaviest, el más pesado
hectare, hectárea
height, altura
 height of a cone,
 altura del cono
 height of a cylinder,
 altura del cilindro
 perpendicular height
 (of a triangle), altura
 (de un triángulo)
 slant height,
 altura de la pendiente,
 altura inclinada
helix, hélice
help¹, ayudar, auxiliar
help², ayuda, auxilio
hemisphere, hemisferio
heptagon, heptágono
Hermitian, hermítico(a)
 Hermitian conjugate
 matrix,
 matriz adjunta
 Hermitian matrix,
 matriz hermítica
 Hermitian product,
 producto hermítico
 Hermitian space,
 espacio hermítico
Heron's formula,
 fórmula de Herón
hexagon, hexágono
hexagram, hexagrama
hexahedron, hexaedro
hidden conditional,
 condicional oculta

high, alto
high school,
 escuela preparatoria
higher, más alto, superior
 higher terms,
 términos superiores
 higher than,
 más alto que
 higher-order
 derivative,
 derivada de
 orden superior
highest, máximo(a),
 el más alto
 highest common
 divisor, máximo
 común divisor
 highest common
 factor, factor común
 máximo
hill, colina, cerro, cuesta
histogram, histograma
 cumulative frequen-
 cy histogram,
 histograma de fre-
 cuencia acumulativa
hold, tener, agarrar,
 sostener, retener
 hold back,
 retener, hacer a
 uno repetir un año
hole, hoyo
hollow, hueco
homework, tarea
homogeneity,
 homogeneidad
homogeneous, homogéneo
 homogenous
 polynomial,
 polinomio homogéneo
 non-homogenous,
 no homogéneo
horizontal, horizontal

horizontal axis,
 eje horizontal
horizontal distance,
 distancia horizontal
horizontal format,
 formato horizontal
horizontal line,
 línea horizontal
horizontal line sym-
 metry, línea horizontal de simetría
horizontal-line test,
 prueba de la línea
 horizontal
hour, hora
 half-hour, media hora
 hour hand, manecilla
 de las horas
hundred, ciento, cien
hundreds, centenas
 hundreds place,
 posición de las cente-
 nas, centenas
hundredth, centésimo,
 unidad de centésima
hundred-thousands,
 centenas de millar
hundred-thousandth,
 cienmilésima
hyperbola, hipérbola
 rectangular hyper-
 bola, hipérbola
 rectangular
hyperbolic, hiperbólico
 hyperbolic function,
 función hiperbólica
 hyperbolic geometry,
 geometría hiperbólica
 hyperbolic spiral,
 espiral hiperbólica
hypotenuse, hipotenusa
 hypotenuse triangle
 congruence,

hipotenusa congruente
hypothesis (pl. hypotheses), hipótesis
    alternative hipothesis, hipótesis alternativo
    hypothesis testing, prueba de hipótesis, comprobación de una hipótesis, verificación de una hipótesis
    null hypothesis, hipótesis nula
hypothetical, hipotético
    hypothetical proposition, proposición hipotética

I

icosahedron, icosaedro
ideal, ideal
idealize, idealizar
identical, idéntico
    identical quantities, cantidades idénticas
    identical relation, relación idéntica
    identical substitution, sustitución idéntica
    identical transformation, transformación idéntica
identically vanishing, desaparición idéntica
identifiable, identificable
identify, identificar
identity, identidad
    additive identity,

identidad aditiva
    algebraic identity, identidad algebraica
    identity element, elemento de identidad
    identity element for addition, elemento de identidad aditiva
    identity element for multiplication, identidad multiplicativa
    identity matrix, matriz identidad, matriz unitaria
    identity property, propiedad de identidad
    identity property of addition, propiedad neutro de la suma, característica de identidad de la suma
    identity property of multiplication, propiedad neutro de la multiplicación, característica de identidad de la multiplicación,
    identity relation, relación de identidad
    identity symbol, símbolo de identidad
    multiplicative identity, identidad multiplicativa
    Pythagorean identity, teorema de Pitágoras
    quotient identity, identidad de cociente
    reciprocal identity, identidad recíproca

trigonometric identity, identidad trigonométrica
if, si
if and only if (iff), si y solamente si
illogical, ilógico
illustrate, ilustrar
illustration, ilustración, dibujo
image, imagen
image point, punto imagen
image set, conjunto imagen
inverse image, imagen inversa
preimage, preimagen
reflected image, imagen reflejada
imaginary, imaginario
conjugate imaginary lines, líneas imaginarias conjugadas
imaginary axis, eje imaginario
imaginary circle, círculo imaginario
imaginary component, componente imaginario
imaginary line, línea imaginaria
imaginary number, número imaginario
imaginary plane, plano imaginario
imaginary point, punto imaginario
imaginary root, raíz imaginaria
imaginary unit, unidad imaginaria
pure imaginary number, número imaginario puro
immeasurable, inmensurable
immense, inmenso
impartial, imparcial
imperfect, imperfecto
implausible, inverosímil
implication, implicación
implicit, implícito
implicit differentiation, diferenciación implícita
implicit function, función implícita
imply, implicar
important, importante
impossible, imposible
impossible case, caso imposible
impossible event, evento imposible
impossible outcome, resultado imposible
impractical, impráctico
imprecise, impreciso
improbable, improbable
improper, impropio
improper fraction, fracción impropia
improper integral, integral impropia
improve, mejorar
in, en
in. (inch), pulgada
inaccurate, impreciso
inalterable, inalterable
incalculable, incalculable
incenter, encentrar
inch (in.), pulgada
cubic inch,

pulgada cúbica
square inch,
pulgada cuadrada
incircle, círculo inscrito
inclination, inclinación
incline[1], inclinar
incline[2], pendiente
inclined lines,
rectas inclinadas
inclined plane,
plano inclinado
include, incluir
included angle,
ángulo contenido
included side,
lado contenido
inclusion, inclusión
inclusive, inclusivo
inclusive disjunction,
disyunción inclusiva
income, ingresos,
ganancias
income values,
valores de ingreso
incommensurable
number, número
inconmesurable
incomparability,
incomparabilidad
incomparable,
incomparable
incomplete, incompleto(a)
incomplete
quadratic equation,
ecuación cuadrática
incompleta
incompleteness,
deficiencia
incomprehensible,
incomprensible
inconclusive,
inconcluyente
incongruent,

incongruente
inconsistency,
inconsistencia
inconsistent, inconsistente
inconsistent
equations,
ecuaciones
inconsistentes
inconsistent
inequality,
desigualdad
inconsistente
incorporate, incorporar
incorrect, incorrecto
increase[1], incrementar,
aumentar
increase exponen-
tially, crecer exponencialmente
increase logarithmi-
cally, crecer logarítmicamente
increase[2], incremento,
aumento
percent increase,
por ciento de aumento,
incremento porcentual
increasing, creciente
increasing function,
función creciente
increasing sequence,
secuencia creciente
increasing serie,
serie crecientes
increment[1], incrementar
increment[2], incremento
indefinite, indefinido
indefinite equation,
ecuación indefinida
indefinite form,
forma indefinida
indefinite integral,
integral indefinida

indirecta
indirect proof,
prueba indirecta
indistinguishable,
indistinguible
individual, individual
indivisible, indivisible
induce, inducir
induced mapping,
barrido inducido
induction, inducción
induction by
simple enumeration,
inducción por
enumeración simple
mathematical induc-
tion, inducción mate-
mática
inductive, inductivo
inductive reasoning,
razonamiento induc-
tivo
inequality, desigualdad
absolute inequality,
desigualdad absoluta
absolute value
inequality,
desigualdad de
valor absoluto
addition property
of inequality,
propiedad aditiva
de la desigualdad
conditional inequal-
ity, desigualdad
condicional
equivalent inequal-
ity, desigualdad equivalente
first-degree inequal-
ity, desigualdad de
primer grado
inconsistent inequal-

indefinitely,
indefinidamente
independence,
independencia
linear independence,
independencia lineal
independent,
independiente
independent event,
evento independiente
independent trial,
prueba independiente
independent variable,
variable independiente
indeterminate,
indeterminado
indeterminate coef-
ficient, coeficiente
indeterminado
indeterminate
equation, ecuación
indeterminada
indeterminate form,
forma indeterminada
index¹, indexar
index², exponente, índice
index laws,
leyes de los
exponentes
index in statistics,
índice de estadísticas
index of a radical,
índice de un radical
rational index,
índice racional
indicate, indicar, señalar
indicated demonstration,
demostración indirecta
indicated root,
raíz indicada
indirect, indirecto
indirect measure-
ment, medida

ity, desigualdad inconsistente
inequality containing one variable, desigualdad con una variable
inequality involving fractions, desigualdades que envuelven fracciones
inequality sign, signo de desigualdad
inequality symbol, símbolo de desigualdad
linear inequality, desigualdad lineal
linear inequality in two variables, desigualdad lineal con dos variables
multiplication property of inequality, propiedad multiplicativa de la desigualdad
quadratic inequality, desigualdad cuadrática
rational inequality, desigualdad racional
transitive property of inequality, propiedad transitiva de las desigualdades
triangle inequality, desigualdad de triángulos
inertia, inercia
inexact, inexacto
inexpensive, barato
inexplicable, inexplicable
infer, inferir
inference, inferencia

inference of immediate, inferencia de lo inmediato
inference of mediate, inferencia de lo mediato
law of disjunctive inference, ley de inferencia disyuntiva
law of inference, ley de inferencia
statistical inference, inferencia estadística
inferible, inferible
infinite, infinito
infinite decimal, decimal infinito
infinite extension, extensión infinita
infinite limit, límite infinito
infinite set, conjunto infinito
infinitely, infinitamente
infinitely great, infinitamente grande
infinitely increasing, aumentar infinitamente
infinitely many, infinitamente mucho
infinitesimal, infinitesimal
infinity, infinito
inflection, inflexión
inflection point, punto de inflexión
point of inflection, punto de inflexión
inflexible, inflexible
inform, informar
informal indirect proof, prueba indirecta informal

informally, informalmente
information, información
    information technology (IT), tecnología de la información
    irrelevant information, información irrelevante, información inaplicable, información sin importancia
    relevant information, información relevante
informative, informativo
infrequent, infrecuente
inhomogeneous, inhomogéneo
initial, inicial
    initial capital, capital inicial
    initial column, columna inicial
    initial condition, condición inicial
    initial data, información inicial
    initial ray, rayo inicial
    initial row, fila inicial
    initial segment, segmento inicial
    initial side of an angle, lado inicial de un ángulo
    initial solution, solución inicial
    initial term, término inicial
    initial value, valor inicial
inner, interior, interno
    inner center, centro interno, centro interior
    inner point, punto interno, punto interior
    inner product, producto interior
    inner scale, escala interior
    inner term, término interno
input[1]**,** capturar, introducir
input[2]**,** entrada de datos, datos
    input values, valores de entrada
inquisitive, inquisitivo, curioso
inscribe, inscribir
inscribed, inscrito
    inscribed angle, ángulo inscrito
    inscribed circle, círculo inscrito
    inscribed figure, figura inscrita
    inscribed polygon, polígono inscrito
    inscribed sphere, esfera inscrita
inseparable, inseparable
insert, insertar
insertion, inserción
inside, dentro, adentro
insignificant, insignificante
inspect, inspeccionar
inspection, inspección
insphere, esfera inscrita
installment, plazo
instead of, en lugar de
instruct, enseñar, instruir

instruction, instrucción
instrument, instrumento
insufficient, insuficiente
intact, intacto
integer, entero,
  número entero
  **consecutive even
  integers,** enteros
  pares consecutivos
  consecutive integers,
  enteros consecutivos
  **consecutive odd
  integers,** enteros im-
  pares consecutivos
  even integer,
  entero par
  integer coefficient,
  coeficiente entero
  negative integer,
  entero negativo
  odd integer,
  entero impar
  positive integer,
  entero positivo
  signless integers,
  enteros sin signos
integrability,
  integrabilidad
integral, integral
  definite integral,
  integral definida
  double integral,
  integral doble
  indefinite integral,
  integral indefinida
  improper integral,
  integral impropia
  integral calculus,
  cálculo integral
  integral coefficient,
  coeficiente integral
  integral exponent,
  exponente integral

  integral factor,
  factor integral
  integral part,
  parte integral
  integral point,
  punto integral
  integral power,
  potencia integral
  integral radicand,
  radicando integral
  integral root,
  raíz de número
  integrales
  integral value,
  valor integral
  Riemann integral,
  integral de Riemann
  surface integral,
  integral de superficie
  upper integral,
  integral superior
  volume integral,
  integral de volumen
integrate, integrar
integrated mathematics,
  matemática integrada
integration, integración
  integration by parts,
  integración por partes
  **numerical integra-
  tion,** integración
  numérica
intent, intento
interact, interactuar
interaction, interacción
intercept[1], interceptar
intercept[2], intercepto,
  intercepción
  intercept point,
  punto de intercepción
  slope-intercept form,
  forma pendiente inter-
  cepto

slope-intercept method, método pendiente intercepto

x-intercept of a line, intercepto de x de una línea

y-intercept of a line, intercepto de y de una línea

intercepted arc, arco interceptado

interchange, intercambiar

interchangeable, intercambiable

interconnect, interconectar, comunicar

interconnection, interconexión

interest, interés

compound interest, interés compuesto

interest compounded annually, interés compuesto anual

interest compounded continuously, interés compuesto continuamente

interest compounded quarterly, interés compuesto trimestral

interest compounded semiannually, interés compuesto semestral

interest rate, tasa de interés

simple interest, interés simple

interface, interfaz

interior, interior

interior angle, ángulo interior

interior angle of a triangle, ángulo interior de un triángulo

interior of an angle, interior de un ángulo

interior point, punto interior

interior region, región interior

interior region of a circle, región interior de un círculo

intermediate, intermedio

intermediate value, valor intermedio

interminable, interminable

intermittent, intermitente

internal bisector, bisector interno

internal division, división interna

internal tangent, tangente interna

internally tangent circles, círculos de tangencia interna

interpolate, interpolar

interpolation, interpolación

inverse interpolation, interpolación inversa

trigonometric interpolation, interpolación trigonométrica

interpret, interpretar

interpretation, interpretación

interquartile range, rango intercuartílico

interrupt, interrumpir

interrupted, interrumpido

intersect, intersectar,

cruzar, hacer esquina
intersecting, intersectante
intersecting lines,
líneas intersectantes
intersecting point,
punto de intersección
intersection,
cruce, traslape
**intersection of
graphs,** intersección
de gráficas
intersection of loci,
intersección de punto
geométricos
intersection of sets,
intersección de
conjuntos
interval, intervalo
class interval,
intervalo de clase
closed interval,
intervalo cerrado
confidence interval,
intervalo de confianza
**consecutive inter-
vals,** intervalos
consecutivos
interval notation,
notación por intervalos
modal interval,
intervalo modal
open interval,
intervalo abierto
**sequence of inter-
vals,** secuencia
de intervalos
intput/output table, tabla
de entradas y salidas
intransitive, intransitivo
intro (introduction),
introducción
introduce,
introducir, presentar

introduction, introducción
intuit, intuir
intuition, intuición
intuitive, intuitivo
invalid, inválido
invalid approach,
enfoque inválido
invariable, invariable
invariance, invariedad
**orientational invari-
ance,** invariabilidad
orientacional
invariant, invariante
invent, inventar
invention,
invento, invención
inventor, inventor
inverse, inverso
additive inverse,
inverso aditivo
inverse correlation,
correlación inversa
**inverse cosine func-
tion,** función inversa
del coseno
inverse curve,
curva inversa
inverse element,
elemento inverso
inverse equation,
ecuación inversa
inverse form,
forma inversa
inverse function,
función inversa
**inverse function
under composition,**
función inversa en
composición
inverse image,
imagen inversa
inverse interpolation,
interpolación inversa

inverse logarithm,
logaritmo inverso
inverse mapping,
barrido inverso
inverse matrix,
matriz inversa,
matriz recíproca
inverse number,
número inverso
**inverse of a state-
ment,** inversa de
un enunciado
inverse operation,
operación inversa
inverse property,
propiedad de inversa
inverse proportion,
proporción inversa
inverse proposition,
proposición inversa
inverse ratio,
razón inversa
inverse relation,
relación inversa
**inverse sine
function,** función
inversa del seno
inverse square,
cuadrado inverso
inverse statement,
declaración inversa
**inverse tangent
function,** función
inversa de la tangente
inverse theorem,
teorema inverso
**inverse transforma-
tion,** transformación
inversa
**inverse trigonomet-
ric function,**
función trigonométrica
inversa

inverse trihedron,
triedro inverso
inverse variation,
variación inversa
**multiplicative
inverse,** inverso
multiplicativo
**inversely proportional
quantities,** cantidades
inversamente propor-
cionales
invert, invertir
invertibility, invertibilidad
investigate, investigar
investigation,
investigación
involve, involucrar,
implicar
inward, hacia adentro
irrational, irracional,
absurdo
irrational number,
número irracional
irrational root,
raíz irracional
irreducible, irreducible
**irreducible algebraic
equation,** ecuación
algebraica irreducible
irreflexive, irreflexiva
irreflexive relation,
relación irreflexiva
irrefutable, irrefutable
irregular, irregular
irregular polygon,
polígono irregular
irregular shape,
forma irregular
irregularity, irregularidad
irrelevant, irrelevante
**irrelevant informa-
tion,** información irre-
levante, información

inaplicable, informa-
ción sin importancia
irreplaceable,
irreemplazable,
no reemplazable
irreversibility,
irreversibilidad
irreversible, irreversible
irreversible process,
proceso irreversible
irrotational field,
campo irrotacional
isogonal, isogonal
isogonal line,
línea isogonal
isogonal mapping,
barrido isogonal
**isogonal transforma-
tion,** transformación
isogonal
isogonality,
isogonabilidad
isolate, aislar
isolate a variable,
despejar (la variable)
isolate the radical,
aislar el radical
isometric, isométrico(a)
isometric chart,
tabla isométrica
isometric circle,
círculo isométrico
**isometric correspon-
dence,** corresponden-
cia isométrica
**isometric graph pa-
per,** papel para hacer
dibujos isométricos
isometry, isometría
direct isometry,
isometría directa
opposite isometry,
isometría opuesta

isomorphic, isomórfico
isosceles, isósceles
isosceles trapezoid,
trapezoide isósceles,
trapecio isósceles
isosceles triangle,
triángulo isósceles
issue, tema, cuestión,
punto en debate
**IT (information technol-
ogy),** tecnología de
la información
item, ítem, cosa, objeto
iterate, iterar
iteration, iteración
iterative, iterativo
iterative function,
función iterativa

J

join, unir
joint, conjunto(a)
joint variation,
variación conjunta
jointly, juntamente, juntos
judge, juzgar
jump, saltar
junior high school,
escuela secundaria
justify, justificar
**justify the state-
ment,** justificar la
afirmación

keep track of,
llevar cuenta de
Kelvin (K), Kelvin
key¹, llave
key², leyenda
key³, clave, esencial
key sequence,
secuencia de pasos
kilo, kilo, kilogramo
kilogram (kg),
kilo, kilogramo
kiloliter (kl), kilolitro
kilometer (km), kilómetro
kite, cometa, papalote
knot (kt.), nudo
know, saber, conocer
known, conocido
known function,
función conocida
known quantity,
cantidad conocida
Kronecker delta,
delta de Kronecker
Kronecker tensor,
tensor de Kronecker

L

l (liter), litro
label¹, etiquetar, identificar
label work,
identificar los pasos
del trabajo
label², etiqueta
label the solution

set, etiquetar el
conjunto solución
laboratory, laboratorio
land mile, milla terrestre,
milla ordinaria
language, lenguaje
algebraic language,
lenguaje algebraico
language of logic,
lenguaje de la lógica
**programming lan-
guage,** lenguaje
de programación
verbal language,
lenguaje verbal
written language,
lenguaje escrito,
lenguaje gráfico
Laplacian operator,
laplaciano escalar,
laplaciano de un
campo escalar
lapse, lapso
large, grande
larger, más grande
larger than,
más grande que
largest, el más grande
last, último
last term,
último término
late, tarde
later, más tarde
later than,
más tarde que
latest, más reciente
lateral, lateral
lateral area of a cone,
área lateral del cono
lateral edge,
extremo lateral,
borde lateral
lateral edge

of a prism,
arista lateral
del prisma
lateral face,
cara lateral
lateral point,
punto lateral
lateral surface,
superficie lateral
lateral surface area,
área de superficie
lateral
latitude, latitud
lattice points,
red de puntos
latus rectum, lado recto
law, ley
    associative law,
    ley asociativa
    cancellation law,
    ley de cancelación
    cancellation law
    of addition,
    ley de cancelación
    de la suma
    cancellation law
    of multiplication,
    ley de cancelación
    de la multiplicación
    commutative law,
    ley conmutativa
    cosine law,
    ley del coseno
    De Morgan's law,
    ley de De Morgan
    detachment law, ley
    del desprendimiento
    distributive law,
    ley distributiva
    index laws,
    leyes de los
    exponentes
    law of chain rule,

    ley de la regla de
    cadena
    law of conjunction,
    ley de conjunción
    law of contradiction,
    ley de contradicción
    law of contrapositive,
    ley de contrapositivo
    law of cosines,
    ley de cosenos
    law of De Morgan,
    ley de De Morgan
    law of detachment,
    ley del desprendimien-
    to
    law of disjunctive
    addition, ley de
    adición disyuntiva
    law of disjunctive
    inference, ley de
    inferencia disyuntiva
    law of double
    negation, ley de
    la negación doble
    law of exponents,
    ley de exponentes
    law of inference,
    ley de inferencia
    law of large numbers,
    ley de los grandes
    números
    law of logarithms,
    ley de logaritmos
    law of Modus Tollens,
    ley de Modus Tollens
    law of positive
    integral exponents,
    ley de exponentes
    integrales positivos
    law of reasoning,
    ley de razonamiento
    law of simplification,
    ley de simplificación

law of sines,
ley de senos
law of substitution,
ley de sustitución
monotonic law,
ley de monotonía
power-of-product law,
ley de potencia de un
producto
**power-of-quotient
law,** ley de la potencia
de un cociente
**right cancellation
law,** ley de cancelación
derecha
trichotomy law,
ley de tricotomía
lb. (pound), libra
**LCD (lowest common
denominator),**
menor denominador
común
lead¹, conducir a
lead², primer(a), principal
lead coefficient,
coeficiente principal
leading coefficient,
coeficiente conductor
leading diagonal,
diagonal principal
leading element,
elemento guía
leading variable,
variable principal
least, el mínimo, el menor
**least common de-
nominator (LCD),**
mínimo común de-
nominador, menor
denominador común
least common factor,
factor común mínimo
least common mul-

tiple (LCM), mínimo
común múltiplo
**least squares
regression line,**
línea de ajuste óptimo
leave, dejar, salir
left¹, izquierda
to the left,
a la izquierda,
hacia la izquierda
left², restante
left-hand,
de mano izquierda
**left-hand cancella-
tion,** cancelación
del lado izquierdo
left-hand number,
numero del lado
izquierdo
left-hand operation,
operación del lado
izquierdo
left-handed, zurdo
left-over, sobrante
leg, lado, cateto
**leg of a right
triangle,** cateto de
un triángulo recto
**leg of an isosceles
triangle,** cateto de
un triángulo isósceles
**leg triangle congru-
ence,** catetos con-
gruentes
lemma, lema
lend, prestar
length, largo, longitud
length of arc,
longitud de arco
**length of semi-
circle,** longitud
de semicírculo
lens, lente

less, menor
>**less than,**
>menor que, menor de
>**less than symbol,**
>signo de menor que
>**less than or equal
>to symbol,** signo de
>menor o igual

lesser, menor
let, dejar
lettered, rotulado
level¹, nivelar, emparejar
level², nivel
>**eye level,**
>altura de los ojos,
>nivel de la vista
>**level of precision,**
>nivel de precisión

L'Hôpital's Rule,
>regla de L'Hôpital

lie, yacer, mentir
>**lie on the graph of,**
>yacer sobre el gráfico
>**lie on the line,**
>yacer sobre la línea

light wave, onda de luz
light year, año luz
lighter, más ligero(a),
>más liviano(a)
>**lighter than,**
>más ligero(a) que,
>más liviano(a) que

lightest, el más ligero,
>el más liviano

like, semejante
>**like denominators,**
>denominadores seme-
>jantes, denominadores
>comunes
>**like monomials,**
>monomios semejantes
>**like numbers,**
>números semejantes
>**like radicals,**
>radicales semejantes
>**like terms,**
>términos similares,
>términos semejantes

likelihood, probabilidad
likely, probable, posible-
>mente
limit¹, limitar
limit², límite
>**central limit
>theorem,**
>teorema central
>del límite
>**infinite limit,**
>límite infinito
>**lower limit,**
>límite inferior

limitless, sin límite
limitation,
>limitante, limitación
limitless, sin límite
line, línea
>**auxiliary line,**
>línea auxiliar
>**concentric lines,**
>líneas concéntricas
>**concurrent lines,**
>líneas concurrentes
>**congruent line
>segments,**
>segmento de línea
>congruentes
>**conjugate
>imaginary lines,**
>líneas imaginarias
>conjugadas
>**coplanar lines,**
>líneas coplanares
>**curved line,**
>línea curva
>**dashed line,**
>línea entrecortada

dotted line,
línea de puntos,
línea punteada
line graph,
gráfica de líneas
equidistant lines,
líneas equidistantes
horizontal line,
línea horizontal
imaginary line,
línea imaginaria
intersecting lines,
líneas intersectantes
isogonal line,
línea isogonal
line of best fit,
línea de mejor ajuste
line of equidistance,
línea de equidistancia
line of reflection,
línea de reflección
line of sight,
campo visual,
línea visual
line of symmetry,
línea de simetría
line plot,
diagrama lineal
line segment,
segmento de una línea
number line,
línea numérica
parallel line segments, segmentos
de rectas paralelas
parallel lines,
líneas paralelas
perpendicular lines,
líneas perpendiculares
proportional line segments, segmentos de
líneas proporcionale
remaining line,

línea restante
scalar line element,
elemento escalar de
línea
sense of a line,
sentido de una línea
skew lines,
líneas oblicuas,
rectas oblicuas
skewed lines,
rectas oblicuas,
líneas oblicuas
straight line,
recta, línea recta
terminal line,
línea terminal
trend line,
línea de tendencia,
línea de rumbo
vector line element,
elemento vectorial de
línea
line up, alinear
linear, lineal
linear algebra,
álgebra lineal
linear coordinates,
coordenades lineales
linear dependence,
dependencia lineal
linear equation,
ecuación lineal
**linear equation in
one variable,**
ecuación lineal de
una variable
linear estimation,
estimación lineal
linear form,
forma lineal
linear function,
función lineal
linear growth,

crecimiento lineal
linear independence,
independencia lineal
linear inequality,
desigualdad lineal
**linear inequality in
two variables,**
desigualdad lineal con
dos variables
linear measure,
medida lineal
**linear measure of an
arc,** medida lineal de
un arco
linear open sentence,
oración lineal abierta
linear pair,
par lineal
linear pair of angles,
par lineal de ángulos
linear regression,
regresión lineal
linear relationship,
relación lineal
**linear transforma-
tion,** transformación
lineal
linear unit,
unidad lineal
linearly, linealmente
linearly dependent,
linealmente depen-
diente
linearly independent,
linealmente indepen-
diente
**linear-quadratic
system,** sistema
cuadrático lineal
link[1], enlazar, vincular
link up,
conectar con
link[2], enlace, vínculo

list[1], hacer una lista, enumerar, incluir en una
lista, sentar en una
lista
list[2], lista
listen, escuchar
liter (l), litro
literal, literal
literal coefficient,
coeficiente literal
literal constant,
constante literal
literal equation,
ecuación literal
literal expression,
expresión literal
literal notation,
notación literal
little[1], pequeño
little[2], poco
loan[1], prestar
loan[2], préstamo
local, local
local maximum,
máximo local,
máximo parcial
localize, localizar
locate, encontrar, ubicar,
localizar, situar
location, lugar, ubicación
locus (pl. loci), locus
compound locus,
locus compuesto
locus of points,
locus de puntos
logarithm (log),
logaritmo
inverse logarithm,
logaritmo inverso
law of logarithms,
ley de logaritmos
logarithmic form,
forma logarítmica

logarithm function, función logarítmica
natural logarithm (natural log), logaritmo natural, logaritmo neperiano
logarithmic, logarítmico
logarithmic form, forma logarítmica
reciprocal logarithmic curve, curva logarítmica recíproca
logarithmically, logarítmicamente
increase logarithmically, crecer logarítmicamente
logic, lógica
algebra of logic, álgebra de lógica
language of logic, lenguaje de la lógica
logic proof, prueba lógica
mathematical logic, lógica matemática
logical, lógico
logical argument, argumento lógico
logical conclusion, conclusión lógica
logical equivalent, equivalente lógico
logical operation, operación lógica
logical order, orden lógico
logical reasoning, razonamiento lógico
logical sequence, secuencia lógica
logical system,

sistema lógico
logically, lógicamente
logically equivalent, lógicamente equivalente
logically equivalent statements, frases lógicamente equivalentes
long, largo
long division, división de casilla
longer, más largo
longer than, más largo que
longest, el más largo
longitude, longitud
longitudinal axis, eje longitudinal
look for, buscar
loop, arco, lazo
loose, flojo
loosen, aflojar
lopsided, ladeado
lose, perder
loss, pérdida
lower, inferior, menor
lower base, base inferior
lower base of a cylinder, base inferior del cilindro
lower bound, límite inferior
lower case, minúscula
lower limit, límite inferior
lowest, mínimo
lowest common denominator (LCD), mínimo común divisor, mínimo común

denominador, menor
denominador común
lowest common multiple, mínimo común múltiplo
lowest terms, términos mínimos
lowest terms fraction, fracción de términos simplificados
lucky, afortunado

machine, máquina
magnet, imán, magneto
magnetic, magnético
   magnetic field, campo magnético
magnetism, magnetismo
magnitude, magnitud
   absolute magnitude, magnitud absoluta
   order of magnitude, orden de magnitud
main, principal
   main diagonal, diagonal principal
   main normal, normal principal
mainstream¹, convencional, comercial
mainstream², corriente principal, corriente dominante
major, importante, mayor
   major arc, arco mayor
   major axis,

eje mayor
   major segment, segmento mayor
make, hacer
   make a mistake, equivocarse
malleable, maleable
manipulate, manipular
manipulation, manipulación
   algebraic manipulation, manipulación algebraica
manipulative materials, materiales manipulativos, materiales prácticos
mantissa, mantisa
many, mucho
   many-to-one correspondence, correspondencia de muchos a uno
map¹, mapear
map², mapa
   map legend, leyenda del mapa
   map scale, escala de mapa
mapping, mapeo, barrido
   induced mapping, barrido inducido
   inverse mapping, barrido inverso
   isogonal mapping, barrido isogonal
   one-to-one mapping, barrido biunívoco
   sense-preserving mapping, proyección de dirección preservada
marbles, canicas

mark, marcar, señalar
  mark correct,
  palomear
  mark wrong,
  tachar
marker, marcador
mass, masa
match¹, cotejar, emparejar,
  hacer asociaciones,
  hacer concordancias,
  asociar, concordar,
  encontrar la respuesta
  más adecuada, juz-
  gar igual, buscar la
  correspondencia
match², cotejo, igual
mathematical,
  matemático
  mathematical
  analysis,
  análisis matemático
  mathematical
  conjecture,
  conjetura matemática
  mathematical idea,
  idea matemática
  mathematical
  induction,
  inducción matemática
  mathematical lan-
  guage,
  lenguaje matemático
  mathematical logic,
  lógica matemática
  mathematical
  operation,
  operación matemática
  mathematical
  phenomena,
  fenómeno
  matemático
  mathematical
  relationships,

  relaciones
  matemáticas
  mathematical
  representation,
  representación
  matemática
  mathematical
  sentence,
  frase matemática
  mathematical
  statements,
  enunciados
  matemáticos
  mathematical
  symbol,
  símbolo matemático
  mathematical
  system,
  sistema matemático
  mathematical visual,
  visual matemático
mathematician,
  matemático
mathematics,
  matemáticas
  integrated
  mathematics,
  matemática integrada
matrix (pl. matrices),
  matriz
  column matrix,
  matriz columna
  diagonal matrix,
  matriz diagonal
  Hermitian conjugate
  matrix, matriz
  adjunta
  Hermitian matrix,
  matriz hermítica
  identity matrix,
  matriz identidad,
  matriz unitaria
  inverse matrix,

matriz inversa,
matriz recíproca
invertible matrix,
matriz invertible
matrix algebra,
álgebra matricial
positive definite matrix, matriz
definida positiva
regular matrix,
matriz regular
row matrix,
matriz fila
singular matrix,
matriz singular
square matrix,
matriz cuadrada
symmetric matrix,
matriz simétrica
transpose matrix,
matriz transpuesta
unit matrix,
matriz unitaria
unitary matrix,
matriz unitaria
zero matrix,
matriz nula
matter[1], importar
matter[2], sustancia, materia
maxima, máximo
maximal, máximo(a)
maximize, maximizar
maximum (max), máximo
absolute maximum,
máximo absoluto
global maximum,
máximo global
local maximum,
máximo local,
máximo parcial
maximum point,
punto máximo
maximum value,

valor máximo
mean[1], significar,
querer decir
mean[2], media
arithmetic mean,
media aritmética
assumed mean,
valor medio asumido
geometric mean,
media geométrica
harmonic mean value, valor medio
armónico
mean absolute deviation, desviación
absoluta media
mean proportional,
proporcional media
mean terms,
términos medios
mean terms of proportion,
términos medios
de una proporción
mean value,
valor medio
Mean Value Theorem, teorema de
valor medio
means of a proportion, medios de
una proporción
sample mean,
media modelo
weighted mean,
media ponderada
working mean,
media provisional,
media de trabajo
meaning, significado,
sentido
meaningful, significativo
meaningless, sin sentido

means, sistema, manera
  by means of,
  mediante,
  por medio de
measurability,
  mensurabilidad
measurable, que se puede medir, medible,
  mensurable
measure¹, medir
  measure capacity,
  medir la capacidad
measure², medida
  angle measure,
  medida de ángulo
  degree measure,
  medida en grados
  direct measure,
  medida dirigida
  linear measure,
  medida lineal
  **measure of a central
  angle,** medida de
  ángulo central
  measure of angle,
  medida del ángulo
  **measure of disper-
  sion,** medida de la
  dispersión
  measure of precision,
  medida de precisión
  measure of radians,
  medida de radianes
  measure of variance,
  la medida de variación
  **measures of central
  tendency,** medidas
  de tendencia central
  **nonstandard mea-
  sure,** medida no
  estándar
  radian measure,
  medida del radián

  standard measure,
  medida estándar
  tape measure, cinta
  métrica, flexómetro
  unit measure,
  unidad de medida
measurement, medida
  **customary measure-
  ment system,**
  sistema anglosajón
  de medidas
  direct measurement,
  medida directa
  **indirect
  measurement,**
  medida indirecta
  **measurement
  system,** sistema
  de medición
  **precision
  measurement,**
  medida de precisión
mechanics, mecánica
  quantum mechanics,
  mecánica cuántica
median, mediana
medium¹, medio
medium², mediano
meet¹, cumplir con, reunir
  los requisitos, encon-
  trarse, conocerse
meet², intersección de
  conjuntos
mega, mega
member, miembro
memorize, aprender
  de memoria
memory, memoria
  memory capacity,
  capacidad de memoria
mental, mental
  mental math,
  cálculo mental

Mersenne primes, números primos de Mersenne

meter, metro

cubic meter, metro cúbico

square meter, metro cuadrado

method, método

cancellation method, método de cancelación

combined method, método combinado

deductive method, método deductivo

extrapolation method, método de extrapolación

factorization method, método de factorización

graphical method, método gráfico

method of elimination, método de eliminación

method of exhaustion, método del agotamiento

method of interpolation, método de interpolación

method of proof, método de prueba

method of successive substitution, método de los coeficientes indeterminados

method of trial and error, método de aproximaciones

method of undeter-

mined coefficients, método de los coeficientes indeterminados

Newton's method, método de Newton

operational method, método operativo, método operacional

short-out method, método corto

slope-intercept method, método pendiente intercepto

square root method, método de la raíz cuadrada

substitution method, método de sustitución

successive method of elimination, método sucesivo de eliminación

tangential approximation method, método de aproximación tangencial

trial and error method, método de aproximación, aproximaciones sucesivas

methodical, metódico

meticulous, meticuloso

metric, métrico

metric system, sistema métrico

metric unit, unidad métrica de medición, unidad métrica de medida

mg (milligram), miligramo

mi. (mile), milla

mid, medio

middle, medio, en el centro, en medio
   middle school, escuela secundaria
   middle term, término medio
midpoint, punto medio
   midpoint preserved, punto medio conservado
mid-range, alcance medio
mid-term exam, examen parcial
midway, a mitad de
mile (mi.), milla
   land mile, milla terrestre, milla ordinaria
   miles per gallon (mpg), millas por galón
   miles per hour (mph), millas por hora
   nautical mile, milla marina, milla náutica
   statute mile, milla terrestre, milla ordinaria
milli, mili
milligram (mg), miligramo
milliliter (ml), mililitro
millimeter (mm), milímetro
million, millón
   millions, las unidades de millón
   millions place, las unidades de millón
millionth, millonésima
minima, mínimo

minimal, mínimo(a)
   minimal surface, superficie mínima
minimize, minimizar
minimum, mínimo
   absolute minimum, mínimo absoluto
   minimum point, punto mínimo
   minimum solution, solución mínima
   minimum value, valor mínimo
minor, menor, de poco importancia
   minor arc, arco menor
   minor axis, eje menor
   minor segment, segmento menor
minuend, minuendo
minus[1], restar
minus[2], menos
   minus sign, signo de sustracción, signo menos
minuscule, minúsculo
minute[1], minuto
   minute hand, manecilla de los minutos
minute[2], diminuto
mirror[1], reflejar
mirror[2], espejo
misleading, engañoso
mismatch[1], emparejar mal, unir mal
mismatch[2], unión desajustada, desajuste
miss, faltar
misshape, malformar

missing, faltante
mix, mezclar
mixed, mezclado, mixto
  mixed decimal,
  decimal mixto
  mixed fraction,
  fracción mixta
  mixed number,
  número mixto
ml (milliliter), mililitro
mm (millimeter),
  milímetro
Möbius strip,
  cinta de Möbius
mod system,
  sistema de módulo
modal, modal, del modo
  modal interval,
  intervalo modal
mode, moda
model¹,
  demostrar, modelar
model², maqueta, modelo
  model problem,
  problema modelo
  model situation,
  situación modelo
  number model,
  modelo númerico
  physical model,
  modelo físico
  quantitative model,
  modelo cuantitativo
  regression model,
  modelo de regresión
modify, modificar
modular, modular
module system,
  sistema de módulo
modulus of a complex
  number, módulo de
  un número complejo
Modus Ponens,

Modus Ponens
Modus Tollens,
  Modus Tollens
momentum, inercia
monitor¹,
  monitorear, observar
  atentamente
monitor², monitor
monomial, monomio
  common monomial
  factor, factor común
  del monomio
  greatest monomial
  factor, factor común
  mayor del monomio
  monomial square
  root, raíz cuadrada
  monómica
monotonic law,
  ley de monotonía
month, mes
  months of the year,
  meses del año
monthly, mensualmente
more, más
  more than,
  más de, más que
morning, mañana
most, el más grande,
  el mayor
mostly, mayormente,
  las más de las veces
motion, movimiento
  motion problems,
  problemas de móviles,
  problemas del movi-
  miento
  uniform motion,
  movimiento uniforme
move, mover, moverse
movement, movimiento
mpg (miles per gallon),
  millas por galón

mph (miles per hour),
millas por hora
multidimensional,
multidimensional
multi-fold,
doblaje múltiple
multilateral, multilateral
multinomial, multinomial
multinomial coefficient,
coeficiente multinómico
multiple[1], múltiple
multiple-choice,
opción múltiple
multiple representations, representaciones múltiples
multiple roots,
raíces múltiples
multiple variables,
de varias variables
multiple[2], múltiplo
common multiple,
múltiplo común
lowest common multiple, mínimo común múltiplo
multiplicand,
multiplicando
multiplication,
multiplicación
associative property of multiplication,
propiedad asociativa de multiplicación
cancellation law of multiplication,
ley de cancelación de la multiplicación
Closure Axiom of Multiplication,
axioma de clausura de

multiplicación, axioma de clausura de la multiplicación
commutative property of multiplication,
propiedad conmutativa de la multiplicación
cross-multiplication,
multiplicación cruzada, producto cruzado de términos, producto de la primera fracción por la inversa de la segunda
distributive property of multiplication over addition,
propiedad distributiva de la multiplicación respecto a la suma
identity property of multiplication,
propiedad neutro de la multiplicación, característica de identidad de la multiplicación,
multiplication property of inequality,
propiedad multiplicativa de la desigualdad
multiplication property of zero,
propiedad multiplicativa del cero
multiplication sign,
signo de multiplición
multiplication table,
tabla de multiplicación, tabla de multiplicar, tabla pitagórica
nested multiplication, multiplicación anidada

scalar multiplication,
multiplicación escalar
**zero property of mul-
tiplication,** propiedad
multiplicativa del cero
multiplicative,
multiplicativo
**multiplicative
identity,** identidad
multiplicativa
**multiplicative
inverse,** inverso
multiplicativo
multiplicity, multiplicidad
multiplier, multiplicador
multiply, multiplicar
cross-multiply,
usar la multiplicación
cruzada, multiplicar la
primera fracción por la
inversa de la segunda
mutually disjoint,
recíprocamente
desligados
mutually exclusive,
mutuamente excluidos
**mutually exclusive
events,** eventos que se
excluyen mutuamente
**mutually exclusive
sets,** conjuntos mu-
tuamente excluyentes
mutually perpendicular,
perpendiculares recí-
procas

N

nabla operator,
operador nabla
name[1], llamarse, nombrar,
denominar
name[2], nombre
Napier's bones,
ábaco de Napier
narrow, estrecho
natural, natural
**natural logarithm
(natural log),**
logaritmo natural,
logaritmo neperiano
natural number,
número natural
nature, naturaleza, índole
nature of the roots,
naturaleza de las raí-
ces
naught, nada, cero
nautical, náutico
nautical mile,
milla marina,
milla náutica
navigate, navegar
navigation, navegación
**n-dimensional vector
space,** espacio vecto-
rial de n dimensiones,
espacio vectorial
n-dimensional
near, cerca, cercano,
próximo
nearer than,
más cercano que,
más próximo que
nearest, el más cercano,
el más próximo

nearest degree,
grado más cercano
nearest tenth,
décima más cercana
necessary, necesario
necessary and sufficient condition,
condición necesaria
y suficiente
necessary but not sufficient condition,
condición necesaria
pero no suficiente
necessary condition,
condición necesaria
negate, negar
negation, negación
negative, negativo
false negative,
falsa negación,
falso negativo
negative carry,
acarreo negativo
negative correlation,
correlación negativa
negative exponent,
potencia de exponente
negativo
negative integer,
entero negativo
negative number,
número negativo
negative proposition,
proposición negativa
negative real number, número
real negativo
negative reciprocal,
recíproco negativo
negative slope,
pendiente negativa
negative sign,
signo negativo

negligible, insignificante
neighboring, de al lado
nested multiplication,
multiplicación anidada
net[1], ganar neto
net[2], red
net[3], limpio, neto
net earnings,
ingresos limpios,
ingresos netos
network, red
neutral element,
elemento neutro
never, nunca, jamás
never-ending,
interminable, sin fin
new, nuevo
Newton's method,
método de Newton
next, siguiente, próximo
next to,
al lado de
next-to-last,
penúltimo
nickel, moneda de cinco
centavos
night, noche
nine, nueve
ninth, noveno
node, nódulo
nominal, nominal
nominal value,
valor nominal
nonadjacent,
no adyacente
nonadjacent angles,
ángulos no adyacentes
nonadjacent side,
lado no adyacente
nonadjacent side of a triangle,
lado no adyacente de
un triángulo

nonagon, nonágono
non-centered conic,
  cónica no centrada
noncollinear, no colineal
  **noncollinear set
  of points,** conjunto de
  puntos no colineales
non-conventional,
  no convencional
non-coplanar,
  no coplanar
non-degenerate,
  no degenerado
non-dense, no denso
non-denumerable set, conjunto no numerable
none, ninguno
non-empty set,
  conjunto no vacio
non-enumerable set, conjunto no enumerado
non-Euclidean geometry, geometría no
  euclidiana
non-homogenous,
  no homogéneo
non-mathematical sentence, oración no
  matemática
non-negative numbers,
  números no negativos
non-periodic function,
  función no periódica
non-positive numbers,
  números no positivos
non-reflexive relation,
  relación no reflexiva
non-repeating decimal,
  decimal no periódico
nonstandard, no estándar
  **nonstandard
  analysis,** análisis
  no estándar

**nonstandard
measure,** medida
  no estándar
**nonstandard
representations,**
  representaciones
  no estándares
nonstandard units,
  unidades no estándares
non-symmetric relation,
  relación asimétrica
non-terminating continued fraction,
  fracción continua
  interminable
non-terminating decimal,
  decimal infinito
non-transitive relation,
  relación no transitiva
non-zero, no cero
noon, mediodía
norm, norma, regla
normal, normal
  main normal,
  normal principal
  normal curve,
  curva normal
  normal distribution,
  distribución normal
normalize, normalizar
normalized form,
  forma normalizada
north, norte
northeast, noreste
northwest, noroeste
not equal to,
  no igual a, no equivalente a, distinto de
notation, anotación,
  notación
  contracted notation,
  notación contraída

decimal notation, notación decimal

expanded notation, notación desarrollada, notación explícita

function notation, notación de la función

interval notation, notación por intervalos

literal notation, notación literal

set-builder notation, notación de construcción de conjuntos

scientific notation, notación científica

sigma notation, notación sigma

standard notation, notación estándar

note[1], notar, anotar

note[2], apunte, nota

notebook, cuaderno

nothing, nada

notice, darse cuenta, percatarse

notion, noción

nowhere dense, considerablemente denso

nth, enésimo

nth root, raíz elevada a un exponente n

nth term, término elevado a un exponente n

null, nulo

null circle, círculo nulo

null divisor, divisor nulo

null element, elemento nulo

null hypothesis, hipótesis nula

null set, conjunto nulo

number, número

approximate number, número aproximado

binary number, número binario

borrowed number, número prestado

cardinal number, número cardinal

compatible numbers, números compatibles

complex number, número complejo

composite number, número compuesto

compound number, número compuesto

counting number, número de cuenta

cubic number, número cúbico

decimal number, número decimal

decimal number system, sistema númerico decimal

directed number, número dirigido

even number, número par

even whole number, número entero par

fractional number, número fraccionario

imaginary number, número imaginario

incommensurable number, número in-

conmesurable
inverse number,
número inverso
irrational number,
número irracional
mixed number,
número mixto
natural number,
número natural
negative integer,
entero negativo
**negative real
number,** número
real negativo
number axis,
eje numérico
number in words,
número escrito en
palabras
number line,
línea numérica
number model,
modelo númerico
number sentence,
oración numérica
number system,
sistema númerico
number theory,
teoría de números,
teoría numérica
number of strokes,
número de golpes
odd number,
número impar,
número non
odd whole number,
número entero impar
one-digit number,
número de un dígito
opposite number,
número opuesto
ordinal number,
número ordinal

perfect number,
número perfecto
prime number,
número primo
positive number,
número positivo
**positive rational
number,** número
racional positivo
positive real number,
número positivo real
**pure imaginary
number,** número
imaginario puro
pure real number,
número real puro
random number,
número al azar
rational number,
número racional
real number,
número real
rounded number,
número redondeado
scale number,
número de escala
square number,
número cuadrado
Sterling number,
número de Sterling
summed numbers,
sumandos
three-digit number,
número de tres dígitos
**transcendental
number,** número
trascendental
triangle number,
número triangular
triangular number,
número triangular
unknown number,
número desconocido

unsigned number,
número sin signo
whole number,
número entero
numbered, numerado
numeral, numérico(a),
numeral
   Roman numeral,
   número romano
numeration, numeración
numerator, numerador
numerical, numérico
   **numerical calcula-
   tion,** cálculo numérico
   **numerical coef-
   ficient,** coeficiente
   numérico
   numerical constant,
   constante numérica
   **numerical expres-
   sion,** expresión
   numérica
   numerical function,
   función numérica
   **numerical integra-
   tion,** integración
   numérica
   numerical order,
   orden numérico
   numerical pattern,
   patrón numérico
   numerical problem,
   problema númerico
   numerical sentence,
   oración numérica
   numerical solution,
   solución numérica
   numerical symbol,
   símbolo numérico
   numerical table,
   tabla numérica
numerically,
   numéricamente

object, objeto
objective, objetivo
oblique, oblicuo
   oblique triangle,
   triángulo oblicuo
oblong, oblongo
observation, observación
observe, observar, ver,
darse cuenta
obsolete, obsoleto,
fuera de uso
obtain, obtener
obtuse, obtuso
   obtuse angle,
   ángulo obtuso
   obtuse triangle,
   triángulo obtuso
obvious, obvio
occasional, de vez en
cuando, esporádico
occur, ocurrir
occurrence, ocurrencia
octadic, octádico
octagon, octágono
octahedron, octaedro
octal system, sistema octal
odd, extraño, raro,
impar, non
   odd function,
   función impar
   odd integer,
   entero impar
   odd number,
   número impar,
   número non
   odd whole number,
   número entero impar
odds, probabilidad

old, viejo, mayor,
   más grande
omit, omitir
on, en, sobre
once, una vez
one, uno
   one at a time,
   de uno a uno,
   uno a la vez
**one cycle of a trigonomet-
ric function,**
   un ciclo de una fun-
   ción trigonométrica
one-by-one, de uno en uno
one-digit number,
   número de un dígito
one-dimensional,
   unidimensional,
   de una dimensión
   **one-dimensional
   space,** espacio
   unidemensional
one-half method,
   método de la mitad
**one-half the circumfer-
ence of a circle,**
   la mitad de la circun-
   ferencia de un círculo
ones, unidades
   ones place,
   posición de las unida-
   des, las unidades
one-sided, (de) un lado
one-tailed test,
   prueba de una cola
**one-to-many correspon-
dence,** corresponden-
   cia de uno a muchos
**one-to-one correspon-
dence,** correspon-
   dencia de uno a uno,
   correspondencia
   biunívoca

one-to-one function,
   función de uno a uno
one-to-one mapping,
   barrido biunívoco
onto, en, sobre
open[1], abrir
open[2], abierto
   open arc,
   arco abierto
   open circle,
   círculo abierto
   open curve,
   curva abierta
   open downward,
   abrir hacia abajo
   open expression,
   expresión abierta
   open figure,
   figura abierta
   open half-plane,
   medio plano abierto
   open interval,
   intervalo abierto
   **open number
   sequence,**
   secuencia de
   números abiertos
   open polygon,
   polígono abierto
   open region,
   región abierta
   open sentence,
   proposición abierta
   open set,
   conjunto abierto
   open upward,
   abrir hacia arriba
operation, operación
   **addition as a binary
   operation,** suma como
   operación binaria
   additive operation,
   operación aditiva

arithmetic operation, operación aritmética

base operation, operación básica

binary operation, operación binaria

biconditional binary operation, operación binaria bicondicional

inverse operation, operación inversa

left-hand operation, operación del lado izquierdo

logical operation, operación lógica

mathematical operation, operación matemática

operation with basic numbers, operación con números elementales

operation with decimals, operación con decimales

operation with fractions, operación con fracciones

operation with monomial, operación con monomio

operation with set, operación de conjunto

one-half method, método de la mitad

order of operations, orden de operaciones

operational method, método operativo, operación, método operacional

operative symbol, símbolo operativo

operator, operador

Laplacian operator, laplaciano escalar, laplaciano de un campo escalar

nabla operator, operador nabla

opposite, opuesto(a), contrario, de lado opuesto, frontero

opposite angles, ángulos opuestos

opposite isometry, isometría opuesta

opposite leg, cateto opuesto

opposite number, número opuesto

opposite orientation, orientación opuesta

opposite point, punto opuesto

opposite rays, rayos opuestos

opposite sequence, secuencia opuesta

opposite side, lado opuesto

opposite side in a right triangle, lado opuesto de un triángulo recto

opposite transformation, transformación opuesta

opposite vertex, vértice opuesto

oppositely directed, dirigidos opuestamente

optics, óptica

optimal approximation,

aproximación óptima
optimum, óptimo
option, opción
optional, opcional
oral representations,
representaciones
orales
orbit¹, orbitar
orbit², órbita
order¹, ordenar, poner
en orden
order², orden
alphabetical order,
orden alfabético
ascending order,
orden ascendente
cyclic order,
orden cíclico
descending order,
orden descendente
logical order,
orden lógico
numerical order,
orden numérico
order of magnitude,
orden de magnitud
order of operations,
orden de operaciones
order preserved,
orden mantenido
**order-preserving
map,** mapa del orden
preservado
order property,
propiedad del orden
order relation,
relación de orden
out of order,
fuera de orden
reverse order,
orden inverso
uniqueness of order,
singularidad de orden

ordered, ordenado, metódico, disciplinado
ordered field,
campo ordenado
ordered pair,
par ordenado
ordering, orden, arreglo
ordinal, ordinal
ordinal number,
número ordinal
ordinary, ordinario
ordinate, ordenada
organize, organizar
organized chart,
gráfico organizado
orient, orientar
orientation, orientación
orientation angle,
ángulo de orientación
orientational invariance,
invariabilidad orienta-
cional
oriented, orientado(a)
oriented curve,
curva orientada
oriented surface,
superficie orientada
origin, origen
shift of origin,
traslado del origen
**turn about the ori-
gin,** girar alrededor
del origen
original, original
orthocenter, ortocentro
orthogonal, ortogonal
**orthogonal projec-
tion,** proyección
ortogonal
orthonormal, ortonormal
orthonormal base,
base ortonormal
oscillate, oscilar

oscillation, oscilación
oscilloscope, osciloscopio
osculating plane,
　　plano osculador
ostacle, obstáculo
ounce (oz.), onza
out, fuera
　　out of order,
　　fuera de orden
　　out of sequence,
　　fuera de secuencia
outcome, resultado, conse-
　　cuencia, respuesta
　　favorable outcome,
　　resultado favorable
　　outcome set,
　　conjunto resultado
　　possible outcome,
　　resultado posible
outer, externo, exterior
　　outer term,
　　término exterior
outlier, valor atípico,
　　valor extremo
outline, bosquejo, reseña
outmost, el más externo,
　　el más exterior
outpace, sobrepasar,
　　exceder
output, datos de salida,
　　salida, potencia
outside, fuera, exterior
outstanding, sobresaliente
outward, hacia afuera
oval, óvalo
over¹, terminado
over², sobre, por encima de
overlap¹, traslapar
overlap², traslape
overlapping triangles,
　　triángulos intercalados
overtaking, alcance
oz. (ounce), onza

P

pace, paso, ritmo
pair¹, asociar, emparejar
pair², par
　　angle pairs,
　　pares de ángulos
　　conjugate pairs,
　　pares conjugados
　　coordinate pairs,
　　pares coordenados
　　linear pair,
　　par lineal
　　ordered pair,
　　par ordenado
　　pair of factors,
　　par de factores
　　prime pair,
　　par primo
palindrome, palíndromo
pan balance,
　　balanza de platillos
paper, papel
parabola, parábola
parabolic, parabólica
paraboloid, paraboloide
paradox, paradoja
paradoxical, paradójico
paragraph proof,
　　prueba de párrafo
parallel, paralelo
　　**parallel line
　　segments,**
　　segmentos de
　　rectas paralelas
　　parallel lines,
　　líneas paralelas
　　parallel postulate,
　　postulado del paralelo
　　de Euclides

parallel projection,
proyección paralela
parallel section,
sección paralela
parallel symbol,
signo de paralelismo
parallel shift,
traslado paralelo
parallelepiped,
paralelepípedo
parallelism, paralelismo
**parallelism pre-
served,** paralelismo
mantenido
parallelogram,
paralelogramo
parameter, parámetro
parametric, paramétrico
parametric curve,
curva paramétrica
**parenthesis (pl. parenthe-
ses),** paréntesis
parity, paridad
part, parte
corresponding parts,
partes correspondien-
tes
integral part,
parte integral
partial, parcial
partial derivative,
derivada parcial
**partial differential
equation,** ecuación
en derivadas parciales
partial product,
producto parcial
partial summation,
sumatoria
particular, particular
particular case,
caso particular
partition, división,

partición
partition postulate,
postulado de la parti-
ción
part-to-part ratio,
razón parte-parte,
cociente parte-parte,
relación parte-parte
part-to-whole ratio,
razón parte-todo,
cociente parte-todo,
relación parte-todo
Pascal's triangle,
triángulo de Pascal
pass through, atravesar
**pass through a
given point,** pasar
por un punto dado
paste[1], pegar
paste[2], pegamento
path, trayectoria, camino,
sendero
closed path,
contorno cerrado
open path,
contorno abierto
straight path,
recta
pattern[1], seguir un patrón
pattern[2], patrón
algebraic pattern,
patrón algebraico
geometric pattern,
patrón geométrico
numerical pattern,
patrón numérico
pattern of numbers,
patrón de números
patternless, sin patrón,
irregular
peculiar, peculiar
peg, estaca
pendulum, péndulo

penny, centavo
pentadecagon, pentadecágono
pentagon, pentágono
per, por
percent, por ciento
   percent decrease, por ciento de disminución, disminución porcentual
   percent increase, por ciento de aumento, incremento porcentual
   percent of a quantity, porcentaje de una cantidad
   percent of decrease, porciento de disminución
   percent of increase, porciento de incremento
percentage, porcentaje
   annual percentage rate (APR), tasa de interés anual
   percentage change, cambio percentil
   percentage error, error de porcentaje
   percentage point, punto de porcentaje
percentile, percentil
   percentile rank, rango percentil
perceptive, perspicaz
perfect, perfecto
   perfect cubic expression, expresión cúbica perfecta
   perfect number, número perfecto

perfect square, cuadrado perfecto
perfect square trinomial, trinomio cuadrado perfecto
perform, desempeñar, realizar, rendir, actuar
   perform the operation, ejecutar la operación
performance, desempeño
performing computation, realización de cálculos
perimeter, perímetro
period, período
   period of a repeating decimal, período de un decimal periódico
   recurring period, período recurrente
periodic, periódico
   periodic curve, curva periódica
   periodic decimals, decimales periódicos
   periodic fraction, fracción periódica
   periodic function, función periódica
periodicity, periodicidad
peripheral, periférico
permutation, permutación
   alternate permutation, permutación alterna
   permutation with repetition, permutación con repetición
perpendicular, perpendicular
   common perpendicular, perpendicular común

perpendicular bisector, mediatriz, bisector perpendicular
perpendicular bisector concurrence, concurrencia de bisectrices perpendiculares
perpendicular height (of a triangle), altura (de un triángulo)
perpendicular lines, líneas perpendiculares
perpendicular planes, planos perpendiculares
perpendicular segment, segmento perpendicular
perpendicularity, perpendicularidad
personal references for capacity, referencias personales de capacidad
personal references for units of mass, referencias personales de unidades de masa
perspective, perspectiva
persuade, persuadir
persuasive, persuasivo
per-unit rate, tasa por unidad
phase, fase
be in phase, estar en fase
be out of phase, discordar en fase
phase angle, ángulo de fase
phase displacement, desplazamiento de fase

phase lag, retraso de fase
phase lead, avance de fase
phase shift, desplazamiento de fase
phenomena (sing. phenomenon), fenómeno
mathematical phenomena, fenómeno matemático
social phenomena, fenómeno social
phrase, frase
physical, físico
physical constant, constante física
physical model, modelo físico
physical object, objeto físico
physical phenomena, fenómeno de la física
physics, física
pi, pi
pick, elegir, escoger
pick up, recoger
pictogram, pictograma, pictografía
pictorial representation, representación pictórica
picture, dibujo
picture graph, gráfica de dibujos
pie chart, gráfica de pastel, gráfica circular
piece, parte, segmento, pedazo

piecewise, en pedazos
    piecewise continuous, continuidad por piezas, continuidad en piezas continuas
pile, pila
pint (pt.), pinta
pivot[1], girar, pivotar
pivot[2], pivote
pivoting, girando, de giro
place[1], poner
place[2], posición, lugar
    place holder, en lugar de
    place value, valor posicional, valor del espacio
placeholder, marcador de posición
plan, plano
planar, planar
plane, plano(a)
    Cartesian coordinate plane, plano coordenado cartesiano
    collinear planes, planos colineales
    complex plane, plano complejo
    concurrent planes, planos coexistentes
    coordinate plane, plano coordenado
    half-plane, medio plano
    imaginary plane, plano imaginario
    inclined plane, plano inclinado
    open half-plane, medio plano abierto
    osculating plane, plano osculador
perpendicular
planes, planos perpendiculares
plane geometric figures, figuras geométricas planas
plane geometry, geometría plana, geometría euclidiana
plane of symmetry, plano de simetría
plane section, sección planar
tangent plane, plano tangente
plausibility, verosimilitud
plausible, creíble, verosímil, plausible
plenty, mucho, más que suficiente
pliable, flexible
plot[1], plotear, dibujar en un plano, trazar puntos, asentar, ubicar
    plot points, asentar puntos
plot[2], plano, trama, representación gráfica
    box plot, gráfico de caja, gráfica de caja
    box-and-whisker plot, diagrama de caja y bigotes
    line plot, gráfica de líneas
    scatter plot, gráfico de dispersión
    stem and leaf plot, diagrama de tallo y hoja
plotting, plano
plus, más

plus sign, signo de adición
point[1], indicar, apuntar,
    señalar, dirigirse hacia
point[2], punto
    collinear points,
    puntos colineales
    concyclic points,
    puntos cocíclicos
    coplanar points,
    puntos coplanares
    corner point,
    esquina, punto
    de esquina
    critical point,
    punto crítico
    crossing point,
    intersección
    decimal point,
    punto decimal
    distinct points,
    puntos distintos
    endpoint,
    extremo,
    punto extremo,
    punto final
    external point,
    punto externo
    fixed point,
    punto fijo
    focal point,
    punto focal
    image point,
    punto imagen
    imaginary point,
    punto imaginario
    inflection point,
    punto de inflexión
    inner point,
    punto interno,
    punto interior
    integral point,
    punto integral
    interior point,

punto interior
intersecting point,
punto de intersección
lateral point,
punto lateral
lattice points,
red de puntos
locus of points,
locus de puntos
maximum point,
punto máximo
midpoint,
punto medio
minimum point,
punto mínimo
opposite point,
punto opuesto
percentage point,
punto de porcentaje
point at infinity,
punto en el infinito
point of concurrency,
punto de concurrencia
point of contact,
punto de contacto
point of inflection,
punto de inflexión,
point of intersection,
punto de intersección
point of reflection,
punto de reflexión
point of symmetry,
punto de simetría
point of tangency,
punto de tangencia
point reflection,
reflexión de puntos
point space,
espacio de puntos
**point-slope
equation of a line,**
ecuación punto-pen-
diente de una recta

point-slope form of line, forma pendiente-punto de una línea

radiant point, punto radiante

sample point, punto modelo

trisection point, punto de trisección

turning point, punto de giro

vanishing point, punto tendiente a cero

pointed, afilado, filoso, dirigido a

pointy, afilado, filoso

Poisson distribution, distribución de Poisson

polar, polar

polar coordinate, coordenada polar

polar vector, vector polar

pole, polo

poll, encuesta

polygon, polígono

circumscribed polygon, polígono circunscrito

concave polygon, polígono cóncavo

congruent polygons, polígonos congruentes

convex polygon, polígono convexo

equiangular polygon, polígono equiangular

equilateral polygon, polígono equilátero

frequency polygon, polígono de la frecuencia

inscribed polygon, polígono inscrito

irregular polygon, polígono irregular

open polygon, polígono abierto

polygon circumscribed about a circle, polígono circunscrito a un círculo

polygon circumscribed in a circle, polígono circunscrito en un círculo

regular polygon, polígono regular

similar polygons, polígonos similares

polygonal line, línea poligónica

polyhedron, poliedro

circumscribed polyhedron, poliedro circunscrito

concave polyhedron, poliedro cóncavo

face of a polyhedron, cara de un poliedro

regular polyhedron, poliedro regular

polynomial, polinomio, polinomial

homogenous polynomial, polinomio homogéneo

polynomial equation, ecuación polinómica

polynomial expression, expresión polinomial

polynomial function, función polinómica

population, población
position¹, posicionar
position², posición
position angle,
ángulo de posición
position vector,
posición de vector
standard position,
posición estándar,
posición normal
positive, positivo
false positive,
falsa afirmación, falso
positivo
positive correlation,
correlación positiva
**positive definite
matrix,** matriz defini-
da positiva
positive exponent,
potencia de exponente
positivo
positive integer,
entero positivo
positive number,
número positivo
positive power of 10,
potencia positiva en
base 10
**positive rational
number,** número
racional positivo
positive real number,
número positivo real
positive sign,
signo positivo
positive slope,
pendiente positiva
possibility, posibilidad
possible, posible
possible event,
evento posible
possible outcome,

resultado posible
post meridian (p.m.),
post merídiem,
postmeridiano (p.m.)
postulate¹, postular
postulate², postulado
**angle addition
postulate,**
postulado de la
suma de los ángulos
distance postulate,
postulado de la dis-
tancia
equality postulates,
postulados de la
igualdad
**Euclidean Parallel
Postulate,** paralelo
postulado de Euclides
**Euclid's Fifth Postu-
late,** quinto postulado
de Euclides
parallel postulate,
postulado del paralelo
de Euclides
partition postulate,
postulado de la parti-
ción
reflective postulate,
postulado reflexivo
**substitution postu-
late,** postulado en la
sustitución
transitive postulate,
postulado transitivo
**trichotomy postu-
late,** postulado de
tricotomía
postulational,
postulacional
postulational system,
sistema postulacional
potential, potencial

vector potential, potencial vectorial
pound (lb.), libra
power, exponente, potencia, poder, electricidad
  integral power, potencia integral
  positive power of 10, potencia positiva en base 10
  power of 10, en base 10
  power series, serie de potencias
  power-of-product law, ley de potencia de un producto
  power-of-quotient law, ley de la potencia de un cociente
  powers of i, potencias de i
powerful, poderoso
powerless, sin poder
practical, práctico
practice¹, practicar, ensayar
practice², práctica
praise¹, halagar
praise², halago
precede, preceder
precedence, precedencia
precedent, precedente
preceding, precedente
precise, preciso
precision, precisión
  precision measurement, medida de precisión
predict, predecir, prever
predictable, predecible
predicted, previsto
prediction, predicción

prefix, prefijo
preimage, preimagen
prejudiced, parcial
premise, premisa
prepare, preparar
prescribe, prescribir
preserved, preservado(a)
pressure, presión
  barometric pressure, presión barométrica
previous, previo, anterior
price, precio
primary, principal, primario
prime, primo
  Mersenne primes, números primos de Mersenne
  prime factor, factor primo
  prime factorization, factorización prima
  prime number, número primo
  prime pair, par primo
  prime polynomial, polinomio primo
  relatively prime, relativamente primo
primitive triangle, triángulo primitivo
principal¹, director de la escuela
principal², principal
  principal angle, ángulo principal
  principal cubic root, raíz cúbica principal
  principal diagonal, diagonal principal
  principal nth root of k, raíz principal enési-

ma de (k)
principal root,
raíz principal
principal solution,
solución principal
principal square root,
raíz cuadrada principal
principle, principio
  counting principle,
  principio de cuenta
  **Fundamental
  Counting Principle,**
  principio básico
  de conteo
  principle of duality,
  principio de dualidad
  substitution principle, principio de
  sustitución
prism, prisma
  antiprism,
  antiprisma
  rectangular prism,
  prisma cuadrangular
  regular prism,
  prisma regular
  right prism,
  prisma recto
  triangular prism,
  prisma triangular
  truncated prism,
  prisma truncado
prismatic, prismático
probability, probabilidad
  **binomial probability
  formula,** fórmula de
  probabilidad binomial
  calculated probability, probabilidad
  calculada
  conditional probability, probabilidad

condicional
  empirical probability,
  probabilidad empírica
  experimental probability, probabilidad
  experimental
  **probability of an
  event,** probabilidad
  de un evento
  probability scale,
  escala de probabilidad
  probability theory,
  teoría de la probabilidad
  probability with replacement, probabilidad con reemplazo
  **probability without
  replacement,** probabilidad sin reemplazo
  simple probability,
  probabilidad simple
  theoretical probability, probabilidad
  teórica
  uniform probability,
  probabilidad uniforme
problem, problema
  algebraic problem,
  problema algebraico
  model problem,
  problema modelo
  motion problems,
  problemas de móviles, problemas del
  movimiento
  numerical problem,
  problema númerico
  verbal problem,
  problema verbal
  word problem,
  problema escrito,
  problema verbal

problem solving, solución de problemas

problem solving strategies, estrategias para resolver los problemas

problematic, problemático

procedure, procedimiento

step-by-step procedure, procedimiento sistemático

trial and error procedure, aproximaciones sucesivas

process¹, procesar

process², proceso

process of elimination, proceso de eliminación

produce, producir

product, producto

algebraic product, producto algebraico

cross product, producto transversal

dyadic product, producto diádico

Hermitian product, producto hermítico

inner product, producto interior

power-of-product law, ley de potencia de un producto

product of binomials, producto de binomios

product property of proportions, propiedad de multiplicación de las proporciones

zero product property, propiedad del producto cero

profit, utilidades, renta, ganancias netas, beneficio

program¹, programar

program², programa

programmable calculator, calculadora programable

programming language, lenguaje de programación

progression, progresión

arithmetic progression, progresión aritmética

geometric progression, progresión geométrica

project¹, proyectar

project², proyecto

projection, proyección

proof, prueba, evidencia

analytical proof, prueba analítica

deductive proof, prueba deductiva

direct proof, prueba directa

formal proof, prueba formal

indirect proof, prueba indirecta

informal indirect proof, prueba indirecta informal

logic proof, prueba lógica

proof by contradiction, prueba por contradicción

proof by exhaustion, prueba por agotamiento de opciones

proof by induction,
prueba por inducción
transformational proof, prueba de transformación
two-column proof,
prueba a dos columnas
visual proof,
prueba visual
proper, propio
proper fraction,
fracción propia,
quebrado propio
proper set,
conjunto propio
proper subset,
subconjunto propio
property, propiedad,
atributo, característica, efectos, bienes
addition property of inequality,
propiedad aditiva
de la desigualdad
addition property of zero, propiedad
de la suma del cero
additive property of equality,
propiedad aditiva
de la igualdad
angle properties of circles, propiedades
de los ángulos en
círculos, propiedades
angulares de círculos
associative property,
propiedad asociativa
associative property of addition, propiedad
asociativa de la suma
associative property

of multiplication,
propiedad asociativa
de multiplicación
closure property,
propiedad de clausura
commutative property, propiedad conmutativa
commutative property of addition,
propiedad conmutativa de la suma
commutative property of multiplication,
propiedad conmutativa de la multiplicación
distributive property,
propiedad distributiva
distributive property of multiplication over addition,
propiedad distributiva
de la multiplicación
respecto a la suma
general associative property, propiedad
general asociativa
general commutative property, propiedad
general conmutativa
identity property,
propiedad de identidad
identity property of addition, propiedad
neutro de la suma,
característica de identidad de la suma
identity property of multiplication,
propiedad neutro de la
multiplicación, característica de identidad
de la multiplicación,

inverse property,
propiedad de inversa
multiplication property of inequality,
propiedad multiplicativa de la desigualdad
multiplication property of zero,
propiedad multiplicativa del cero
order property,
propiedad del orden
product property of proportions,
propiedad de multiplicación de las proporciones
properties preserved,
propiedades mantenidas
property of an operation, propiedad de una operación
property of density,
propiedad de densidad
reflexive property of congruence,
propiedad reflexiva de la congruencia
reflexive property of equality, propiedad reflexiva de la igualdad
substitution property, propiedad de sustitución
substitution property of equality,
principio de sustitución de la igualdad
symmetric property of equality,
propiedad simétrica de la igualdad

symmetrical property, propiedad simétrica
transitive property,
propiedad transitiva
transitive property of equality,
propiedad transitiva de la igualdad
transitive property of inequality,
propiedad transitiva de las desigualdades
trichotomy property,
propiedad de tricotomía
zero product property, propiedad del producto cero
zero property of addition, propiedad del cero de la suma
zero property of multiplication,
propiedad multiplicativa del cero
proportion, proporción
direct proportion,
proporción directa
inverse proportion,
proporción inversa
product property of proportions, propiedad de multiplicación de las proporciones
proportion by addition, proporción por adición
proportion by alternation,
proporción por alternación
proportion by

subtraction, proporción por resta
simplified proportion, proporción simplificada
proportional, proporcional
inversely proportional quantities, cantidades inversamente proporcionales
mean proportional, proporcional media
proportional line segments, segmentos de líneas proporcionale
proportional quantities, cantidades proporcionales
proportional reasoning, razonamiento proporcional
proposal, propuesta, proposición
propose, proponer
proposition, proposición, propuesta
hypothetical proposition, proposición hipotética
inverse proposition, proposición inversa
negative proposition, proposición negativa
protractor, transportador
prove, probar, comprobar, verificar
proven, probado
provide, proporcionar, proveer
pseudo-scalar, pseudoescalar
pt. (pint), pinta

pulley, polea
purchase, comprar
pure, puro
pure imaginary number, número imaginario puro
pure math, matemáticas puras
pure quadratic equation, ecuación cuadrática pura
pure real number, número real puro
put, poner, colocar
put together, juntar, unir
puzzle, puzle, rompecabezas
puzzling, extraño, misterioso
pyramid, pirámide
rectangular pyramid, pirámide rectangular
right pyramid, pirámide recta
triangular pyramid, pirámide triangular
pyramidal surface, superficie piramidal
Pythagorean, pitagórico
Pythagorean identity, teorema de Pitágoras
Pythagorean theorem, teorema pitagórico
Pythagorean triple, triple pitagórico

Q

qt. (quart), cuarto de galón
quadrangle, cuadrángulo
quadrant, cuadrante
quadrantal angle,
   ángulo cuadrantal
quadratic, cuadrático
   **linear-quadratic
   system,** sistema
   cuadrático lineal
   **pure quadratic
   equation,** ecuación
   cuadrática pura
   quadratic curve,
   curva cuadrática
   quadratic equation,
   ecuación cuadrática
   quadratic formula,
   fórmula cuadrática
   quadratic function,
   función cuadrática
   quadratic inequality,
   desigualdad cuadráti-
   ca
   **quadratic-linear
   equation system,**
   sistema de ecuación
   cuadrático-lineal
   quadratic trinomial,
   trinomio cuadrático
   **standard form of a
   quadratic equation,**
   forma regular de una
   ecuación cuadrática
quadratrix, cuadratriz
quadrature of a conic,
   cuadratura de una
   sección cuadrático-
   lineal

quadrilateral, cuadrilátero
quadruple, cuadruple
quality, calidad, cualidad
quantifier, cuantificador
quantify, cuantificar
quantitative, cuantitativo
   quantitative model,
   modelo cuantitativo
quantity, cantidad
quantum mechanics,
   mecánica cuántica
quart (qt.), cuarto de galón
quarter, cuarto, moneda de
   25 centavos
   quarter-circle,
   cuarto de círculo
   quarter-turn,
   giro de un cuarto
quartile, cuartil
quaternion, cuaternión
question[1], preguntar,
   cuestionar
question[2], pregunta,
   cuestión
   clarifying questions,
   preguntas aclaratorias
questionable,
   cuestionable, dudoso
quintupling,
   quintuplicación
quiz, prueba
quota, cuota
quotient, cuociente
   quotient identity,
   identidad de cociente

R

radian, radián
   radian measure,

medida del radián
radiant, radiante
    radiant point,
    punto radiante
radical¹, raíz cuadrada
radical², radical
    radical equation,
    ecuación radical
    radical form,
    forma radical
    radical sign,
    signo radical
    radical symbol,
    símbolo radica
radicand, radicando
    integral radicand,
    radicando integral
radius (pl. radii), radio
    radius of a circle,
    radio de un círculo
    **radius of a circum-
    scribed circle,**
    radio del círculo
    circunscrito
    radius of a sphere,
    radio de una esfera
    **radius of an inscribed
    circle,** radio del círcu-
    lo inscrito
    radius vector,
    vector radial
raise, elevar, aumentar
    raise doubts,
    sublevar dudas
    raise to a power,
    elevar a una potencia
random,
    aleatorio, al azar
    random arrangement,
    ordenamiento al azar
    random event,
    evento al azar
    random number,

número al azar
    random process,
    proceso al azar
    random sample,
    muestra aleatoria,
    muestra al azar
    random selection,
    selección al azar
randomly, al azar
randomness, azar
range, rango
    interquartile range,
    rango intercuartílico
    range of a function,
    variación de una fun-
    ción, fluctuación de
    una función
    range of data,
    intervalo de datos,
    fluctuación de los
    datos
rank, rango
rate, velocidad, ritmo,
    paso, tasa
    **annual percentage
    rate (APR),** tasa de
    interés anual
    at the rate of,
    a razón de
    exchange rate,
    tipo de cambio,
    tasa de cambio
    **foreign exchange
    rate,** tipo de cambio
    de divisas
    interest rate,
    tasa de interés
    per-unit rate,
    tasa por unidad
    rate of change,
    tasa de cambio
    rate of depreciation,
    índice de depreciación

rate of exchange, tipo de cambio

unit rate, tarifa unitaria

ratio, proporción, razón

continued ratio, razón continua

cosecant ratio, razón cosecante

cosine ratio, razón del coseno

cotangent ratio, razón cotangente

part-to-part ratio, razón parte-parte, cociente parte-parte, relación parte-parte

part-to-whole ratio, razón parte-todo, cociente parte-todo, relación parte-todo

ratio of division, razón de la división

ratio of equality, razón de la igualdad

ratio of similitude, razón de similtud

ratio scale, escala de la razón

reciprocal ratio, razón recíproca

scale ratio, razón de la escala

secant ratio, razón secante

sine ratio, razón del seno

rational, racional

rational coefficient, coeficiente racional

rational expression, expresión racional

rational fraction, fracción racional

rational function, función racional

rational index, índice racional

rational inequality, desigualdad racional

rational number, número racional

rational root, raíz racional

rational root theorem, teorema de raíces racionales

rational thought, pensamiento racional

rationale, fundamento lógico

rationality, racionalidad

rationalization, racionalización

rationalize, racionalizar

rationalize the denominator, racionalizar el denominador

rationalizing factor, factor racionalizante

raw data, datos base, datos de fundamento, datos crudos, datos originales

ray, rayo, semirecta

initial ray, rayo inicial

opposite rays, rayos opuestos

reach[1], alcanzar, lograr

reach[2], alcance, extensión

reachable, alcanzable

reaffirm, reafirmar

reaffirmation, reafirmación

real, real

real axis,
eje real
real density,
densidad real
real domain,
dominio real
real exponent,
exponente real
real number,
número real
real number axis,
eje de los números
reales
real part,
parte real
real solution,
solución real
real square root,
raíz cuadrada real
real variable,
variable real
real world math,
matemática del
mundo real
real world situation,
situación del mundo
real
realize, darse cuenta,
percatarse
rearrange, reordenar
rearrangement,
reordenamiento
reason[1], razonar
reason[2], razón
reasonable, razonable
reasonable estimate,
estimación razonable
reasonableness,
racionabilidad
**reasonableness
of a solution,**
racionabilidad de
una solución

reasoning, razonamiento
deductive reasoning, razonamiento
deductivo
inductive reasoning, razonamiento
inductivo
law of reasoning,
ley de razonamiento
logical reasoning,
razonamiento lógico
proportional reasoning, razonamiento
proporcional
spatial reasoning,
razonamiento espacial
recalculate,
volver a calcular
reciprocal, recíproco
negative reciprocal,
recíproco negativo
reciprocal identity,
identidad recíproca
reciprocal logarithmic curve,
curva logarítmica
recíproca
reciprocal ratio,
razón recíproca
reciprocal relation,
relación recíproca
reciprocal trigonometric function,
función trigonométrica
recíproca
recognize, reconocer
recommend, recomendar,
sugerir
record[1], archivar, grabar,
escribir, anotar
record[2], archivo,
expediente
rectangle, rectángulo

golden rectangle, rectángulo áureo, rectángulo dorado

rectangular, rectangular

rectangular coordinate system, sistema rectangular de coordenadas

rectangular coordinate, coordenada rectangular

rectangular hyperbola, hipérbola rectangular

rectangular parallelepiped, paralelepípedo rectangular

rectangular prism, prima rectangular

rectangular pyramid, pirámide rectangular

rectangular solid, sólido rectangular

rectilinear, rectilíneo

rectilinear asymptote, asíntota rectilíneo

rectilinear motion, movimiento rectilíneo

rectilinearity, rectilinealidad

recuperate, recuperar

recur, repetirse, reproducirse

recurring decimal, decimal recurrente

recurring period, período recurrente

recursive, recursivo

recursive definition, definición recursiva

reduce, reducir

reduce to lowest terms, reducir a los términos mínimos

reduced equation, ecuación reducida

reduced form, forma reducida

reduced fraction, fracción reducida

reducibility, reducibilidad

reducible, reducible

reducible equation, ecuación reducible

reducible fraction, fracción reducible

reducible polynomial, polinomio reducible

redundant, redundante

refer, referir

reference angle, ángulo de referencia

reference frame, marco de referencia

reflect, reflejar

reflected image, imagen reflejada

reflecting telescope, telescopio reflector

reflection, reflexión, reflejo

angle of reflection, ángulo de refracción

glide reflection, reflexión por deslizamiento

point of reflection, punto de reflexión

point reflection, reflexión de puntos

reflection in a line, reflexión en una línea

reflective postulate, postulado reflexivo

reflex, reflejo

reflex angle,

ángulo de reflexión,
ángulo reflexivo
reflexive, reflexivo
**reflexive property
of congruence,**
propiedad reflexiva de
la congruencia
**reflexive property of
equality,** propiedad
reflexiva de la igualdad
reflexivity, reflexibilidad
refracting telescope,
telescopio dióptico
refraction, refracción
refuse, negar, rehusar
refutable, refutable
refute, refutar
region, región
   circular region,
   región circular
   critical region,
   región crítica,
   zona crítica
   exterior region,
   región exterior
   **exterior region of a
   circle,** región exterior
   de un círculo
   interior region,
   región interior
   **interior region of a
   circle,** región interior
   de un círculo
   open region,
   región abierta
   shaded region,
   región sombreada
regression, regresión
   **least squares regres-
   sion line,** línea de
   ajuste óptimo
   **regression coeffi-
   cient,** coeficiente de

regresión
   regression equation,
   ecuación de regresión
   regression model,
   modelo de regresión
regroup, reagrupar,
reconstituir
regrouping,
reagrupamiento,
reconstitución,
reagrupación
regular, regular
   **regular dodecahe-
   dron,** dodecaedro
   regular
   regular icosahedron,
   icosaedro regular
   regular matrix,
   matriz regular
   regular polygon,
   polígono regular
   regular polyhedron,
   poliedro regular
   regular prism,
   prisma regular
reinforce, reforzar
reject, rechazar
rejection, rechazo
relate, relacionar
related facts, operaciones
con números elemen-
tales relacionadas,
hechos relacionados
related statement, declaración relacionada
relation, relación
   asymmetric relation,
   relación asimétrica
   **asymmetrical rela-
   tion,** relación asimétrica
   binary relation,
   relación binaria

commutation relation, relación de conmutación
equivalence relation, relación de equivalencia
functional relation, relación funcional
identity relation, relación de identidad
inverse relation, relación inversa
irreflexive relation, relación irreflexiva
non-reflexive relation, relación no reflexiva
non-symmetric relation, relación asimétrica
non-transitive relation, relación no transitiva
reciprocal relation, relación recíproca
relation of equivalence, relación de equivalencia
relation of identity, relación de identidad
relation symbol, símbolo de relación
reversible relation, relación reversible
symmetrical relation, relación simétrica
transitive relation, relación transitiva
relationship, relación
algebraic relationship, relación algebraica
fundamental

relationship, relación fundamental
geometric relationship, relación geométrica
relative, relativo
relative efficiency, eficacia relativa
relative error, error relativo
relatively prime, relativamente primo
relativity, relatividad
theory of relativity, teoría de la relatividad
relevant information, información relevante
reliability, fiabilidad
reliable, confiable, fiable, fidedigno
remainder, restante, resto, sobrante, residuo, remanente
remaining, restante
remaining line, línea restante
remedial, paliativo, remediador, correctivo
remember, recordar, acordarse
remote interior angles, ángulos interiores remotos
remove, quitar
remove parentheses, quitar los paréntesis
rename, renombrar
repeat, repetir
repeated, repetido
repeated addition, suma repetida
repeated root,

raíz repetida
repeated subtraction,
resta repetida
repeated trials,
pruebas repetidas
repeating, repetido
repeating decimal,
decimal periódico
repetend,
factor de repetición
repetition, repetición
rephrase, reformular
replace, reemplazar,
sustituir
replacement, reemplazo
replacement set,
conjunto de reemplazo
replicable, reproducible
replicate, reproducir,
replicar
replication, reproducción,
réplica
report card,
cartilla de calificacio-
nes, boleta de califica-
ciones
report[1], reportar
report[2], informe, reporte
represent, representar
representation,
representación
**algebraic representa-
tion,** representación
algebraica
request, pedir
require, requerir
requirement, requisito
research[1], investigar
research[2], investigación
resemble, parecer
resembling, parecido
residual, residuo
residue, residuo

resolve, resolver
respect, respecto
with respect to,
con respecto a
respectively,
respectivamente
response,
respuesta, reaccción
rest, resto
restrain, impedir
restrict, restringir
restricted domain,
dominio restringido
restriction, restricción
result, resultado
resultant, resultante,
resultado posible
resultant force,
fuerza resultante
resulting, resultante
resulting equation,
ecuación resultante
retain, retener
retrieval, recuperación
retrieve, recuperar
return, volver, regresar,
devolver
reuse, volver a usar
reveal, revelar
revenue, ingresos,
inverso(a)
reverse[1], voltear, girar,
invertir
reverse the process,
invertir el proceso
reverse[2], reverso, al revés
reverse factoring,
técnica de factoriza-
ción inversa
reverse order,
orden inverso
reversibility, reversibilidad
reversible, reversible

reversible process, proceso reversible

reversible relation, relación reversible

reversible transformation, transformación reversible

review[1], examinar, revisar

review[2], examinación, revisión

revolution, revolución

    cone of revolution, cono de revolución

    cylinder of revolution, cilindro de revolución

    revolutions per minute (rpm), revoluciones por minuto

revolve, girar, dar la vuelta

rewrite, reformular, volver a escribir, reescribir

rhombohedron, romboedro

rhomboid, romboide

rhombus, rombo

rid, deshacerse de

riddle, acertijo

Riemann integral, integral de Riemann

right, correcto, derecho, recto

    right angle, ángulo recto

    right cancellation law, ley de cancelación derecha

    right circular cone, cono circular recto

    right circular cylinder, cilindro circular recto

    right cone, cono recto

    right cylinder, cilindro recto

    right prism, prisma recto

    right pyramid, pirámide recta

    right triangle, triángulo recto

    right triangle trigonometry, trigonometría de un triángulo recto

    to the right, hacia la derecha

right-hand, de mano derecha

right-handed, diestro

    right-handed trihedron, triedro directo

rigid, rígido

    rigid motion, movimiento ligero

rise, subir, ascender, aumentar

roll, rodar

roll dice, tirar dados

Rolle's Theorem, teorema de Rolle

Roman numeral, número romano

root, raíz

    common root, raíz común

    complex root, raíz compleja

    conjugate root, raíz conjugada

    cube root, raíz cúbica

    digital root, raíz digital

    distinct root,

raíz distinta
double roots,
raíces dobles
extract a root,
extraer una raíz
extraneous root,
raíz extrínseca
imaginary root,
raíz imaginaria
indicated root,
raíz indicada
integral root,
raíz de número
integrales
irrational root,
raíz irracional
**monomial square
root,** raíz cuadrada
monómica
multiple roots,
raíces múltiples
nth root,
raíz elevada a
un exponente n
principal root,
raíz principal
rational root,
raíz racional
real square root,
raíz cuadrada real
repeated root,
raíz repetida
root of a quadratic,
raíz de un número
cuadrado perfecto
root of an equation,
raíz de una ecuación
root test,
prueba de la raíz
square root,
raíz cuadrada
surd root,
raíz sorda

triple root,
raíz triple
roster form,
lista de presencia
rotate, girar, voltear,
dar vueltas
rotation, rotación
**around in a full
rotation,** una
vuelta completa
axis of rotation,
eje de rotación
body of rotation,
elemento de rotación
center of a rotation,
centro de rotación
clockwise rotation,
rotación similar al
reloj
**counterclockwise
rotation,** rotación
contraria a las agujas
del reloj
rotation axis,
eje de rotación
rotational, rotacional
rotational symmetry,
simetría rotacional
rough, áspero, aproximado,
preliminar
rough draft,
borrador
rough estimate,
estimado aproximado,
estimado preliminar,
cálculo aproximado
round[1], redondear
round off,
redondear
**round off to the
nearest tenth,**
redondear hasta el
decimal más cercano

round², redondo
    round bracket,
    corchete circular
round trip, viaje de ida y
    vuelta, viaje redondo
rounded, redondeado
    rounded number,
    número redondeado
rounding, redondeo
    rounding error,
    error de redondea-
    miento
roundness, redondez
route, ruta
routine, rutina
row, fila
    initial row,
    fila inicial
    row matrix,
    matriz fila
    row vector,
    vector fila
**rpm (revolutions per min-
ute),** revoluciones por
minuto
rule, regla, reglamento
    Chain Rule, regla de
    concatenación
    Cramer's Rule,
    regla de Cramer
    rule of elimination,
    regla de eliminación
rule out, descartar,
eliminar
ruled curve,
    curva reglada
ruler, regla

sale, rebaja, saldo, barata
salient, saliente
same, idéntico, igual,
    mismo
same, similar
sample¹, muestrear, probar
sample², muestra
    biased sample,
    muestra engañosa
    random sample,
    muestra aleatoria,
    muestra al azar
    sample data,
    muestra de datos
    sample mean,
    media modelo
    sample point,
    punto modelo
    sample space,
    espacio modelo
sampling, muestreo
    sampling error,
    error de muestreo
    sampling techniques,
    técnicas de modelaje
SAS Similarity Theorem,
    teorema de semejanza
    SAS
SAS triangle congruence,
    triángulo congruente
    SAS
satisfy, satisfacer
save, ahorrar, archivar
savings, ahorros
scalar, escalar
    pseudo-scalar,
    pseudoescalar
    scalar arc segment,

elemento escalar
de arco
scalar field,
campo escalar
scalar line element,
elemento escalar
de línea
**scalar line integral
oriented,** integral de
línea escalar orientada
scalar multiplication,
multiplicación escalar
scalar quantity,
cantidad escalar
**scalar surface ele-
ment,** elemento
escalar de superficie
scalar triple product,
producto triple esca-
lar, producto mixto
scale[1], escalar
scale[2],
báscula, escala, tama-
ño, rango, abanico
absolute scale,
escala absoluta
inner scale,
escala interior
map scale,
escala de mapa
probability scale,
escala de probabilidad
ratio scale,
escala de la razón
scale drawing,
dibujo a escala
scale number,
número de escala
scale of a graph,
escala de un gráfico
scale ratio,
razón de la escala
scalene, escaleno

scalene triangle,
triángulo escaleno
scatter, esparcir
scatter plot, gráfico
de dispersión
scattergram,
diagrama de disper-
sión, nube de puntos
school, escuela
elementary school,
escuela primaria
high school,
escuela preparatoria
junior high school,
escuela secundaria
middle school,
escuela secundaria
science, ciencia
scientific, científico
scientific calculator,
calculadora científica
scientific notation,
notación científica
scientist, científico
scope, alcance
score[1], calificar
score[2], puntaje, resultado,
tanteo
scrutinize, escudriñar,
examinar
scrutiny, escrutinio
season, estación
secant, secante
secant curve,
curva secante
secant function,
función secante
secant of a circle,
secante de un círculo
secant ratio,
razón secante
secant segment,
segmento secante

secant to a circle, secante a un círculo

second, segundo

second degree, de grado dos

second-degree equation, ecuación de segundo grado

second derivative, segunda derivada

second Green formula, segunda fórmula de Green

second-quadrant angle, ángulo del segundo cuadrante

secondary, secundario

second-to-last, el penúltimo

section, sección

conic section, sección cónica

cross-section, sección recta, muestra representativa

parallel section, sección paralela

plane section, sección planar

sector, sector, sector circular

sector of a circle, sector de un círculo

see, ver, mirar

segment[1], segmentar

segment[2], segmento

congruent line segments, segmento de línea congruentes

initial segment, segmento inicial

segment of a circle, segmento de un círculo

segmental arc, arco segmental

seldom, rara vez

select, seleccionar

selection, selección

random selection, selección al azar

self-conjugate conic, cono autoconjugado

self-corresponding element, elemento autocorrespondiente

self-evident, autoevidente, evidente por sí mismo

semicircle, semicírculo

semicircular, semicircular

sense, sentido, significado

sense of a line, sentido de una línea

sense of orientation, sentido de orientación

sense of rotation, sentido de rotación

sense-preserving, de dirección preservada

sense-preserving mapping, proyección de dirección preservada

sense-reversing, sentido de reversión

senseless, absurdo, sin sentido

sensible, sensato

sentence, frase, oración, enunciado

addition sentence, ecuación de suma

closed sentence,

frase cerrada
compound sentence,
oración compuesta
conditional sentence,
oración condicional
equivalent sentence,
oración equivalente
false sentence,
proposición falsa
linear open sentence,
oración lineal abierta
**mathematical
sentence,**
frase matemática
number sentence,
oración numérica
numerical sentence,
oración numérica
open sentence,
proposición abierta
**subtraction sen-
tence,** enunciado
de resta
verbal sentence,
oración verbal
separate[1], separar
separate[2], separado
sequence[1], poner en
secuencia
sequence[2], secuencia,
sucesión
arithmetic sequence,
secuencia aritmética
decreasing sequence,
secuencia decreciente
Fibonacci sequence,
sucesión de Fibonacci
geometric sequence,
secuencia geométrica
harmonic sequence,
secuencia armónica
increasing sequence,
secuencia creciente

key sequence,
secuencia de pasos
logical sequence,
secuencia lógica
**open number
sequence,**
secuencia de
números abiertos
opposite sequence,
secuencia opuesta
out of sequence,
fuera de secuencia
**sequence of inter-
vals,** secuencia de
intervalos
sequence of points,
secuencia de puntos
sequencing, secuenciar
serial, serial, seriado,
de serie
seriate, seriar
series, serie
alternating series,
series alternas
arithmetic series,
serie aritmética
convergent series,
serie convergente
divergent series,
serie divergente
Fourier series,
serie de Fourier
geometric series,
serie geométrica
harmonic series,
serie armónica
increasing series,
series crecientes
power series,
serie de potencias
**series of increasing
powers,** serie de
potencias crecientes

series of natural numbers, serie de números naturales
series of positive terms, serie de términos positivos
trigonometric series, series trigonométricas
set, conjunto, juego
difference set, conjunto de diferencia
disjoint sets, conjuntos disyuntivos
empty set, conjunto vacío, conjunto nulo
equivalent sets, conjuntos equivalentes
finite set, conjunto finito
image set, conjunto imagen
infinite set, conjunto infinito
intersection of sets, intersección de conjuntos
mutually exclusive sets, conjuntos mutuamente excluyentes
noncollinear set of points, conjunto de puntos no colineales
non-empty set, conjunto no vacío
non-enumerable set, conjunto no enumerado
null set, conjunto nulo
open set, conjunto abierto
outcome set, conjunto resultado
proper set, conjunto propio
replacement set, conjunto de reemplazo
set-builder notation, notación de construcción de conjuntos
set of data, conjunto de datos
set of irrational numbers, conjunto de números irracionales
set of numbers, conjunto de números
set of objects, conjunto de objetos
set of rational numbers, conjunto de números racionales
set of real numbers, conjunto de números reales
simple difference set, conjunto de diferencia simple
solution set, conjunto solución
truth set, conjunto de verdad
union of sets, unión de conjuntos
universal set, conjunto universal
seven, siete
seventh, el séptimo
several, varios
shade[1], sombrear, llenar, marcar
shade[2], sombra
shaded region, región sombreada
shading, sombreado

shadow, sombra
shape¹, formar, dar forma
shape², forma, figura
   geometric shape,
   figura geométrica
   irregular shape,
   forma irregular
share, compartir
sharp, afilado, filoso,
   puntiagudo
   sharp curve,
   curva cerrada
sheet, hoja
shift of origin,
   traslado del origen
short¹, tener un corto
   circuito
short², corto, bajo, breve
   short-circuit,
   cortocircuito, tener un
   cortocircuito
   short-out method,
   método corto
shortcut, atajo
shorten, acortar
shorter, más corto,
   más bajo
   shorter than,
   más corto que,
   más bajo que
shortest, el más corto
show, demostrar, mostrar
   show your work,
   identificar los pasos
   del trabajo
shrink, encoger, disminuir
SI (System International),
   Sistema Internacional
side, lado
   adjacent sides,
   lados adyacentes
   alongside,
   al costado de,

al lado de
   backside,
   revés
   beside,
   al lado de
   common side,
   lado común
   congruent sides,
   lados congruentes
   consecutive sides,
   lados consecutivos
   corresponding side,
   lado correspondiente
   included side,
   lado contenido
   initial side of an
   angle, lado inicial
   de un ángulo
   lopsided,
   ladeado
   nonadjacent side,
   lado no adyacente
   one-sided,
   (de) un lado
   opposite side,
   lado opuesto
   side opposite an
   angle, lado opuesto
   a un ángulo
   side view,
   vista de un lado
   terminal side of an
   angle, lado terminal
   de un ángulo
sideways, lateral
sigma, sigma
   sigma notation,
   notación sigma
sign, signo
   addition sign,
   signo de suma
   division sign,
   signo de división

sign

equal sign,
signo de igual,
signo de igualdad
inequality sign,
signo de desigualdad
minus sign,
signo de sustracción,
signo menos
multiplication sign,
signo de multiplición
negative sign,
signo negativo
plus sign,
signo de adición
positive sign,
signo positivo
radical sign,
signo de extracción
radical
subtraction sign,
signo de resta
summation sign,
signo de suma
signed number,
número sigma
significant, significativo,
importante
significant digit,
dígito significativo
significant figure,
figura significativa
signless integers,
enteros sin signos
similar, similar, semejante
similar decimals,
decimales similares
similar figures,
figuras similares
similar polygons,
polígonos similares
similar terms,
términos similares
similar triangles,

triángulos similares
similarity, similaridad
similarity symbol,
signo de semejanza
similitude, similitud
simple, sencillo
simple closed curve,
curva simple cerrada,
curva cerrada simple
simple difference set,
conjunto de diferencia
simple
simple equation,
ecuación simple
simple event,
evento simple
simple interest,
interés simple
**simple interest
formula,** fórmula
de interés simple
simple probability,
probabilidad simple
simpler, más simple
simpler than,
más simple que
simplest, el más simple
simplest form,
forma más simple
**simplest radical
form,** forma radical
más simple
simplex, simplex
simplification,
simplificación
simplified, simplificado(a)
**simplified propor-
tion,** proporción sim-
plificada
simplified solution,
solución simplificada
simplify, simplificar
simplify a fraction,

simplificar una fracción

simplify a result, simplificar el resultado

simplify an algebraic expression, simplificar una expresión algebraica

simplify an expression, simplificar la expresión

simulate, simular

simulation, simulacro

simultaneous, simultáneo

simultaneous displacement, desplazamiento simultáneo

simultaneous equations, ecuaciones simultáneas

simultaneous inequalities, desigualdades simultáneas

sine, seno

sine function, función del seno

sine ratio, razón del seno

sine wave, onda sinusoidal

single event, evento singular ocurrencia única

single-event experiment, experimento de evento singular, experimento único

singular matrix, matriz invertible, matriz singular

singularity, singularidad

sinusoid, sinusoide

six, seis

sixths, sextos

size, tamaño

sketch, dibujar al trazo, delinear, bosquejar

skew, enchuecar

skew lines, líneas oblicuas

skew symmetry, simetría oblicua

skewed lines, rectas oblicuas

skip count, contar por múltiplos de un número

slant[1], inclinarse

slant[2], inclinación

slant height, altura de la pendiente, altura inclinada

slanted, inclinado

slide, deslizar

slide rule, regla de cálculo

slope, gradiente, pendiente, cuesta

negative slope, pendiente negativa

point-slope equation of a line, ecuación punto-pendiente de una recta

point-slope form of line, forma pendiente-punto de una línea

positive slope, pendiente positiva

slope of a line, pendiente de una línea

slope-intercept form, forma pendiente intercepto

slope-intercept method, método pendiente intercepto

zero slope,
pendiente cero
slow, lento
small, pequeño
smaller, más pequeño
    smaller than,
    más pequeño que
smallest, el más pequeño
smooth curve,
    curva continua
social phenomena,
    fenómeno social
solenoidal field, campo
    solenoidal, campo de
    flujo conservativo
solid, sólido
    geometric solid,
    sólido geométrico
    rectangular solid,
    sólido rectangular
    solid angle,
    ángulo sólido
    solid figure,
    figura sólida
    solid geometry,
    geometría sólida
    solid sphere,
    esfera sólida
solidity, solidez
solidus, barra de fracción
solubility, solubilidad
solution, solución,
    resolución
    algebraic solution,
    solución algebraica
    exact solution,
    soluciones exactas
    initial solution,
    solución inicial
    minimum solution,
    solución mínima
    real solution,
    solución real

    simplified solution,
    solución simplificada
    solution of the
    sentence, solución
    de una oración
    solution set,
    conjunto solución
    solution set of
    system of equations,
    conjunto solución
    de un sistema de
    ecuaciones
    unique solution,
    solución única
solvable, resoluble
solve, resolver
    solve a fractional
    equation, resolver una
    ecuación fraccional
    solve a problem,
    resolver un problema
    solve a quadratic
    equation, resolver una
    ecuación cuadrática
    solve an equation,
    resolver una ecuación
    solve for a variable,
    resolver una variable
    solve graphically,
    resolver gráficamente
sophisticated, sofisticado
sophistication,
    sofisticación
sort, clasificar
sound[1], sonido
    sound wave,
    onda sonora
sound[2], fundado
south, sur
southeast, sudeste
southwest, sudoeste
space, espacio
    Euclidean space,

espacio euclidiano
finite sample space,
espacio muestral finito
Hermitian space,
espacio hermítico
n-dimensional
vector space,
espacio vectorial
de n dimensiones,
espacio vectorial
n-dimensional
one-dimensional
space, espacio
unidemensional
point space,
espacio de puntos
sample space,
espacio modelo
space curve,
curva espacial
space orientation,
orientación del espacio
vector space,
espacio vectorial
spacing, el espacio
span[1], atravesar, cruzar
span[2], lapso, distancia,
extensión
spatial, espacial
spatial reasoning,
razonamiento espacial
spatial relationship,
relación especial
special, especial
special case,
caso especial
special education,
educación especial
specific, específico
specific result,
resultado específico
specification,
especificación

specified, especificado
specify, especificar
spectrum, espectro
speculate, especular
speculative, especulativo
speed, rapidez, velocidad
spend, gastar
sphere, esfera
circumscribed
sphere, esfera
circunscrita
inscribed sphere,
esfera inscrita
solid sphere,
esfera sólida
spherical, esférico
spherical angle,
ángulo esférico
spherical triangle,
triángulo esférico
spin, rotación
spinner, ruleta
spiral, espiral
hyperbolic spiral,
espiral hiperbólica
split, dividir
spread[1], extender, esparcir,
dispersar, desplegar
spread[2], extensión
spreadsheet,
hoja de cálculo
spring, primavera, resorte
square[1], cuadrar,
encuadrar
square both sides,
elevar al cuadrado
ambos lados
square [2] (sq.) ,
cuadrado, cuadro
chi square,
ji cuadrada
complete the square,
completar el cuadrado

difference of two perfect squares, diferencia de dos cuadrados perfectos

difference of two squares, diferencia de dos cuadrados

inverse square, cuadrado inverso

least squares regression line, línea de ajuste óptimo

monomial square root, raíz cuadrada monómica

perfect square, cuadrado perfecto

perfect square trinomial, trinomio cuadrado perfecto

principal square root, raíz cuadrada principal

real square root, raíz cuadrada real

square array, matriz cuadrada

square bracket, corchete, corchete cuadrado

square centimeter, centímetro cuadrado

square foot, pie cuadrado

square inch, pulgada cuadrada

square matrix, matriz cuadrada

square meter, metro cuadrado

square mile, milla cuadrada

square number, número cuadrado

square of a number, el cuadrado de un número

square root, raíz cuadrada

square-root algorithm, algoritmo de la raíz cuadrada

square root method, método de la raíz cuadrada

square root of a fraction, raíz cuadrada de una fracción

square root of a number, raíz cuadrada de un número

square root of the denominator, raíz cuadrada del denominador

square root of the numerator, raíz cuadrada del numerador

square unit, unidad cuadrada

square yard, yarda cuadrada

SSS triangle congruence, triángulo congruente SSS

stabilization, estabilización

stack, pila

stage, etapa

stand for, representar

standard[1], estándar, norma, regla, patrón

standard[2], estándar, normal, típico

angle in a standard position, ángulo en posición normal

standard algorithm, algoritmo estándar

standard deck of cards, juego estándar de barajas

standard deviation, desviación estándar, desviación típica, desviación normal

standard form, forma estándar, forma corriente

standard form of a quadratic equation, forma regular de una ecuación cuadrática

standard measure, medida estándar

standard normal distribution, distribución normal estándar

standard notation, notación estándar

standard position, posición estándar, posición normal

standard representation, representación estándar

standard unit, unidad estándar

standardization, estandarización

standardize, estandarizar, normalizar

state[1], afirmar, declarar, aseverar

state[2], estado

statement, declaración, proposición, enunciado

arithmetic statement, frase aritmética

bank statement, estado financiero

biconditional statement, proposición bicondicionada

compound statement, enunciado compuesto

conditional statement, enunciado condicional

contrapositive statement, oración contrapositiva

converse of a statement, converso de una frase

converse statement, oración conversa

deduced statement, afirmación deducida

geometric statement, declaración geométrica

inverse of a statement, inversa de un enunciado

inverse statement, declaración inversa

logically equivalent statements, frases lógicamente equivalentes

mathematical statement, enunciado matemático

related statement, declaración relacionada

universally quantified statement, frase universalmente cuantificada

statistic, estadística

biased statistic, estadística parcial

test statistic, prueba estadística

statistical, estadístico(a)

five-number statistical summary, resumen estadístico de cinco datos

statistical estimate of error, estimado estadístico del error

statistical frequency, frecuencia estadística

statistical inference, inferencia estadística

statistician, estadístico

statistics, estadísticas

stats, estadística

statute mile, milla terrestre, milla ordinaria

stem and leaf plot, diagrama de tallo y hoja

stencil, plantilla

step, paso, escalón

step curve, curva escalonada

step function, función escalonada

step graph, gráfico escalonado

step-by-step, paso por paso

step-by-step carry, transporte paso a paso

step-by-step procedure, procedimiento sistemático

steradian, estereorradián

Sterling number, número de Sterling

stiff, tieso

Stokes theorem, teorema de Ampère-Stokes, teorema de la circulación

storage, almacenaje

store, almacenar

straight, recto(a)

straight angle, ángulo llano

straight edge, reglón, herramienta para dibujar líneas rectas, regla recta

straightedge, reglón, herramienta para dibujar líneas rectas, regla recta

straight line, recta, línea recta

straight line segment, segmento de línea recta, segmento de recta

straight path, recta

strange, curioso, extraño, raro

strategy, estrategia

stratified, estratificado, en etapas

strength, fortaleza

stretch, extender, alargar, estirar, dar de sí

string, serie, hilo

strip, tira, cinta

strong, fuerte
structure¹, estructurar
structure², estructura
study¹, estudiar
study², estudio
  study guide,
  guía de estudios
subdivision, subdivisión
subgroup, subgrupo
subject¹, tema, materia,
  asignatura
subject², sujeto a
subjective, subjetivo
subscript, subíndice,
  suscrito
  subscripted variable,
  variable suscrito
subset, subconjunto
  proper subset,
  subconjunto propio
subsidiary, subsidiaria
subspace, subespacio
substance, sustancia
substantial, sustancial
substitute, sustituir
substitution, sustitución
  identical substitu-
  tion, sustitución
  idéntica
  law of substitution,
  ley de sustitución
  substitution method,
  método de sustitución
  substitution postu-
  late, postulado en la
  sustitución
  substitution
  principle, principio
  de sustitución
  substitution prop-
  erty, propiedad de
  sustitución
  substitution prop-

  erty of equality,
  principio de sustitu-
  ción de la igualdad
  successive substi-
  tution, sustitución
  sucesiva
subtend, subtender
  subtend an angle,
  subtender un ángulo
subtended, subpuesto
  subtended angle,
  ángulo subpuesto
subtract, restar, sustraer
subtraction,
  resta, sustracción
  proportion by
  subtraction,
  proporción por resta
  repeated subtraction,
  resta repetida
  subtraction sen-
  tence, enunciado
  de resta
  subtraction sign,
  signo de resta
subtrahend, sustraendo
succeed, lograr, tener éxito
succeeding, sucediente
success, éxito, logro
successful, exitoso
succession, sucesión
successive, sucesivo
  successive approxi-
  mation, aproximación
  sucesiva
  successive displace-
  ments, deplazamien-
  tos sucesivos
  successive division,
  división sucesiva
  successive elimina-
  tion, eliminación
  sucesiva

successive method of elimination, método sucesivo de eliminación

successive reduction, reducción sucesiva

successive repetitions of the curve, repeticiones sucesivas de la curva

successive steps, pasos sucesivos

successive substitution, sustitución sucesiva

successive terms, términos sucesivos

successive trials, pruebas sucesivas

successively, sucesivamente

successor, sucesor

sufficient, suficiente

necessary and sufficient condition, condición necesaria y suficiente

necessary but not sufficient condition, condición necesaria pero no suficiente

sufficient condition, condición suficiente

suffix, sufijo

suggest, sugerir, recomendar

suitable, adecuado, idóneo

sum, suma

algebraic sum, suma algebraica

digital sum, suma digital

sum formula for trig-onometric functions, fórmula de suma para funciones trigonométricas

sum of a geometric series, suma de una serie geométrica

sum of an arithmetic series, suma de una serie aritmética

sum of two cubes, suma de dos cubos

summability, sumabilidad

summand, sumando

summarize, resumir

summary, resumen

five-number statistical summary, resumen estadístico de cinco datos

summation, suma

partial summation, sumatoria

summation of series, sumatoria de series

summation sign, signo de suma

upper limit of summation, límite superior de la suma

summed numbers, sumandos

summer, verano

super power, superpotencia

superfluous, superfluo

superior angle, ángulo superior

superior arc, arco superior

superscript, sobreíndice

supplement, suplemento

supplementary,

suplementario
**supplementary
angles,** ángulos
suplementarios
supply¹, abastecer,
proporcionar, proveer,
suministrar
supply², abasto, provisión,
suministro, oferta
supply and demand,
oferta y demanda
support¹,
apoyar, respaldar,
sostener, mantener
support², apoyo, respaldo,
soporte
supported, fundado,
fundamentado, sus-
tentado, sostenido
suppose, suponer
surd root, raíz sorda
sure, seguro
surface, superficie
closed surface,
superficie cerrada
cylinder surface,
superficie cilíndrica
cylindrical surface,
superficie cilíndrica
**lateral surface
area,** área de
superficie lateral
pyramidal surface,
superficie piramidal
**scalar surface
element,** elemento
escalar de superficie
surface area,
área de superficie
surface integral,
integral de superficie
**vector surface ele-
ment,** elemento vecto-

rial de superficie
surround, rodear
surrounding, rodeante,
alrededor
survey¹, sondear
survey², encuesta, sondeo
sustain, sostener
syllabus, plan de estudios,
programa de estudios
syllogism, silogismo
symbol, símbolo
angle symbol,
símbolo de ángulo
congruence symbol,
símbolo de con-
gruencia
currency symbol,
símbolo monetario
**greater or equal
to symbol,** signo
de mayor o igual
greater than symbol,
signo de mayor que
grouping symbol,
símbolo para agrupar,
símbolo de agrupación
inequality symbol,
símbolo de des-
igualdad
identity symbol,
símbolo de identidad
**less than or equal
to symbol,** signo
de menor o igual
less than symbol,
signo de menor que
**mathematical
symbol,** símbolo
matemático
numerical symbol,
símbolo numérico
operative symbol,
símbolo operativo

parallel symbol, signo de paralelismo

radical symbol, símbolo radica

relation symbol, símbolo de relación

similarity symbol, signo de semejanza

symbol for operation, símbolo para operación

symbol in verbal form, símbolos verbales

symbol in written form, símbolo escrito, símbolo gráfico

verbal symbol, símbolo verbal

written symbols, símbolo gráfico

symbolic, simbólico

symbolically, simbólicamente

symbolism, simbolismo

symbolize, simbolizar

symmetric, simétrico(a)

symmetric matrix, matriz simétrica

symmetric property of equality, propiedad simétrica de la igualdad

symmetric tensor, tensor simétrico

symmetrical, simétrico(a)

symmetrical curve, curva simétrica

symmetrical equations, ecuaciones simétricas

symmetrical figure, figura simétrica

symmetrical property, propiedad simétrica

symmetrical relation, relación simétrica

symmetrical tensor, tensor simétrico

symmetry, simetría

axis of symmetry, eje de simetría

center of symmetry, centro de simetría

central symmetry, simetría central

horizontal line symmetry, línea horizontal de simetría

line of symmetry, línea de simetría

plane of symmetry, plano de simetría

point of symmetry, punto de simetría

rotational symmetry, simetría rotacional

skew symmetry, simetría oblicua

symmetry with respect to a line, simetría con respecto a una recta, simetría axial

symmetry with respect to a plane, simetría con respecto a un plano

symmetry with respect to a point, simetría con respecto a un punto

translational symmetry, simetría translacional

vertical symmetry, simetría vertical
synthesize, sintetizar
synthetic, sintético
synthetic division, división sintética, división de Horner
system, sistema
algebraic system, sistema algebraico
base ten number system, sistema de numeración decimal
binary number system, sistema de numeración binaria
Cartesian coordinate system, sistema de coordenadas cartesianas
clock system, sistema de reloj
closed system, sistema cerrado
complete system, sistema completo
coordinate system, sistema de coordenadas
counting system, sistema de conteo
customary measurement system, sistema anglosajón de medidas
decimal number system, sistema númerico decimal
linear-quadratic system, sistema cuadrático lineal
logical system, sistema lógico

mathematical system, sistema matemático
measurement system, sistema de medición
metric system, sistema métrico
mod system, sistema de módulo
module system, sistema de módulo
number system, sistema númerico
octal system, sistema octal
postulational system, sistema postulacional
rectangular coordinate system, sistema rectangular de coordenadas
System International (SI), Sistema Internacional
system of conics, sistema de conos
system of dependent equations, sistema de ecuaciones dependientes
system of equations, sistema de ecuaciones
system of equations with two variables, sistema de ecuaciones con dos variables
system of inequalities, sistema de desigualdades
system of linear equations, sistema de ecuaciones lineales

system of linear inequalities, sistema de desigualdades lineales

system of sentences, sistema de frases

three dimensional coordinate system, sistema coordenado tridimensional

within a given system, dentro de un sistema dado

systematic, sistemático

systematic approach, aproximación sistemática

systematically, sistemáticamente

T (ton), tonelada

t-test, prueba t

table, tabla

cumulative frequency distribution table, tabla de distribución de frecuencias acumuladas

data frequency table, tabla de frecuencia de datos

data table, tabla de información

exchange rate table, tabla de tasas de cambio

frequency distribution table, tabla de distribución de frecuencias

frequency table, tabla de frecuencia

intput/output table, tabla de entradas y salidas

multiplication table, tabla de multiplicación, tabla de multiplicar, tabla pitagórica

numerical table, tabla numérica

truth table, tabla de verdad

tablespoon (tbsp.), cucharada

tabulation, tabulación

tail, cola

tail (of a coin), escudo (de moneda)

take, tomar

take away, sustraer, quitar

take care, cuidarse

take on, asumir

take out, sacar, eliminar

tally[1], computar, calcular, llevar la cuenta, contar

tally[2], cómputo, cálculos, conteo, cuenta

tally mark, conteo con palitos

tangent, tangente

common external tangent, tangente común externa

common internal tangent, tangente común interna

common tangent, tangente común
conjugate tangents, tangentes conjugadas
consecutive tangents, tangentes consecutivas
external tangent, tangente externa
internal tangent, tangente interna
internally tangent circles, círculos de tangencia interna
inverse tangent function, función inversa de la tangente
tangent curve, curva tangente
tangent function, función tangente
tangent of a circle, tangente de un círculo
tangent plane, plano tangente
tangent ratio, razón tangencial
tangent segment, segmento de tangente
tangential, tangencial
tangential approximation method, método de aproximación tangencial
tangential equation, ecuación tangencial
tangible, tangible
tangram, tangrama
tape[1], grabar
tape[2], cinta, cassette, cinta adhesiva
tape measure, cinta métrica,

flexómetro
tautology, tautología
tax, impuesto
Taylor's Theorem, fórmula de Taylor, teorema de Taylor
tbsp. (tablespoon), cucharada
t-distribution, distribución de t
teaspoon (tsp.), cucharadita
technical, técnico
technical writing, redacción técnica
technique, técnica
counting techniques, técnicas de conteo
sampling techniques, técnicas de modelaje
technology, tecnología
information technology (IT), tecnología de la información
telescope, telescopio
reflecting telescope, telescopio reflector
refracting telescope, telescopio dióptico
temperature, temperatura
template, machote, plantilla
ten, diez
ten thousands, decenas de mil, decenas de millar
ten thousands place, decenas de millar
tens, decenas
tens place, posición de las decenas, decenas
tensor[1], tensor

antisymmetric tensor, tensor antisimétrico
Kronecker tensor, tensor de Kronecker
symmetric tensor, tensor simétrico
symmetrical tensor, tensor simétrico
tensor of the second order, tensor de segundo orden
tensor², tensorial
tensor field, campo tensorial
tensor product, producto tensorial
tensor quantity, magnitud tensorial
tenth, décimo
ten-thousandths, diezmilésimas
tenths, décimas
term, término
absolute term, término absoluto
constant term, término constante
defined terms, términos definidos
express in terms of, expresar en términos de
higher terms, términos superiores
initial term, término inicial
inner term, término interno
last term, último término
like terms,
términos similares, términos semejantes
lowest terms, términos mínimos
mean terms, términos medios
middle term, término medio
nth term, término elevado a un exponente n
outer term, término exterior
similar terms, términos similares
successive terms, términos sucesivos
undefined term, término indefinido
unknown term, término desconocido
unlike terms, términos diferentes
terminal, terminal
terminal column, columna terminal
terminal line, línea terminal
terminal side of an angle, lado terminal de un ángulo
terminate, terminar
terminating, que termina, terminable
terminating decimal, decimal finito, decimal terminal
terminology, terminología
tessellation, teselado
test¹, probar, ensayar
test², prueba, ensayo
divisibility test, prueba de divisibilidad

equality test of fractions, prueba de igualdad de fracciones
horizontal-line test, prueba de la línea horizontal
one-tailed test, prueba de una cola
root test, prueba de la raíz
test statistic, prueba estadística
test tube, tubo de ensayo
t-test, prueba t
two-tailed test, prueba de dos colas
vertical-line test for a function, prueba de la línea vertical para una función
testing, prueba, verificación
hypothesis testing, prueba de hipótesis, comprobación de una hipótesis, verificación de una hipótesis
tetrahedron, tetraedro
textbook, libro de texto
then, entonces
theorem, teorema
binomial theorem, teorema del binomio
central limit theorem, teorema central del límite
circulation theorem, teorema de la circulación, teorema de Ampère-Stokes
converse theorem, teorema converso

divergence theorem, teorema de la divergencia
Fermat's Last Theorem, última conjetura de Fermat, último teorema de Fermat
field theorem, teorema del campo
fundamental theorem, teorema fundamental
Fundamental Theorem of Algebra, teorema fundamental del álgebra
Fundamental Theorem of Arithmetic, teorema fundamental de la aritmética
Fundamental Theorem of Calculus, teorema fundamental del cálculo
group theorem, teorema de grupo
inverse theorem, teorema inverso
Mean Value Theorem, teorema de valor medio
Pythagorean theorem, teorema pitagórico
rational root theorem, teorema de raíces racionales
Rolle's Theorem, teorema de Rolle
SAS Similarity Theorem, teorema de semejanza SAS

Stokes theorem, teorema de Ampère-Stokes, teorema de la circulación

Taylor's Theorem, fórmula de Taylor, teorema de Taylor

theoretical, teórico

theoretical framework, marco teórico

theoretical probability, probabilidad teórica

theory, teoría

probability theory, teoría de la probabilidad

number theory, teoría de números, teoría numérica

theory of relativity, teoría de la relatividad

therefore, por ende, por lo tanto, así que

thermal, termal, térmico

thermometer, termómetro

thick, grueso

thickness, espesor, grosor

think, pensar

thinking, pensamiento

critical thinking, pensamiento crítico

third[1], tercera parte, tercio

third[2], tercero, tercer

third degree, de grado tres

third quartile, tercer cuartil

third-quadrant angle, ángulo del tercer cuadrante

thought, pensamiento

thought process, proceso deductivo

thousand, mil, millar

thousands, unidades de millar, unidades de mil, millares

thousands place, posición de millar, posición de mil, unidades de millar, unidades de mil, millares

thousandth, milésimo

thousandths, milésimas

three, tres

three-digit number, número de tres dígitos

three-dimensional, tridimensional, de tres dimensiones

three dimensional coordinate system, sistema coordenado tridimensional

three-dimensional domain, dominio tridimensional

throw, lanzar, tirar

throw away, echar, tirar

ticket, boleto

tie, atar, enlazar, ligar, empatar

tilt[1], inclinar, ladear

tilt[2], inclinación

time[1], cronometrar

time[2], vez (pl. veces)

time[3], tiempo

time lapse, lapso de tiempo

timeline, línea de tiempo, línea cronológica

times[1], multiplicar

times², por, multiplicado por

tiny, pequeñito, diminuto, minúsculo

together, junto

tolerable, tolerable

tolerance, tolerancia

tolerate, tolerar, soportar

tomorrow, mañana

ton (T), tonelada

tool, herramienta

top, cima, parte superior

topological, topológico

topology, topología

total¹, totalizar, sumar

total², total

    total number of outcomes, número total de resultados

    total number of possibilities, número total de posibilidades

touch, tocar, contactar

touching, tocando, en contacto

towards, hacia, rumbo a

    towards the end of, a fines de

trace¹, trazar

trace², trazo, trazado, vestigio, rastro, bosquejo

track¹, seguir, dar seguimiento, rastrear

track², pista, huella

tracking, seguimiento

traditional, tradicional

trajectory, trayectoria

transcendental, trascendental

    transcendental curve, curva trascendental

transcendental function, función trascendental

transcendental number, número trascendental

transcript, boleta de calificaciones

transform, transformar

    transform the formula, transformar la fórmula

transformation, transformación

    coordinate transformation, transformación de coordenadas

    Fourier transformation, transformación de Fourier

    identical transformation, transformación idéntica

    inverse transformation, transformación inversa

    isogonal transformation, transformación isogonal

    linear transformation, transformación lineal

    opposite transformation, transformación opuesta

    reversible transformation, transformación reversible

transformational, transformacional

    transformational geometry, geometría transformacional

transformational proof, prueba de transformación
transformed, transformado
transitive, transitivo(a)
  transitive postulate, postulado transitivo
  transitive property, propiedad transitiva
  transitive property of equality, propiedad transitiva de la igualdad
  transitive property of inequality, propiedad transitiva de las desigualdades
  transitive relation, relación transitiva
transitivity, transitividad
translate, trasladar
translation, traslación, translación
translational symmetry, simetría translacional
transmission, transmisión
transmit, transmitir
transpose, transponer
  transpose matrix, matriz transpuesta
transposition, transposición
transversal, transversal
transverse, transverso(a)
  transverse axis, eje transverso
trapezium, trapecio
trapezoid, trapezoide, trapecio
  isosceles trapezoid, trapezoide isósceles, trapecio isósceles
travel, viajar

tree diagram, diagrama de árbol, diagrama ramificado
trend, tendencia
  trend line, línea de tendencia, línea de rumbo
triad, triplete
trial, intento, ensayo, prueba
  independent trial, prueba independiente
  method of trial and error, método de aproximaciones
  repeated trials, pruebas repetidas
  successive trials, pruebas sucesivas
  trial and error, ensayo y error
  trial and error method, método de aproximaciones, aproximaciones sucesivas
  trial and error procedure, aproximaciones sucesivas
  trial divisor, divisor de prueba
triangle, triángulo
  AA triangle similarity, triángulos semejantes AA
  AAA triangle similarity, triángulo semejante AAA
  AAS triangle congruence, triángulo congruente AAS
  ASA triangle congru-

ence, triángulo congruente ASA
acute triangle, triángulo agudo
circumscribed triangle, triángulo circunscrito
congruent triangles, triángulos congruentes
equiangular triangle, triángulo equiangular
equilateral triangle, triángulo equilátero
hypotenuse triangle congruence, hipotenusa congruente
isosceles triangle, triángulo isósceles
oblique triangle, triángulo oblicuo
obtuse triangle, triángulo obtuso
overlapping triangles, triángulos intercalados
Pascal's triangle, triángulo de Pascal
primitive triangle, triángulo primitivo
right triangle, triángulo recto
right triangle trigonometry, trigonometría de un triángulo recto
SAS triangle congruence, triángulo congruente SAS
scalene triangle, triángulo escaleno
similar triangles, triángulos similares
spherical triangle, triángulo esférico
SSS triangle congruence, triángulo congruente SSS
triangle inequality, desigualdad de triángulos
triangle number, número triangular
vector triangle, triángulo de vectores
triangular, triangular
triangular number, número triangular
triangular prism, prisma triangular
triangular pyramid, pirámide triangular
triangulation, triangulación
trichotomy, tricotomía
trichotomy law, ley de tricotomía
trichotomy postulate, postulado de tricotomía
trichotomy property, propiedad de tricotomía
trick[1], engañar
trick[2], maña, truco, engaño, trampa
trig, trigonometría
trigonometric, trigonométrico
trigonometric approximation, aproximación trigonométrica
trigonometric cofunctions, cofunciones trigonométricas

trigonometric equation, ecuación trigonométrica
trigonometric function, función trigonométrica
trigonometric identity, identidad trigonométrica
trigonometric interpolation, interpolación trigonométrica
trigonometric series, series trigonométricas
trigonometric value, valor trigonométrico
trigonometry, trigonometría
right triangle trigonometry, trigonometría de un triángulo recto
trihedral, triédrico
trihedral angle, ángulo triedro
trihedron, triedro
trillion, trillón, millón de millones, billón
trinomial, trinomio, trinomial
triple¹, triplicar
triple², triple
triple root, raíz triple
triple³, terna, triple
Pythagorean triple, triple pitagórico
trisection, trisección
trisection of an angle, trisección de un ángulo
trisection point, punto de trisección
trisectrix, trisectriz
trivial, trivial
truncate, truncar
truncated prism, prisma truncado
truncation, truncamiento
truncation error, error de truncamiento
true, cierto, veraz, verdadero
truth, verdad
truth set, conjunto de verdad
truth table, tabla de verdad
truth value, valor verdadero, valor de verdad
try¹, intentar, tratar, ensayar, probar
try², intento
tsp. (teaspoon), cucharadita
turn¹, girar, voltear
turn about the origin, girar alrededor del origen
turn², vuelta, giro
turning point, punto de giro
twice, doble, dos veces
two, dos
two-by-two, de dos en dos
two-column proof, prueba a dos columnas
two-digit number, número de dos dígitos
two-dimensional, de dos dimensiones, bidimensional
two-tailed test, prueba de dos colas

type, tipo, clase
type I error,
error tipo I
type II error,
error tipo II
typical, típico

umpteenth, enésimo
unalign, desalinear
unaligned, no alineado
unalike, diferente
unalterable, inalterable
unary, unario
unbalanced, desequilibra-
do, no balanceado
unbelievable, increíble,
inversosímil
unbiased, imparcial
fair and unbiased
object, objeto justo
e imparcial
unbiased objects,
objetos no polarizados,
objetos imparciales
uncertain, dudoso, incierto
uncertain truth
value, valor de verdad
incierto
uncertainty, incertidumbre
unchanged, sin cambio, sin
alteración, inalterado
unclassified, no clasificado
unclear, confuso, no claro,
ambiguo
uncommon, poco común
uncomplicated,
no complicado
unconditional equation,

ecuación incondicional
unconnected, desconec-
tado, inconexo, no
relacionado
uncover, descubrir
uncovered, descubierto
undecidable, que no puede
ser decidido
undefined, indefinido
undefined term,
término indefinido
undeniable, innegable
under, bajo, debajo de,
menor
underline, subrayar
understand, comprender,
entender
understandable, compren-
sible, entendible
undetermined coefficient,
coeficiente indetermi-
nado
undiscovered,
no descubierto
unending, interminable
unequal, desigual
uneven, no balanceado,
disparejo
unexpected, inesperado
unexplainable, inexplicable
unexplored, inexplorado
unidentifiable,
no identificable
uniform, uniforme
uniform motion,
movimiento uniforme
uniform probability,
probabilidad uniforme
uniformemente, evenly
uniformity, uniformidad
unimportant,
sin importancia
uninferible, no inferible

union, unión
    union of sets,
    unión de conjuntos
    union of the graphs,
    unión de gráficos
unique, único, singular
    unique solution,
    solución única
uniqueness, singularidad
    uniqueness of order,
    singularidad de orden
    uniqueness of solution, singularidad de solución
unit, unidad
    appropriate unit,
    unidad apropiada
    corresponding unit,
    unidad correspondiente
    cubic unit,
    unidad cúbica
    customary units of capacity,
    unidades de capacidad anglosajonas
    customary units of mass, unidades de masa anglosajonas
    imaginary unit,
    unidad imaginaria
    linear unit,
    unidad lineal
    metric unit,
    unidad métrica de medición, unidad métrica de medida
    nonstandard units,
    unidades no estándares
    per-unit rate,
    tasa por unidad
    square unit,

    unidad cuadrada
    standard unit,
    unidad estándar
    unit circle,
    círculo unitario
    unit doublet,
    doblete unidad
    unit element,
    elemento de unidad
    unit fraction,
    fracción unitaria
    unit matrix,
    matriz unitaria
    unit measure,
    unidad de medida
    unit normal,
    unidad normal
    unit ramp,
    rampa unitaria
    unit rate,
    tarifa unitaria
    unit segment,
    segmento unitario
    unit step function,
    función escalón unitario
    unit vector,
    vector unitario
    whole unit,
    unidad entera
unitary matrix,
    matriz unitaria
unite, unir
univariate, univariado
    univariate data,
    datos univariados
universal, universal
    universal quantifier,
    cuantificador universal
    universal set,
    conjunto universal
    universal validity,

validez universal
universally quantified statement, frase universalmente cuantificada
universe, universo
university, universidad
unjustifiable, injustificable
unknown, desconocido, incógnito
unknown number, número desconocido
unknown term, término desconocido
unless, a menos que, excepto cuando
unlike, diferente, peculiar
unlike radicals, radicales diferentes
unlike terms, términos diferentes
unlikely, poco probable
unlimited decimal, decimal ilimitado
unlimited extent, extensión ilimitada
unnatural, innatural
unnecessary, innecesario
unobservable, inobservable, no visible
unobserved, no visto, no observado, desapercibido, inadvertido
unoriginal, no original
unpredictable, impredecible
unproven, no probado
unquestionable, incuestionable
unrelated, desconectado, inconexo, no relacionado
unreliable, no fiable, no

fidedigno
unrestricted, irrestringido
unrounded, no redondeado
unscientific, no científico
unsegmented, no segmentado, continuo
unsigned number, número sin signo
unsimplified, no simplificado, complejo
unsmoothed curve, curva áspera
unsolvability, insolucionabilidad
unsolvable, sin solución
unsound, infundado
unspecified, no especificado
unsuitable value, valor inajustable
unsupported, infundado, no fundamentado, no sustentado
unsure, inseguro
unsystematic, no sistemático, no metódico, desordenado
untrue, falso
unusual, inusual, raro, extraño, extraordinario
up, arriba
uphill, cuesta arriba
upper, superior
upper base, base superior
upper base of a cylinder, base superior del cilindro
upper bound, límite superior
upper integral, integral superior

upper limit of summation, límite superior de la suma
upper quartile, cuartil superior
uppercase, mayúscula
use, usar, emplear, utilizar
useful, útil
usefulness, utilidad
user, usuario
usual, usual
utilize, utilizar

vacuum, vacío
vague, vago, impreciso
valid, válido
valid argument, argumento válido
validity, validez
universal validity, validez universal
value, valor
absolute value, valor absoluto
absolute-value of a number, valor absoluto de un número
approximate rational value, valor racional aproximado
approximate value, valor aproximado
assign values, asignar valores
corresponding value for, el valor correspon-

diente de
designated value, valor designado
eigenvalue, valor propio
exact value, valor exacto
extreme value, valor extremo
fixed value, valor fijo
income values, valores de ingreso
initial value, valor inicial
input values, valores de entrada
integral value, valor integral
intermediate value, valor intermedio
maximum value, valor máximo
mean value, valor medio
minimum value, valor mínimo
nominal value, valor nominal
place value, valor posicional, valor del espacio
trigonometric value, valor trigonométrico
truth value, valor verdadero, valor de verdad
unsuitable value, valor inajustable
value added tax (VAT), impuesto sobre el valor agregado (IVA)
value of a function,

valor de una función
value of a variable,
valor de una variable
**value of an algebraic
expression,**
valor de una expresión
algebraica
vanishing point,
punto tendiente a cero
variable, variable
    dependent variable,
    variable dependiente
    independent variable,
    variable independiente
    leading variable,
    variable principal
    multiple variables,
    de varias variables
    real variable,
    variable real
    subscripted variable,
    variable suscrito
variance, varianza,
variación
variation, variación
    combined variation,
    variación combinada
    inverse variation,
    variación inversa
vary, variar
VAT (value added tax),
IVA (impuesto sobre
el valor agregado)
vector^1, vector
    axial vector,
    vector axial
    eigenvector,
    vector propio
    polar vector,
    vector polar
    position vector,
    posición de vector
    radius vector,

vector radial
row vector,
vector fila
vector field,
campo vectorial
vector line element,
elemento vectorial
de línea
vector path element,
elemento vectorial
de arco
vector potential,
potencial vectorial
vector product,
producto vectorial,
producto externo
vector quantity,
cantidad del vector
vector space,
espacio vectorial
**vector surface
element,**
elemento vectorial
de superficie
vector triangle,
triángulo de vectores
unit vector,
vector unitario
vector^2, vectorial
velocity, velocidad
    angular velocity,
    velocidad angular
Venn diagram,
diagrama de Venn
verbal, verbal
    verbal explanation,
    explicación verbal
    verbal expression,
    expresión verbal
    verbal language,
    lenguaje verbal
    verbal problem,
    problema verbal

verbal process,
proceso verbal
verbal sentence,
oración verbal
verbal symbol,
símbolo verbal
verbally, verbalmente
verification, comprobación, verificación
verified, verificado
verify, verificar, comprobar
verify results,
verificar los resultados
verify the claims of others,
verificar afirmaciones de otros
vertex (pl. vertices),
vértice
common vertex,
vértice común
consecutive vertices,
vértices consecutivos
cyclic vertices of a quadrilateral,
vértices cíclicos de un cuadrilátero
opposite vertex,
vértice opuesto
vertex angle,
ángulo del vértice
vertex of a cone,
vértice de un cono
vertical, vertical
vertical angles,
ángulos verticales
vertical asymptote,
asíntota vertical
vertical axis,
eje vertical
vertical distance,
distancia vertical
vertical format,
formato vertical
vertical line,
línea vertical
vertical symmetry,
simetría vertical
vertical-line test for a function,
prueba de la línea vertical para una función
vertices (sing. vertext),
vértice
view, vista
visual, visual
mathematical visual,
visual matemático
visual proof,
prueba visual
visualization, visualización
visualize, visualizar
void[1], vacío
void[2], inválido, nulo, desprovisto de
volume, volumen
volume change,
cambio de volumen
volume element,
elemento de volumen
volume integral,
integral de volumen
volume of a cone,
volumen de un cono
volume of a solid,
volumen de un sólido
volume of a solid figure, volumen de una figura sólida

W

warp, combar, deformar
wave, onda
  light wave,
  onda de luz
  sine wave,
  onda sinusoidal
  sound wave,
  onda sonora
  wave function,
  función de onda
weak, débil
weakness, debilidad
week, semana
weekly, semanalmente
weigh, pesar, sopesar
weight[1], dar valor
weight[2], peso
weighted, ponderado(a)
  weighted inner product, producto interno ponderado
  weighted mean, media ponderada
well-formed, bien formado
west, oeste, poniente
whenever,
  siempre y cuando
whirl, giro
whitespace,
  espacio en blanco
whole, entero
  coherent whole,
  conjunto coherente
  even whole number,
  número entero par
  odd whole number,
  número entero impar
  part-to-whole ratio,

razón parte-todo, cociente parte-todo, relación parte-todo
  whole number,
  número entero
  whole unit,
  unidad entera
wide, amplio, ancho
width, ancho, anchura, envergadura
  width of an interval, anchura de un intervalo
winter, invierno
wire, alambre
wired, alámbrico
wireless, inalámbrico
with, con
  with repetition, con repetición
  with replacement, con reemplazo
  with respect to, con respecto a
within a given system, dentro de un sistema dado
without, sin
  without repetition, sin repetición
  without replacement, sin reemplazo
word problem, problema escrito, problema verbal
work[1], trabajar, funcionar
  work backwards, trabajar de atrás para adelante
work[2], trabajo
workbook, libro de ejercicios, cuaderno de ejercicios

working mean,
    media provisional,
    media de trabajo
write, escribir
written, escrito(a)
    written explanation,
    explicación escrita
    written form of rea-
    soning, forma gráfica
    de razonamiento
    written language,
    lenguaje escrito,
    lenguaje gráfico
    written representa-
    tions, representacio-
    nes gráficas
    written symbols,
    símbolo gráfico
wrong, equivocado,
    erróneo, incorrecto

X-Z

x-axis, eje de las x, eje x
x-coordinate, coordenada x
x-intercept of a line,
    intercepto de x
    de una línea
yard (yd.), yarda
    square yard,
    yarda cuadrada
y-axis, eje de las y, eje y
y-coordinate, coordenada y
yd. (yard), yarda
year, año
yield[1], producir, rendir
yield[2], rendimiento,
    producción, interés
y-intercept of a line,
    intercepto de y de una

    línea
young, joven
z-angle, ángulo z
zero, cero
    above zero,
    encima de cero
    addition property of
    zero, propiedad de la
    suma del cero
    below zero,
    bajo cero
    multiplication
    property of zero,
    propiedad multiplicati-
    va del cero
    non-zero,
    no cero
    zero degree,
    grado cero
    zero-divergence field,
    campo solenoidal,
    campo de flujo conser-
    vativo
    zero divisor,
    divisor cero
    zero exponent,
    exponente cero
    zero matrix,
    matriz nula
    zero of a function,
    cero de una función
    zero product prop-
    erty, propiedad del
    producto cero
    zero property of ad-
    dition, propiedad del
    cero de la suma
    zero property of mul-
    tiplication, propiedad
    multiplicativa del cero
    zero slope,
    pendiente cero

Velázquez Press

For over 150 years, *Velázquez Spanish and English Dictionary* has been recognized throughout the world as the preeminent authority in Spanish and English dictionaries. Velázquez Press is committed to developing new bilingual dictionaries and glossaries for children, students, and adults based on the tradition of *Velázquez Spanish and English Dictionary*.

We invite you to go to www.AskVelazquez.com to access online services such as our free translator, irregular verb conjugator, and member forum. We also invite you to add on to the glossary. If you know of a K-12 mathematics term that is not included, please let us know at info@academiclearningcompany.com for future editions.

Por más de 150 años, *Velázquez Spanish and English Dictionary* ha sido reconocido como la máxima autoridad en diccionarios de español e inglés en todo mundo. Velázquez Press está comprometido a eleborar diccionarios y glosarios bilingües para niños, estudiantes y adultos en la tradición del *Velázquez Spanish and English Dictionary*.

Lo invitamos a visitar www.AskVelazquez.com para acceder a los servicios en línea como nuestro traductor automático, información sobre ortografía de verbos irregulares en español y el foro. Si sabe de algún término de matematica de los grados escolares kinder a 12 que no está incluido, por favor, mande un correo electrónico a info@academiclearningcompany.com para ediciones futuras.